Beyond Control

Law and Social Theory

Series editors:
PETER FITZPATRICK
Professor of Law, Queen Mary and Westfield College
University of London
COLIN PERRIN
Law School and Department of Philosophy
University of Kent at Canterbury

Also available

Law and the Senses
EDITED BY LIONEL BENTLY AND LEO FLYNN

The Wrongs of Tort
JOANNE CONAGHAN AND WADE MANSELL

Delimiting the Law
'Postmodernism' and the Politics of Law
MARGARET DAVIES

Dangerous Supplements
EDITED BY PETER FITZPATRICK

Disabling Laws, Enabling Acts
Disability Rights in Britain and America
CAROLINE GOODING

The Critical Lawyers' Handbook
EDITED BY IAN GRIGG-SPALL AND PADDY IRELAND

Foucault and the Law
ALAN HUNT AND GARY WICKHAM

The Critical Lawyers' Handbook 2
EDITED BY PADDY IRELAND AND PER LALENG

Family Law Matters
KATHERINE O'DONOVAN

False Images
Law's Construction of the Refugee
PATRICIA TUITT

Contract
A Critical Commentary
JOHN WIGHTMAN

BEYOND CONTROL
Medical Power and Abortion Law

SALLY SHELDON

Pluto  **Press**

LONDON • CHICAGO, IL

First published 1997 by Pluto Press
345 Archway Road, London N6 5AA
and 1436 West Randolph
Chicago, Illinois 60607, USA

British Library Cataloguing in Publication Data
A catalogue record for this book is available from the British Library

ISBN 0 7453 1168 7 hbk

Library of Congress Cataloging in Publication Data
Sheldon, Sally.
    Beyond control: medical power and abortion law/Sally Sheldon.
        p.   cm. — (Law and social theory)
    Includes bibliographical references and index.
    ISBN 0–7453–1168–7 (hbk)
    1. Abortion—Law and legislation—Great Britain—History.
I. Title. II. Series.
KD3340.S53   1997
344.41'04192—dc21   96–51823
                                                                    CIP

Designed and produced for Pluto Press by
Chase Production Services, Chadlington, OX7 3LN
Typeset from disk by Stanford DTP Services, Northampton
Printed in Great Britain

Contents

Table of Statutes

Table of Cases

Acknowledgements

This book results from doctoral research conducted at the European University Institute in Florence from 1990 to 1994. I would like to thank my two thesis supervisors, Peter Fitzpatrick and Gunther Teubner for their enthusiasm, accessibility, support and constructive criticism throughout those years. Carol Smart was also kind enough to read and provide useful comments on a first draft of Chapter 6, and to give me the benefit of more general thoughts on the thesis as a whole. Over and above this, I have been greatly influenced by her published work.

One of the many advantages of preparing a doctoral thesis at the European University Institute is the existence of a large body of postgraduate researchers and visiting fellows with whom it is possible to discuss work in progress. It is impossible to list all the people who have helped and influenced the present effort, but I would like particularly to thank Eugene MacNamee, John Stanton-Ife, Mary Daly, Maria Drakopoulou, Liz Kingdom, Yota Kravaritou, Barbara MacLennan, Katherine O'Donovan and Joyce Outshoorn. Most of all, I am greatly indebted to Julia Sohrab who provided constructive and incisive comments on almost every chapter as it appeared.

Since leaving the EUI, I have faced the task of attempting to translate my thesis into a book. Certain people have made this process a good deal less painful than it might otherwise have been. My colleagues at Keele University have provided a working environment which has been both intellectually stimulating and very supportive. The arrival of Michael Thomson in the office next door to mine has proved less of a distraction than I feared, and even more rewarding than I had hoped in terms of the possibility to share and to develop ideas. I continue to learn a lot from him. Since returning to the UK, I have also greatly benefited from the possibility to discuss research in progress with friends at other universities, especially Sue Millns and Wade Mansell. Peter Fitzpatrick has proved to be every bit as kind and as encouraging an editor as he was a supervisor. I would also like to thank Anne Beech and Robert Webb at Pluto for their help and Jeanne Brady of Cove Publishing Support Services for her attention to detail.

Finally I would like to thank Nick, Hil and Kenneth who put up with me during the writing and rewriting of this book and have always been on hand to provide humour, support and gin and tonic, each at the appropriate time and always mixed in the perfect quantities.

Earlier versions of parts of this book have appeared in the following places:

Chapter 2 (1994) *The British Abortion Act 1967: A Permissive Reform?* EUI Working paper Law no. 94/2 (Florence: European University Institute)

Chapter 3 (1993) '"Who is the Mother to Make the Judgment?": Constructions of Woman in UK Abortion Law', 1 *Feminist Legal Studies* 3–22

Chapter 5 (1996) '"Subject Only to the Attitude of the Surgeon Concerned": Judicial Protection of Medical Discretion', 5 *Social and Legal Studies* 93–109

Chapter 6 (1995) 'Abortion Law and the Politics of Medical Control', in Bridgeman, J. and Millns, S. (eds), *Law and Body Politics: Regulating the Female Body* (Aldershot: Dartmouth Publishing Company)

Chapter 7 (1996) 'The Abortion Pill, RU486: Problems of Access and Control', in Feminist Legal Research Unit (ed.), *Women's Access to Healthcare: Law, Society and Culture* Working paper no. 4 (Liverpool: Liverpool University).

Part of Chapter 5 also appeared in (1997) 'Multiple Pregnancy and Re(pro)ductive Choice', 5 *Feminist Legal Studies* 99–107.

I would like to dedicate this book to the memory of my father, Alfred Thomas Sheldon (1927–1990) and my brother, David John Sheldon (1954–1996), both of whom taught me a great deal.

Sally Sheldon
October 1996

1
Abortion in Britain: Thirty Years On

Conscious activity to control human fertility is as intrinsic to the social being of human groups as the activity to control and organize the production of food. What changes over time and from one social context to another is who controls fertility, under what conditions, through what means, and for what purposes (Petchesky, 1984a, p. 25).

The rights and interests of the mother emerge, not now solely concerned with her protection from unsafe abortions, but instead also with her autonomy and ability to determine what should happen to her body. This development has marched hand in hand with the emergence of a strong medical profession and with the phenomenon of science-based medicine ... Until Parliament or the European Court of Human Rights intervenes, the supremacy of the English medical profession, coupled with its increased (and continually increasing) ability to provide safer and less risky abortion procedures, have resulted in the legal acceptance of the medicalization of abortion (Grubb, 1990, pp. 156–7).

In the 1960s, women's movements across Europe took to the streets to claim the abortion issue as their own. A key contention was that the question of who controls female fertility is a political one, involving fundamental choices as to the position and role of women within society. Restrictive controls over access to abortion services were seen as indicative of attempts to exercise control over women's sexuality and fertility and to enforce certain roles and life-style choices which reflected particular moral assumptions regarding appropriate female conduct. Access to safe, legal abortion on demand was advanced as a prerequisite for the full and equal participation of women in society and an essential part of any feminist reformist agenda. As Madeleine Simms of the first British reforming group, the Abortion Law Reform Association, put it: 'no true state of equality can exist for women in a society which denies them freedom and privacy in respect of fertility control' (1981, p. 183).

In many other countries across the world, abortion has retained this high political profile and remains as the most fundamental locus of feminist campaigning. Finding a satisfactory reconciliation of two very different abortion laws almost brought the German unification process to a standstill. In the United States, the 'abortion wars' have been still more fierce. The American anti-choice movement has adopted such violent tactics that it is not unknown for American doctors working in abortion clinics to arrive at work wearing bullet-proof vests. The availability of safe, legal abortion hangs like a pendulum, liable to swing violently as a result of fine shifts in the composition of the Supreme Court. The fact that the judges who sit on that court are political appointees, and the significance their position on abortion will have in their selection, enhances the construction of abortion as a matter of politics. The fiery rhetoric of American radical feminist writers seems to gain some credence when the regulation of abortion is so explicitly a political matter.

Much criticised within the US,[1] such analysis transfers still less happily to the British context. Thirty years on, the feminist claim that the regulation of abortion is intrinsically in some undefined way about attempting to control women or to impose a particular brand of morality upon us seems increasingly difficult to sustain in Britain. Indeed, whatever disagreement or struggle there is regarding abortion in this country has become increasingly muted. Over the past thirty years, doctors' interpretation of the Abortion Act appears to have become gradually more liberal, and access to safe, legal abortion services has, as a result, greatly improved. In this climate of access to safe, legal abortion services, it seems that abortion has lost its high place on progressive agendas for reform. Rather, it appears a status quo with regard to the regulation of abortion services has been established, and those who continue to kick against it – be they pro- or anti-choice activists – are cast as marginal extremists.

For this reason, attempts to export the more violent American anti-choice campaigning tactics across the Atlantic have proved largely unsuccessful. 'Operation Rescue', the US group which besieges abortion clinics, harassing women seeking termination services and chaining themselves to operating tables, has been subject to condemnation from liberals and conservatives alike in Britain. Indeed, it was ministers of the Conservative Government who were most active in attempting to prevent the radical leader of Operation Rescue, Don Tresham, from travelling to Britain, on the grounds that his presence was not conducive to the public good. Meanwhile in Parliament, a stream of attempts to reform the 1967 Act has fallen at the first hurdle (see Millns and Sheldon, forthcoming). Whilst the anti-choice movement has vowed to flag abortion as an important issue for the 1997 election, founding a Pro-Life Alliance to contest parliamentary seats where there is no anti-choice candidate, this move seems unlikely to have any real effect other than to ensure them the possibility of making a party political broadcast (Millns and Sheldon, forthcoming).

If the anti-choice movement has been unsuccessful in challenging the 1967 Act, so too have pro-active, pro-choice campaigns failed to capture the public imagination. Currently, the fiercest battles for feminists seem likely to be waged not around the issue of whether women should have the right *not* to become mothers, but rather around how they must act once they have chosen maternity. Media attention and political debate are focused not so much on abortion as on a range of other issues: whether children should be fostered by lesbian and gay male couples or parents of a different ethnic origin to their own, the problems of single-parent families and parents who provide inadequate care or supervision of their children, control of access to reproductive technologies, the right to use corporal punishment and so on. Moreover, the responsibility owed to children is extended ever backwards through pregnancy, with more attention paid to the woman's conduct when pregnant.[2] And this discourse of 'responsible parenting' is not confined to women – rather the establishment of the Child Support Agency illustrates its extension to men (albeit that male responsibility is conceived of primarily in terms of a duty to contribute financially).

It is true that sometimes abortion does catch the public attention. Most notable in recent years are the case of the 'Carlisle baby' (allegedly a late termination resulting in a living abortus), the X case (a 14-year-old Irish rape victim, forbidden to travel to terminate her pregnancy in Britain) and the case of the anonymous woman who had chosen selective reduction of a pregnancy of twins (see pp. 90–5 for more discussion of this last case). However, such issues seem to dominate headlines and chat shows for a maximum of a week before dropping out of the public consciousness. Moreover, they do not seem to have any more than an extremely limited effect in Britain in terms of engendering a climate for statutory reform or judicial change.

In this book, I aim to trace how and why the regulation of abortion seems increasingly to have lost a high political profile in this country. Focusing on the development of the law, I will argue that the regulation of abortion has increasingly shifted from the political public realm into the private sphere, where it has been constructed as a matter for the discretion of the medical profession. This recodification as a technical problem to be discussed by experts, which has become increasingly clear in recent years, has defused the most fierce debates around abortion and has militated against any attempt to radically reform the law, that is, whether to make it more or less restrictive. In this sense, my focus will be on the medicalisation of the law in this area. 'Medicalisation' here refers to the pre-eminence of a medical discourse or narrative, and the marginalisation of other understandings or knowledges. It is important to bear in mind that such medical discourse is itself in a constant state of flux and development and that this will also have an effect on the availability of abortion services.[3]

With this aim in mind, in the pages that follow I will examine some aspects of the regulation of abortion services in England and Wales from 1967 onwards. In doing this, I also make a second claim: despite this *apparent* depoliticisation, it does still make sense to talk of the regulation of abortion as a political matter and, in particular, as an important feminist issue. I believe this to be true in three senses. First, the regulations governing the availability of abortion are underpinned by quite specific, discernable values which reflect particular attitudes to women and a clear value judgement as to who should control female fertility. Second, whilst this is well concealed, the regulation of abortion continues to serve as a focal point for the deployment of power over women. Third, whilst the medicalisation of abortion law has had substantial benefits for ensuring women's access to abortion services, it also poses substantial problems for that access, and these have been inadequately addressed. The paradox between an apparent depoliticisation and the underlying deeply political nature of who controls access to abortion services will be at the crux of the present work.

Before going on to set out exactly what will be discussed in this book, it is probably worth mentioning what will not be covered. First, discussion will be confined to the law as it applies to England and Wales. With some few exceptions, this analysis will also be of relevance to Scotland. Northern Ireland is not dealt with here: it presents legal and political issues which are very different from those raised by mainland Britain (see Furedi, 1995). Second, there is no discussion in the current work as to the ethics of abortion. It will no doubt already be clear what my position would be in the abortion debate as it is currently constructed. This position does not derive from any belief that the decision to terminate a pregnancy is not a morally serious one, but rather from the conviction that in the final analysis, any system of legal regulation of abortion must decide on one person who should be empowered to make such a decision. It seems to me that this can only be the pregnant woman.

OUTLINE OF CHAPTERS

I begin my analysis, in the next two chapters, with some consideration of the statute which partially decriminalised abortion in Britain: the 1967 Abortion Act. To develop the argument that the regulation of abortion remains an important political issue, I argue that the Abortion Act cannot be adequately understood in abstraction from a context of gendered power relations. In Chapter 2, I look in detail at the motivation for the partial decriminalisation of abortion in 1967 and question the accuracy of the received representation of the Act as a *permissive* piece of legislation. Whilst the Act undoubtedly represented an advance for women, this is a partial vision. Rather than being seen as a loosening of power, motivated by a desire to carve out a greater free space for female reproductive autonomy, I argue that the Act can be better understood as an adoption of more continuous, regulatory and corrective mechanisms of controlling individuals and populations. The Act is a landmark in the medicalisation of the law, and close analysis of it clearly reveals the relationship between such medicalisation and the institution of a network of medical control over women.

It is important that the Abortion Act should not be understood just as part of a general (genderless) shift towards a different mode of regulation. In Chapter 3, I indicate the importance of viewing this reform within a context of gender, outlining the clearly gendered constructions of the woman seeking abortion which underlay the reform and justified the need for and appropriateness of the particular regulatory framework which was introduced. The very nature of the subject to be regulated – the woman seeking abortion – legitimates and grounds the need for medical control and supervision over her. Thus, while the reform may be seen within a general movement towards what Foucault has described as 'governmentality', this should be understood here as a broad brush-stroke which maps a multiplicity of interconnecting, fine techniques of control which operate to construct different (gendered) subjectivities.

In the following chapters, I move on to consider the current regulation of abortion in Britain. The Abortion Act has carved out and legitimated a broad area for the free exercise of medical discretion. In Chapter 4, I take a closer look at the workings of medical practice in the case of a request for a termination, assessing whether and how one can see power being deployed over women and the role of legal regulation in encouraging and facilitating this exercise of power. I argue that although there is clearly an increasingly liberal attitude within the medical profession towards requests for terminations, the regulation of abortion remains a site which provides a particular opportunity for the deployment of power over women. I identify four analytically distinguishable operations of power, which I call technical control, decisional control, paternalistic control and normalising control. To distinguish between the various ways in which power is deployed in this context seems to me to be important, first in order to better understand the feminist claim that the regulation of abortion in some way involves the operation of power over women, and second to flesh out what exactly this 'in some way' actually means. A more refined analysis of power may also provide useful insights for the development of goals and strategies for reform.

In Chapters 5 and 6, the focus shifts to the interaction between legal and medical regulation. Here the apparent depoliticisation resulting from the medicalisation of abortion becomes clearly visible. In Chapter 5, I take a fresh look at some of the relevant decisions which the British courts have made in this area. Most striking here is the judges' tremendous respect for and deference to medical opinion and their unwillingness to 'second-guess' or supervise the exercise of medical opinion under the Abortion Act. Abortion is constructed as a medical event and the doctors' power to define is accepted and reinforced, with other accounts pushed to the margins. This depoliticises the judicial decision which can be legitimated with reference to scientific truth. Judges intervene only to correct excesses or substantial departures from 'good medical practice' (a standard determined by the medical profession) in such a way as to legitimate the normal run of such practice. Whilst judicial reluctance to interfere with medical discretion has, in other areas of law, left (potential) plaintiffs without redress for various infringements of bodily autonomy, it is here seen to have worked to the advantage of women seeking to terminate a pregnancy. For example, women have been protected from claims for injunctions to prevent proposed abortions brought by their sexual partners or parents. I argue that this highlights a peculiar difficulty of the situation which feminists face with regard to the medical control of abortion, which will be developed in subsequent chapters. The principled arguments against medical control (and the implicit paternalism upon which it is predicated) may prove to be in direct conflict with considerations of the practical and concrete benefits it has provided and the security which it may continue to give on the level of entrenching and extending women's access to abortion services. Notwithstanding this, I also hope to show that whilst doctor and woman acting in conjunction are relatively well protected from outside challenge, women are less well protected within the medical relationship itself.

The same tension regarding the medical control of abortion emerges equally clearly in Chapters 6 and 7. In Chapter 6, I come to consider the most recent statutory development regarding abortion: the reforms introduced by the Human Fertilisation and Embryology Act. A most significant feature of the parliamentary debates surrounding the reform is the pre-eminence of medical discourse and the marginalisation of other knowledges or ways of structuring dispute. Thus it seems that whilst the pro-choice movement has been successful in fending off the various attacks made on the 1967 Act, ground may have been lost with regard to popular assumptions about abortion. The agenda is unmistakably set within a medical framework and the issue of what is at stake in abortion debates centres essentially around the medical development of the foetus to the exclusion of broader social issues.

Moreover, the acceptance of a medical framework further entrenches and legitimates the medical control of abortion and would stand against any initiative to claim decisional control for women.

In Chapter 7, I discuss the decision to license the 'abortion pill', RU486, for use in Britain and examine the debates (both in and outside of Parliament) surrounding its introduction and the regulations introduced to regulate its use. This provides further illustration of many of the arguments made earlier in the book. The fact that RU486 was licensed for use in Britain with a minimum of public debate is again indicative of the extent to which abortion has become viewed as a medical phenomenon and the depoliticisation effected by such a construction. Many other countries have refused to consider licensing the drug or, where it has been licensed, this has typically excited fierce debate. In Britain, on the other hand, the drug was licensed with a minimum of controversy and media attention, but only within a framework of medical control which is tighter even than that required for surgical terminations. Emphasising again that the depoliticisation of abortion is only apparent, I argue that what debate occurred concerning the introduction of RU486, although played out in a largely medical rhetoric, can only be understood within the context of a struggle over the control of abortion (and female fertility). Likewise, only fears regarding who will control abortion can explain the stringent regulations introduced to govern the drug's use. Finally, I consider how drugs like RU486 may help to challenge commonly held assumptions about abortion.

In the concluding chapter, I draw together the strands of my argument in order to offer some thoughts on the implications of the medicalisation of abortion law. Here I will attempt to tease out two tensions which run throughout this work. First of these is an awareness that medicalisation has simultaneously brought both advantages and disadvantages. Whilst helping to secure women's access to the provision of abortion services, many of the problems which women now face in obtaining such services relate to medical control, rather than to legal prohibition. This, of course, poses the problem of how to respond to medicalisation and medical control. This second tension also raises difficult issues regarding the use of law in feminist campaigns. What role should legal reform now have in pro-choice campaigns? And what options for reform are now available?

A NOTE ON LANGUAGE

Throughout this work, I have adopted the now popular convention of referring to the individual or patient in the abstract as 'she'. I have been in some doubt as to how I should refer to the doctor. Whilst feminist writers have undoubtedly been right in challenging the sexist conventions which are embedded in our language, in some cases merely to change the convention obscures the issue. Part of the argument which follows rests on the claim that the doctor has been constructed as a male figure (as is particularly clear in Chapters 2 and 3). In this context, it would seem misleading to refer to the doctor as 'she': use of such a convention only serves to further conceal the implicitly gendered nature of this role. Consequently, I have adopted the masculine form when referring to the doctor or consultant. This is maintained throughout, notwithstanding the fact that this clearly gendered construction of the doctor has become less explicit over the last thirty years and many more women have entered the medical profession.

2
The Abortion Act 1967:
A Permissive and Liberatory Reform?

Permissive legislation is the characteristic of a free people
(Benjamin Disraeli).

It is generally accepted that the law relating to abortion is widely
disregarded, and that stricter enforcement would be difficult, and not
necessarily a deterrent when women are desperate, and prepared, if
no help is available, to operate upon themselves with instruments
or drugs. Legal sanctions do little more than provide an abortionist
with incentives to avoid detection, and so drive the offence
underground to an extent where a small fragment of 1 per cent of
abortionists is detected. On the other hand illegal abortion is
associated with deaths counted in hundreds each year, and causes
ill-health and serious damage to many women. Modest estimates of
illegal operations range between 50,000 and 100,000 annually, and
the figure of a quarter of a million has authority. It may appear that
the present law drives abortion into the most undesirable and
dangerous channels, without eliminating it (Dickens, 1966, p. 165).

INTRODUCTION

The 1960s saw a tidal wave of permissive indulgence, homosexual
as well as heterosexual. One-parent families, a huge boom in
contraceptives, a crusade for sexual indulgence in whatever form,
became accepted (Morgan in Thompson, 1993, p. 137).

The Oxford English Dictionary defines permissive as: 'Having the quality
of permitting or giving permission; that allows something to be done
or to happen; not forbidding or hindering. In modern use freq.:
tolerant, liberal, allowing freedom, *spec.* in sexual matters; freq. in phr.
permissive society' (emphasis in original). A permissive measure is thus
one which permits or tolerates certain behaviour, which limits the
potential of external bodies to intervene in the life of an individual to
correct or to punish certain acts, especially in sexual matters. Further,
in general usage, permissive would also seem to have acquired a more
specific meaning of describing something which loosens control over

sexuality and reproduction, and which contributes to the constitution of a 'private' sphere where sex (and its potential reproductive consequences) can be enjoyed free from external interference, regardless of the (lack of) procreative intention of the participants.

Against such a definition, it seems self-evident that the partial lifting of criminal controls over abortion in 1967 was a permissive measure which brought greater freedom for women. Such an understanding seems to be shared both by the liberals who condoned the passage of the Act and the conservatives who condemned it. However, such an account is problematic. Freedom seems to emerge as no more than a space for action created by the absence or limitation of repressive (criminal) legislation. One is free only in the sense of being free from one particular manifestation of repressive power which emanates from the state; other forms of power are ignored and no room is left for analysis of the quality or type of freedom which one may exercise.

Foucault and 'Governmentality'

In this chapter, I reread the Abortion Act, drawing on the writings of Michel Foucault. Behind the formally constituted egalitarian juridical framework of modern society, Foucault identified a foundational network of micro-powers or disciplines. He argued that the formal legal and political structures of the society are predicated upon relations of power which both guarantee a submission of forces and bodies, yet evade and undermine the formally constituted juridical limitations on the exercise of power. Modern society, Foucault argued, is a 'society of normalization, a society governed less by legal rights than by the authority of the human sciences' (1980b, p. 107).

Seen in this light, it becomes necessary to question in more detail to what extent the lifting or restriction of criminal prohibitions entails an increase in human freedom. What forms of power may continue to operate within the space which has been cleared by the drawing back of legal boundaries? What kind of freedom do women exercise under the Abortion Act? In his 1979 Tanner lectures, Foucault linked his ideas on disciplinary forms of power with the increasing governmentalisation or 'governmentality' of western society from the eighteenth century onwards. He argued that the same style of analysis which had been used to study techniques and practices addressed to individual human subjects within particular, local institutions could be addressed to techniques and practices for governing populations of subjects at the level of a political sovereignty over an entire society. These links between the macrophysics and microphysics of power developed his earlier idea of 'biopower': the explosion of numerous and diverse techniques for achieving the subjugation of bodies and the control of populations (1979b, pp. 140–1). Methods of power and knowledge here 'assumed responsibility for the life processes and undertook to manage them' (1979b, p. 144).

In the Tanner lectures, Foucault describes forms of power exercised over subjects as members of a population, within which issues of individual sexual and reproductive conduct interconnect with issues of national policy and power. Through statistics, the phenomenon of population was shown to have its own regularities, such as birth and death rates, characteristic ailments, age profiles, social groupings and so on, knowledge of which allowed it to be 'managed' more efficiently. Government became more 'pastoral', with a concern for the welfare of the population, and a range of new tactics and techniques of power emerged. Implicated here are social welfare programmes which, in aiming to provide for basic individual needs, instigate new, decentralised modalities of control, operating through state-sanctioned experts (social workers, doctors, psychiatrists, child care experts, teachers and so on). These experts are empowered to function as 'parallel judges' able to dispense justice at the local level after a close and minute examination of the individual case in hand. Political problems are thus recast in the neutral language of science, and then are debated and managed by specialists. Power is legitimated here by expert knowledge, and operates through surveillance, normalisation and judgement with the individual constructed as a subject for study and observation. Power develops at the micro level of such practices and is subsequently colonised, extended, overlaid and entrenched by more global forms of domination such as law. I hope to demonstrate that the regulation of abortion can be usefully viewed as one site within such a broader network of control.

A Permissive Reform?

The Abortion Act represented a liberalisation of the draconian terms of sections 58 and 59 of the Offences Against the Person Act 1861. It took English statute law from an almost complete ban on the performance of abortions to a system whereby terminations might be performed in certain circumstances given the approval of two doctors. The Abortion Act thus decreased repressive criminal controls and was seen to facilitate a greater degree of individual (especially female) autonomy in sexual and reproductive matters. Henceforth, it seems, a woman would be guaranteed a greater degree of privacy, autonomy and freedom in her decision to terminate a pregnancy. Such an understanding of the Act fits neatly with a prevalent tendency to assume a rather linear notion of progress with regard to the law. In such a perspective, masculine bias in law is seen as a kind of lingering anachronism: something which has been gradually eroded and (so the story goes) which will continue to be worn down, until the day that perfect formal and substantive equality and gender neutrality is achieved. Moreover, such a vision accords with a broader, often unstated view of society, and state power within that society: society is not yet perfect, but it is gradually getting better, the standard of living is always rising, people are healthier and wealthier than they were in the past, and the individual is gradually accorded more rights and more liberty as she achieves more protection from infringements on her private life. For an analysis of the Abortion Act, this rather linear concept could only state the Act to be an advance, albeit one which did not go far enough. The point is now to continue to push in the same direction to extend the good work already begun. Veteran pro-choice campaigner Madeleine Simms writes that 'the 1967 Abortion Act was a half-way house. It handed the abortion decision to the medical profession. The next stage is to hand this very personal decision to the woman herself' (1985, p. 94).

This vision of the Abortion Act as a permissive measure fits neatly into a powerful and dominant story which has been told about the late 1960s in Britain (see Weeks, 1989, Chapter 13). The latter half of the 'Swinging Sixties' is remembered not only for its permissive social mores, but also for the influence of these values on social policy, and the introduction of increasingly liberal, permissive legislation and humanising reform. A Labour Government, headed by Harold Wilson, was voted into power in 1964 and, having secured a larger majority of seats in 1966, it embarked on a substantial programme of social reform. The voting age was lowered to 18, divorce was made easier, access to contraception was facilitated, the death penalty was largely abolished, a more liberal attitude was taken towards the censorship of plays and gay male sex was decriminalised (albeit in very restricted circumstances). Many have seen these reforms in extravagant terms as signalling a shift to a new and more permissive Britain.

The reform of abortion law was a central piece of this programme. Although the Abortion Act results from a Private Member's Bill introduced by a young, Liberal MP, David Steel (Tweeddale, Ettrick and Lauderdale), it is clear that it could never have succeeded without Government help.[1] The dispute over abortion reform was seen in the light of a contest between enlightenment and obscurantism, its protagonists being cast respectively as 'the prisoners of the past' and 'forward looking minds'.[2] The Abortion Act was thus heralded as a crucial step in the process of women's emancipation,[3] and as a result of 'millions of women up and down the country . . . saying, "We will no longer tolerate this system whereby men lay down, as though by right, the moral laws, particularly those relating to sexual behaviour."'[4]

The vision of the Act as a permissive measure which liberalised, humanised and modernised the previous law provided the basis for both the liberal approbation and the conservative fears which greeted its passing. Conservative concern at the likely result of the liberalisation of abortion law were expressed as long ago as 1939, when the Birkett

Committee (an inter-departmental committee appointed by the Minister of Health and chaired by Norman Birkett QC) had concluded that abortion should be available only on medical grounds.[5] The Committee's feeling that to provide abortion at the woman's request would only aggravate the disturbing trend of the decline in the birth rate and prove an added temptation to loose and immoral conduct was still very much present in the late 1960s. In his book, *The Nameless*, published the year before the Abortion Act was passed, Paul Ferris wrote that

> one often meets the feeling that abortion, like contraception, is the thin end of a decadent wedge, a dangerous device to make sex easy for all. The trouble with protectives (says this argument) is that they can be bought by promiscuous bachelors as well as by prudent husbands. Similarly, even those who favour a more liberal attitude to abortion may be inhibited by the thought that any conceivable system short of one founded on explicit moral sanctions, can be used by tarts as well as by tired housewives (1966, pp. 10–11).

The extravagant language of a broadsheet put out in the late 1960s illustrates these concerns well.

> WANTED: for loitering with intent to murder innocent, unborn Children, a black-hearted monster going by the name of Abortion Bill, and last seen in the House of Commons where it was harboured, supported and assisted by a large number of M.P.s . . . If this Bill is not defeated it will be the beginning of the end of traditional Christian morality in this country. It will be followed by attempts to make divorce easier than at present and to legalize homosexuality – even to the extent of legal homosexual 'marriages'. There is no doubt whatever that once Abortion becomes legal there will be moves on foot for the sterilization of the unfit, and the killing of the sick and old and the socially useless . . . (Lamp Society of Bebington broadsheet, cited in Hindell and Simms, 1971, p. 89).

Liberals, however, welcomed the perceived permissive character of the reforms. Brian Lapping purports to identify a common theme running throughout a great many of the 'civilising measures' introduced during these years: the right to privacy. He writes that

> The Abortion and Family Planning Acts sought to ensure the right to privacy of a man and a woman who chose to make love. If they did not want to seek the public acknowledgement and approval of their conduct, called for by having a baby, these new measures helped to protect their privacy (1970, p. 218).

It seems that both liberal and conservative commentators share a similar view of the abortion law reforms, a view which I will argue falls victim to the same misapprehension. To see the Abortion Act as a permissive measure which decreases the deployment of power over women is at best a partial vision. In the rest of this chapter, I will give an account of the partial decriminalisation of abortion, concentrating on the arguments expressed in favour of reform. I will begin by briefly sketching the background to the Abortion Act by way of an overview of the development of the law and medical practices until 1967. My claim is that the Abortion Act, rather than being a 'permissive' measure which sought to delineate space for autonomous female action, was actually largely motivated by the legislator's desire to facilitate a closer control over this private and hitherto inaccessible sphere. Such an analysis provides a much clearer explanation for the form of the regulation which the Abortion Act introduces than can be gleaned from any understanding of the reform as a permissive measure.

THE DEVELOPMENT OF THE LAW UNTIL 1967

Statute Law

Abortion law was an area where reform seemed long overdue. Inside and outside of Parliament, there was widespread desire for change and modernisation. Indeed in the 15 years preceding the introduction of the Abortion Act 1967, there had been no fewer than five parliamentary initiatives aiming at reform.[6] The Offences Against the Person Act 1861 which governed the regulation of abortion, had been widely criticised as anachronistic and archaic. That Act provides that

s.58 Every woman being with child, who, with intent to procure her own miscarriage shall unlawfully administer to herself any poison or other noxious thing, or shall unlawfully use any instrument or other means whatsoever with the like intent, and whosoever, with intent to procure the miscarriage of any woman, whether she be or be not with child, shall unlawfully administer to her or cause to be taken by her any poison or other noxious thing, or shall unlawfully use any instrument or other means whatsoever with the like intent, shall be guilty of an offence and being convicted thereof shall be liable to imprisonment.

s.59 Whosoever shall unlawfully supply or procure any poison or other noxious thing, or any instrument or thing whatsoever, knowing that the same is intended to be unlawfully used or employed with intent to procure the miscarriage of any woman, whether she be or be not with child, shall be guilty of an offence, and being convicted thereof shall be liable to imprisonment for a term not exceeding five years.

These sections contained no time limit, made no distinction between abortions early and late in pregnancy[7] and contained no explicit exception for therapeutic abortion.

A time limit was later read into the Offences Against the Person Act by virtue of the Infant Life (Preservation) Act 1929. The latter statute had not been introduced in order to deal with abortion. Rather it was intended to close a legal loophole whereby the killing of the foetus/baby in the actual process of being born was covered neither by the Offences Against the Person Act (which foresaw an offence only where miscarriage was procured) nor by the law of murder (which requires the unlawful killing of 'a person in being' – a legal status only acquired upon birth). Where a baby was killed during the process of (spontaneous) birth, but before being fully separated from the body of the pregnant woman, no offence was committed. The Infant Life (Preservation) Act introduced the offence of child destruction, s.1(1) prohibiting the destruction of a child 'capable of being born alive', making an exception only for the case where its destruction was carried out in good faith for the purpose of preserving the life of the pregnant woman.[8] The Act included a rebuttable presumption that this capacity for life was acquired at 28 weeks of gestation. This limit was read into the Offences Against the Person Act (and later the Abortion Act) as prohibiting abortion after this time, except where the additional requirements of the Infant Life (Preservation) Act were also fulfilled.[9]

Medical Practice and Jurisprudence
However, access to legal abortion prior to 1967 was not nearly so restricted in practice as it might appear from a reading of statute. Medical practitioners had long found some room for manoeuvre in the prescription and performance of abortions and the decision in *R* v. *Bourne* (1938)[10] had given explicit judicial approval to the exercise of medical discretion for therapeutic terminations. Dr Bourne had aborted a 15-year-old girl who had been raped by a group of soldiers. Rather than basing his case on an appeal to humanity, he defended himself on grounds of good medical practice, asserting that the girl's mental and physical health might have suffered had the pregnancy continued. Macnaghten J, who presided over the case, linked the 1861 and 1929 statutes, and ruled that the burden rested on the Crown to satisfy the jury that the defendant did not procure the miscarriage of the girl for the purpose of preserving her life. He reasoned (very creatively) that although these words were contained in the Infant Life (Preservation) Act and not in the Offences Against the Person Act (under which Bourne was charged), they were *implied* in the latter by the presence

there of the word 'unlawful' (which logically presupposed that in certain circumstances abortion must, on the contrary, be lawful). He told the jury that they should take a broad view of what was meant by preserving the life of the mother:

> If the doctor is of the opinion, on reasonable grounds and with adequate knowledge, that the probable consequences of the continuance of the pregnancy will be to make the woman a physical and mental wreck, the jury are quite entitled to take the view that the doctor, who, in those circumstances, and in that honest belief, operates, is operating for the purpose of preserving the life of the woman.[11]

In 1948, *R* v. *Bergmann and Ferguson*[12] clarified this decision. Here, the judge held that it was not relevant whether Dr Ferguson (the psychiatrist who had certified the need for termination) held a *correct* opinion as to the existence of such grounds for termination, so long as it was *honestly held*. This was emphasised again in *R* v. *Newton and Stungo*:

> use of an instrument is unlawful unless the use is made in good faith for the purpose of preserving the life or health of the woman. When I say health I mean not only her physical health but also her mental health. But I must emphasise that the burden of proof that it was not used in good faith is on the crown.[13]

Thus, as long as the doctor acted in good faith, therapeutic abortion was legal. Indeed, even before the *Bourne* judgment, it is clear that abortions had been performed by doctors for therapeutic purposes, according to criteria established by themselves (Keown, 1988, p. 78). Provided that practitioners abided by professional ethics, there seems to have been little risk of prosecution. The bringing of a case against Dr Bourne was no exception to this as Bourne seems to have actively courted his prosecution, informing the police of the operation himself and inviting them to arrest him (Bourne, 1962). Of the four doctors involved in the other two cases mentioned above, the only conviction was of one who was clearly acting outside the terms of what was accepted to be good medical practice (see Chapter 5, pp. 81–2 for a more detailed consideration of these cases). A 1884 report in the *Lancet* commented that the strongest evidence should be forthcoming before a doctor was brought to account for carrying out the operation or even for the death of his patient, for, 'Even if a medical practitioner is known to have procured abortion, the presumption is that it was done in the legal exercise of his calling.'[14]

The combination of a climate of social reform with very restrictive legislation (and wide variation in medical interpretation of it) formed the backdrop for the introduction of the 1967 Abortion Act.

THE NEED FOR REFORM

The Abortion Act represents the outcome of struggles between different groups expressing competing interests and opinions. Particularly important in the process of instigating reform was the work of women's campaign groups, notably the Abortion Law Reform Association, and the influence of professional medical bodies. Various factors contributed to a climate sympathetic to reform: the role of illegal abortions in sustaining high figures of maternal mortality, concern and sympathy for the situation of women facing unwanted pregnancy, an unequal application of the law (with a thriving private sector in the provision of abortion) and the lack of a well-organised opposition to reform were all vital. Whilst recognising the significance of such activity, it is also important that state and law should not be viewed merely as neutral sites where struggle between these groups might be played out. Here, I give greater weight to a government interest in managing the social problem of abortion and bringing under control a situation of widespread illegality and *de facto* female resistance to the law. Below I group the motivations for reform which I believe to have been the most important into two major categories: the protection of medical discretion and autonomy and a desire to bring women out of the backstreets and into contact with their GPs. The former of these has already received some attention (see especially Keown, 1988; Thomson, forthcoming) and so will be covered in less detail here. The latter has been largely neglected.

Protection of Medical Autonomy and Discretion

Groups representing the interests of the medical profession exerted considerable influence on the development of the Abortion Act (as indeed they have done with earlier and later abortion legislation). Keown notes that none of the major medical bodies opposed reform as such, but that the profession was firmly opposed to any reform which compromised clinical freedom either by taking the final decision out of the hands of the doctor or by specifying the indications for abortion too exactly (1988, p. 87). In the late 1960s, many prominent members of the medical profession were opposed to what they saw as the intrusion of the law into the sphere of medical power. Moreover, the situation of semi-legality of many abortions left them in a position of uncertainty with regard to potential prosecution. There were also feelings of anger and resentment amongst many that whereas some doctors desisted from performing any abortions, less timid colleagues in the higher echelons of the profession were collecting large fees.

Restriction of Professional Autonomy
There had long been resentment within the medical profession that the law should restrict their freedom to act in the best interests of their patients. John Keown (1988) argues that the desire to protect professional autonomy was central to the position adopted by the various groups. This led medical professionals to call for the law to ensure the elimination of abortion by untrained and unskilled personnel. As Michael Thomson has cogently argued, this relates directly to the occupational concerns of a profession keen to entrench its own position and to establish its own dominance in the area of reproduction (forthcoming). Further, doctors opposed any rigid codification of the indications for abortion which might lead patients to expect a right to termination where given circumstances were met (see below, pp. 27–8).

Fear of Prosecution
There seems to have been very little real risk of prosecution of a qualified medical practitioner who performed abortions prior to 1967 so long as he acted in conformity with medical practice. As has already been seen, this was especially true after the case of *R* v. *Bourne* had clarified the operation of the law. However, for the medical profession the protection offered by the law seemed fragile and ambiguous, granting only 'a tenuous and ill-defined right to induce abortion' (Hordern, 1971, p. 9). *Bourne* seemed to have carried the law far beyond the intention and the letter of the statutes. Moreover, it had been decided not in the House of Lords or Court of Appeal, but merely in the High Court (and might consequently have been overruled by a subsequent decision at a higher level). Finally, a great deal rested on whether the doctor could establish that a pregnancy had been terminated in good faith and that it was his honest opinion that unless he had done so the consequences would have been grave.

Many practitioners thus remained reluctant to carry out terminations for fear of prosecution (Harvard, 1958; Ferris, 1966). Harley Street doctors would take precautions to cover their backs by obtaining a second opinion, normally from a psychiatrist who would testify to the effect of continuing a pregnancy on the woman's mental health. Other less wealthy doctors would operate in semi-clandestinity. Such secrecy was in itself dangerous however as it could be taken as a sign of bad faith. It was such doctors who were more open to prosecution. Moreover, doctors were restricted from charging high fees, given that this in itself could be taken as an indication of bad faith (Harvard, 1958, p. 609; Ferris, 1966).[15]

'Legal', Private Abortions
Large numbers of abortions of dubious legality were occurring in the private sector for those women who could afford them. Francome estimates that in 1966, 15,000 pregnancies were terminated in the private sector and 5,700 in the National Health Service (1986, p. 27). In her minority opinion to the Birkett Report, Dorothy Thurtle noted that it was not difficult 'for any woman of moderate means to find a medical man willing to relieve her of an unwelcome pregnancy regardless of the state of her health' (in Brookes, 1988, p. 124). It seems that by the late 1960s, a 'legal' termination was available to any woman who had a certain amount of persistence and the necessary 100 or so guineas to pay for one. The price could rise even higher than this. Ferris notes that,

> where the surgeon considers that a woman, her husband or her lover can afford more, the fees go up. Hearsay puts them as high as £400 or £500, though the highest I heard anyone admit to was £250 – 'If they can afford to pay,' he said, 'I have no hesitation in jacking up my fee' (1966, p. 103).

Inevitably there were allegations of social inequality in the operation of the law with Alice Jenkins giving her 1960 book on abortion the title of *Law for the Rich*. Introducing his own (failed) attempt to reform the law in 1961, Kenneth Robinson MP (Lab., St Pancras N) said

> It is a perfectly simple matter for anyone who has sufficient money to get a pregnancy terminated today by a qualified medical practitioner on the flimsiest of medical grounds . . . This leads in the simplest possible terms to a situation in which there is one law for the rich and one law for the poor. If there were no other arguments for amending the law, I submit that is a very powerful one.[16]

This failure to prosecute senior obstetricians and gynaecologists who collected large fees for performing terminations also provoked resentment amongst their more junior colleagues. One doctor told the Birkett Committee that 'patients for whom I have without difficulty refused to evacuate the uterus have had the operation performed in London' (Simms, 1980, p. 1).

Bringing Women from the Backstreets to the GP's Surgery

Reducing Maternal Mortality
The major aim of the pressure group most active in pushing for reform seems to have been to bring some relief to the suffering of those women who experienced unwanted pregnancy. The formation of the

Abortion Law Reform Association in 1936 had been provoked by the plight of women who had previously faced risky backstreet abortions, and who had often suffered serious physical complications as a result of having them.[17] Official estimates showed that 35–40 women died each year as a result of botched abortions, but unofficial sources guessed at a far higher figure.[18] The parliamentary debates preceding the introduction of the 1967 Act are littered with tragic examples of women who have died either during illegal abortions or as a result of being forced to continue with an unwanted pregnancy, and who leave families behind them. A particularly distressing account is given by Lena Jeger MP (Lab., Holborn and St Pancras S), who relates the story of an 'honest young woman' who was refused a termination on the grounds that 'she did not seem quite depressed enough'. Forced to continue with the pregnancy, the woman's depression following the birth of the child was so great that she killed it. She was sent to Holloway prison, and her other five children were put into care.[19] However, the desire to improve the situation of women facing unwanted pregnancy was not translated into a desire to give women greater autonomy. Rather, as is shown in the next chapter, these women were not seen as sufficiently stable or rational to make important reproductive decisions. Whilst the reformers believed that women seeking abortion had been wrongly stigmatised as criminals, they represented them as victims who needed help and guidance.

The difficulty of legally terminating a pregnancy was implicated in sustained high maternal mortality figures, which had consistently refused to improve in line with other health statistics. Indeed by 1966 illegal abortion had become the chief cause of avoidable maternal death (Brookes, 1988, p. 133) at a time when four women in a thousand died for reasons relating to maternity (Jenkins, 1960, p. 47). According to Mason (1990, p. 105), pathologists of the period taught that in cases of the unexpected death of a young woman, pregnancy should be suspected until its existence was positively disproved. Likewise, Francome relates that at the beginning of the nineteenth century, women of childbearing age were routinely examined for a blue line on the gums which was indicative of lead poisoning (1984, p. 33). Taking lead-based products was a common way of trying to provoke a miscarriage.

The Threat to the Family
The related threat to the family was another powerful argument for reform. Many examples are given in the parliamentary debates of cases where the family had suffered as a result of losing the wife and mother who was its central focus and binding force. The abortion reformer Joan Malleson wrote:

it happens that with the invalidism or death of these mothers, the family disintegrates; for around their health and their capacity to tend the children the whole home revolves: and therefore these mothers are the very last who should be permitted to jeopardize their well-being (1938, cited in Jenkins, 1960, p. 37).

This loss of mother and wife might result from the woman's death following an unsafe, illegal abortion or as a result of the suicide of the woman faced with an unwanted pregnancy (Jenkins, 1960, pp. 76–7).[20] Equally, the effective loss of the mother might be caused by the additional strain which she faced in having another child – particularly a disabled one (see Chapter 3). The thalidomide tragedies of the early 1960s had contributed to the creation of a greater public sympathy for women seeking abortion. As Dr John Dunwoody (Lab., Falmouth and Camborne), himself a GP, told Parliament:

my belief is that in many cases today where we have over-large families the mother is so broken down physically and emotionally with the continual bearing of children that it becomes quite impossible for her to fulfil her real function, her worthwhile function as a mother, of holding together the family unit, so that all too often the family breaks apart, and it is for this reason that we have so many problem families in many parts of the country.[21]

David Owen (Lab., Plymouth, Sutton) outlines the same problem: the woman facing an unwanted pregnancy is

in total misery, and could be precipitated into a depression deep and lasting. What happens to that woman when she gets depressed? She is incapable of looking after those children, so she retires into a shell of herself and loses all feeling, all her drive and affection.[22]

Backstreet Abortions: a Consistent Flouting of the Law
Dickens concludes his book on abortion and the law with the assertion that 'the present law drives abortion into the most undesirable and dangerous channels, without eliminating it' (1966, p. 165). This is symptomatic of the widespread agreement which had been reached by the late 1960s that the regulation of abortion was a failure. This failure was not measured entirely – or even primarily – in humanitarian terms, but rather in functionalist ones: the law was unpopular, ineffective and constantly flouted. As such, an important reason which was advanced for the partial decriminalisation of abortion in Britain was the need to take control of a situation where 'the administration of the law has broken down [and] it is neither respected nor obeyed'.[23]

The Birkett Committee had reported in 1939 that 'We are satisfied that the law in this matter is freely disregarded among women of all types and classes.' Speaking thirty years later to the House of Commons, Roy Jenkins (then Home Secretary) was in agreement. He argued that the present regulations were unable to deal with the problem. Decriminalisation would serve to bring unwanted pregnancy and abortion within the ambit of a medical control, where they might thus be more effectively monitored:

> the existing law on abortion is uncertain and is also, and perhaps more importantly, harsh and archaic and . . . is in urgent need of reform . . . How can anyone believe otherwise when perhaps as many as 100,000 illegal operations per year take place, that the present law has shown itself quite unable to deal with the problem? . . . the law is consistently flouted by those who have the means to do so . . . it causes many otherwise thoroughly law-abiding citizens to act on the fringe, or perhaps on the wrong side of the law. As the Minister responsible for law enforcement, I believe that to be a thoroughly bad thing.[24]

Paul Ferris concurs:

> Britain has been magnificently hypocritical, maintaining that in general abortion is wrong, but fitfully turning a blind eye when the law is interpreted so as to allow abortion for a variety of reasons . . . the result has been to squeeze the law so hard, and make it look so ridiculous, that reform of some kind is now in sight. The authorities' inability to stop illegal abortion brought the law into contempt for a hundred years (1966, p. 14).

Illegal backstreet abortions were not a new phenomenon but media reporting and the growth in public awareness had made it increasingly hard to ignore their widespread occurrence. It was impossible to judge accurately how many illegal abortions per year were performed, but estimates ranged from 10,000 to 250,000 (Dickens, 1966, p. 73).[25] The Birkett Committee found that 'many mothers seemed not to understand that self-induced abortion was illegal. They assumed it was legal before the third month, and only outside the law when procured by another person' (cited in Lewis, 1984, p. 17).

Prosecutions for illegal abortions represented just the very tip of this iceberg, with convictions numbering an average of around 50 per year (Williams, 1958, p. 192). There were 62 prosecutions for illegal abortions in England and Wales in 1966, only 28 of which resulted in prison sentences (Mason, 1990, p. 105). As with all 'victimless crimes', offences were hard to detect. The police were largely tolerant of the activities of abortionists unless they were forced to act – for example, if a woman died during or following an abortion or where she was brought to the hospital with serious complications such as a septic abortion or perforated uterus. From the police's point of view, abortion cases were time-consuming and awkward, since the woman, who was generally required as a witness, was naturally reluctant to bring evidence against the abortionist who had relieved her of an unwanted pregnancy. As one police officer related

> it is gratitude to the person who has relieved them of an unwanted burden that keeps the victims of abortion silent. For this type of help, gratitude wells up in the heart to subdue every other sense. Even when dying they hug their secret gratefully, refusing to divulge the name of the person who has brought them to this impasse (Williams, 1958, p. 190).

Moreover, the public were often unwilling to help with enquiries. David Steel gives the example of a 24-year-old woman found dying in a North London street following an illegal abortion. He quotes from the *Evening Standard*: 'After hearing from the police that they had been unable to find out where the abortion took place, the St. Pancras coroner said: "We are up against a blank wall of unwillingness to know and unwillingness to talk."'[26]

Likewise, Ferris cites several interviews with police officers who spoke of their reluctance to prosecute abortionists. One superintendent told him, 'we know there's lots going on. but we don't prosecute unless we're forced to' (1966, p. 92). Where prosecutions were brought, it was long-established practice to charge only the abortionist.[27] In the rare cases where charges were brought against the pregnant woman, juries were unwilling to convict, probably as a result of sympathy with her situation.

Many of the backstreet abortionists commanded huge popular support, especially where they were known to have acted through sympathy for the woman rather than for pecuniary reasons (Ferris, 1966, p. 88; Simms, 1981, p. 179; Brookes, 1988, p. 140). Simms reports on the funeral of a 'well-known abortionist', Dr Daniel Powell of Tooting, which was attended by women from all parts of the country. When Dr Powell had been prosecuted, his patients had collected the money for his defence. One detective who had been on his trail for some years said, 'he was a great hearted and fearless man whose work was directed by the highest motives' (Simms, 1981, pp. 173–4). Hindell and Simms (1971, pp. 38–9) likewise relate the case of William Tellam, who was sentenced to three years' imprisonment for carrying out illegal abortions in his surgery. Instead of being regarded as a villain, Tellam was a kind of hero figure and 18,000 people signed a petition asking for clemency in his case. Dora Russell, founder of the Abortion Law Reform Association, wrote in the *Guardian* regarding his prosecution:

> Our inhuman and obsolete law against abortion has now claimed a fresh victim in one of the best and ablest medical men practising in Penzance . . . It is tragic that even a skilled practitioner who comes to the help of women pregnant and desperate, is liable to disgrace and punishment (Hindell and Simms, 1971, p. 39).

Brookes reports several other cases where patients collected petitions sometimes with many thousands of signatures in support of doctors convicted for performing abortions (1988, pp. 140–1).

THE PERCEIVED BENEFITS OF REFORM

In such a climate of mass illegality and popular resistance to enforcement of the law, a partial and controlled decriminalisation of abortion had much support in Parliament. Even the staunchest opponents of abortion agreed that some kind of reform was needed.[28] This may have been inspired in part by compassion for the plight of the woman, but more important was the clear need to bring this situation of widespread illegality and *de facto* female resistance to the law under control. Steel, in introducing the second reading of his Bill, emphasised that 'We want to stamp out the back street abortions, but it is not the intention of the Promoters of the Bill to leave a wide open door for abortion on request.'[29] The Abortion Act aimed to abolish backstreet abortion by granting registered medical practitioners a legal monopoly on the termination of pregnancy. This would install the medical profession as the gatekeepers or 'parallel judges' who could grant or refuse access to termination according to how deserving an individual case was felt to be. 'Liberalisation' was thus proposed and accepted (at least in part) to bring under control a situation of mass illegality, and to ensure that the incidence of abortion might be more closely monitored.

The model of legislation adopted in the Abortion Act clearly reflects these aims. It permits women seeking termination to be brought under closer medical control, it safeguards medical autonomy and discretion, and at the same time it renders abortion visible, enabling it to be monitored by way of a system of registration and provisions regulating where terminations might be performed.

Bringing Women under Medical Control

The Abortion Act is fundamentally underpinned by the idea that reproduction is an area for medical control and expertise and that the doctor is the most appropriate expert to deal with abortion. This reflects not merely a belief in his technical expertise, but also the notion that the doctor is in the best position to observe the woman, assess her needs and interests, and take charge of her situation. The doctor is here seen as taking on many of the pastoral functions which have in previous times been associated with the priest: he is a guardian of the social body and a bastion of moral values.[30] Peter Mahon MP (Lab., Preston S) reminds the House of Commons that 'it would be as well if we applauded the work of some of these men to keep our homes and families and the country right.'[31] The Abortion Act accords clear moral authority to the doctor, in that it is he who has the final decision regarding abortion.

The granting of such power to doctors in the field of abortion is often justified by the argument that abortion is essentially a medical matter. However, the actual decision whether or not a given pregnancy should be terminated is not normally one that requires expert medical advice, or the balancing of medical criteria. Further, the doctors' decision-making power is not, according to the terms of the Abortion Act, contained within a narrow, limited medical field. In judging whether or not abortion could be detrimental to the mental or physical health of the pregnant woman or existing children of her family, under s.1(2) of the Act, 'account may be taken of the pregnant woman's actual or reasonably foreseeable environment.' The woman's whole lifestyle, her home, finances and relationships are opened up to the doctor's scrutiny, so that he may judge whether or not the patient is a deserving case for relief. The power given to doctors here far exceeds that which would accrue merely on the basis of a technical expertise.

The terms of the Abortion Act are strongly influenced by the notion that social factors are inseparable from medical ones. After the Act came into force, David Steel argued that 'social conditions cannot be and ought not to be separated from medical considerations. I hope that the Abortion Act by its very drafting has encouraged the concept of socio-medical care' (1971, p. 7). This can be seen as part of an ongoing expansion of the authority of the medical professional over an ever greater area of human life (see, in particular, Illich, 1977; Zola, 1972, 1977).

The casting of abortion as a matter for medicine has had a particular effect in the way abortion has come to be viewed. Science – and especially medicine – has a special role in justifying a particular type of power, and making its exercise seem logical and neutral (Foucault, 1980b, p. 107). Scientific knowledges can legitimate and depoliticise, providing grounds for making what might otherwise be seen as an inherently political decision seem neutral or commonsensical and this will be clearly seen in some of the following chapters. Medicine has played a pivotal role in establishing and legitimating the techniques essential to the operation of such power: it is by identifying individual anomalies medically that the technologies of bio-power are in a position to supervise and administer them. Within medicine, the operation of power becomes justified by the patient's own 'best interests'.

In the case of abortion, it was hoped that mere contact with the responsible and reassuring figure of the doctor might dissuade the woman from seeking to terminate a pregnancy – the need for an abortion often being posited here as a direct consequence of her own hysteria and derangement, rather than a rational decision reflecting a reasoned assessment of her concrete situation. The point is repeatedly made in the parliamentary debates that the rule of the doctor would be one of taking control of the pregnancy and managing it in a responsible way.[32] The Bill's sponsor, David Steel, argues that 'if we can manage to get a [pregnant, unmarried] girl . . . into the hands of the medical profession, the Bill is succeeding in its objective'.[33] Over twenty years later, Steel picks up on this same argument to illustrate the success of the Abortion Act. He relates that doctors have told him that they now have the chance to see women before they abort and to discourage them from doing so. According to one doctor:

> One of the effects of the 1967 legislation has been that people will come to his surgery and discuss abortion with him, whereas pre-1967 they would not have done so and he would have lost control of what was happening, and the patient might have ended up with a backstreet abortion or going into a private clinic.[34]

David Owen (Lab., Plymouth, Sutton) expresses the same sentiment later in the 1966–7 debates, noting that

> If we allow abortion to become lawful under certain conditions, a woman will go to her doctor and discuss with him the problems which arise . . . he may well be able to offer that support which is necessary for her to continue to full term and successfully to have a child.[35]

The same argument also arises in the academic literature. The eminent academic lawyer Glanville Williams was closely involved with the Abortion Law Reform Association and helped with the drafting of the Abortion Act. Asserting the need for reform, he argued that

> An important medical result of legalizing abortion would be that it would enable the patient to take proper professional advice. It is, of course, always open to a doctor to dissuade his patient from the operation by pointing out any harmful effects that he thinks it may have (1958, pp. 203–4).

In short, the Abortion Act would serve to encourage the woman into the hands of the medical profession, who can take control of the situation and manage her pregancy in her best interests.

Medical Autonomy
The law clearly aims to protect medical autonomy and discretion rather than to grant substantive rights to the woman, even where she is in the most extreme circumstances envisaged by the reformers. The severely depressed mother of five, described by Lena Jeger (see p. 20 above), still would have no *right* to a termination. Rather, the regime introduced by the Abortion Act offers the qualified doctor (and only derivatively his patient) a valid defence against the crime of unlawful procurement of miscarriage under the Offences Against the Person Act for a termination where this has been medically authorised and performed. Thus, s.1(1) provides that,

> a person shall not be guilty of an offence under the law relating to abortion when a pregnancy is terminated by a registered medical practitioner if two registered medical practitioners are of the opinion formed in good faith . . . [that certain conditions are fulfilled].

This is important in that the law serves to grant woman and doctor together some rights against the state, but grants the woman no right to privacy or autonomy *vis-à-vis* the doctor.

The clear desire to avoid according any substantive rights to women is most clearly illustrated by the debates centring around whether the Abortion Act should carry a 'social clause' (whereby the need for abortion might be established with regard to socio-economic factors), and/or a clause allowing abortion in case of rape or incest. Steel's original Medical Termination of Pregnancy Bill did carry such clauses, clause 1(c) allowing doctors to authorise abortion where 'the pregnant woman's capacity as a mother will be severely overstrained by the care of a child or of another child as the case may be' and clause 1(d) where 'the pregnant woman is a defective or became pregnant while under the age of sixteen or became pregnant as a result of rape'.

These clauses were, however, opposed by all of the major medical bodies, who felt that women might interpret them to mean they had a *right* to demand abortions where the circumstances outlined were met (Keown, 1988, p. 87). For example, the Royal Medico-Psychological Association warned that

> Spelling out in detail when a doctor should or should not have the right to induce abortion, even if the legislation is cast in permissive terms, would have the effect of introducing an element of coercion in the sense that in each defined situation the patient might

reasonably expect the doctor to acquiesce and the role of the surgeon or gynaecologist would be reduced to that of a technician carrying out an objectionable task (Keown, 1988, p. 89).[36]

As a result of pressure from medical bodies, the two clauses were subsequently removed. It was argued that in case of rape or incest, abortion would already be available under other provisions, notably the risk to the woman's mental health. To remove the clause would mean that women would not feel they had an automatic right to termination in these circumstances and would minimise the risk of their fabricating stories of rape in order to qualify for an abortion.[37] Hindell and Simms comment forcefully:

> David Steel, the medical profession, and the Government were propounding the view that the law must not be made too clear lest the public read it and began to demand their rights. Much better to leave it vague and fuzzy so that doctors would have total discretion in the matter of abortion and so that patients would be unable to argue (1971, p. 185).

The social clause was likewise removed and was replaced with wording which, whilst allowing social and economic factors to be taken into account, made it absolutely clear that they should be evaluated by the doctor and not the woman herself. Thus, under section 1(2), the doctor is now authorised to determine whether continuance of pregnancy would involve such risks to life or to mental and physical health as are specified in section 1(1) to take account 'of the pregnant woman's actual or reasonably foreseeable environment'.[38] This ensures that socio-economic factors are assessed only in so far as they are subject to assessment by a doctor and that the doctor, rather than the woman herself, thus remains the ultimate judge even with regard to such factors.

Both Houses of Parliament debated the possibility of inserting a 'consultant clause' whereby one of the two certifying doctors would need to be a consultant obstetrician/gynaecologist. It was felt that this would provide an additional control on the provision of abortion services and guard against possibility of their becoming too widely available. Ultimately, however, the clause was not included. Lord Kennet speaking in the House of Lords at the final debate on the clause commented that

> The point here is that no Minister of Health has ever arrogated to himself the right to say 'This class of doctor shall carry out a surgical operation and that class of doctor shall not' and the present Minister of Health is unwilling to be the first to arrogate to himself that right.[39]

Monitoring the Incidence of Abortion

Another perceived advantage to the strict medical control was that abortion might be made more visible and hence more easily monitored and controlled. Section 1(3) of the Abortion Act provides that any treatment for the termination of pregnancy must be carried out in a hospital vested in the Minister of Health or the Secretary of State, or in a place approved by either for the purposes of the section.[40] Henceforward, abortions would be performed only in hospitals or specially licensed premises. The Abortion Act foresaw a system where doctors might be made responsible for notifying the performance of abortions, so that their incidence might be better measured and recorded. Under section 2, there is a duty for the Minister of Health (or the Secretary of State for Scotland) to ensure that any practitioner who terminates a pregnancy must provide to the Ministry of Health (or Scottish Home and Health Department), 'such notice of the termination and such other information relating to the termination as may be so prescribed'. Under section 4(1) of the Abortion Regulations, the operating practitioner is required to notify the abortion to the Chief Medical Officer, within seven days.[41] This makes possible the yearly publication of statistics by the Office of Population Censuses and Surveys (OPCS), recording the number of abortions, reasons for performing them, the number of foreign women having abortions in Britain, the method of abortion, the number of weeks of gestation, whether women are married or single, how many children they have already and whether the abortions are performed on the NHS or in private clinics. These statistics also enable comparisons with similar foreign data.

A dark mass of unknowable female criminality which had been perceived as profoundly threatening to the existing social order (and, in particular, to the family) is thus brought into the open, and isolated in the bodies of individual women where it can be contained, monitored and controlled. The problem of abortion is changed from one of widespread and unquantifiable dev*iance*, to one of isolated, identifiable and treatable individual dev*iants*. The construction of these deviants will be further explored in the following chapter where the contraindications justifying a termination of pregnancy will be considered in more detail.

CONCLUSIONS

In passing the Abortion Bill, Parliament may be regarded as having promoted the policies of the social welfare state or the attitudes of a permissive society. Alternatively, it can be considered as a contribution to women's rights. Yet the main outcome of the Bill, welcomed by the sponsors and hated by the opponents, is to give abortion a degree of respectability it lacked before. No longer is it largely hush-hush, back street or Harley Street. Instead it is authorised by statute, subject to conditions that are not unduly restrictive (Richards, 1970, p. 111).

In this chapter, I have marked an important shift in the state's attempts to bring under control women seeking to terminate pregnancies. Here, focusing on the aims of the Abortion Act, I have taken issue with the received understanding of that statute as an essentially permissive measure which envisages a loosening of control over abortion and implicitly over reproduction and (female) sexuality. Viewed in such a light, the Abortion Act has been understood as both interpretative and constitutive of the development of a private sphere where sex may be enjoyed free from public interference and without regard to the (lack of) procreative intention of the participants. I have challenged this representation in arguing that whilst the Abortion Act has facilitated women's access to safer, legal terminations, it also represented a new way of striving to reach a certain social and political end: to increase control over a situation of widespread illegality by implementing a more subtle deployment of power over women and a more efficient way of managing this 'private sphere' of sexuality. Women's sexuality and fertility has in this sense been rendered *more* visible by the passing of the Abortion Act. This 'private' sphere of action is now open to extensive examination by doctors (as will be seen in Chapter 4).

The problematisation of the connection between seemingly humanising reform and a loosening of power which has underpinned this chapter owes a debt to the work of Michel Foucault. Foucault has written that the reduction in penal severity in the last 200 years has long been regarded in an overall way as a quantitative phenomenon: 'less cruelty, less pain, more kindness, more respect, more "humanity"' (1991, p. 16). He argues, however, that these changes are also qualitative in nature, representing a new, more efficient, strategy in the deployment of power. Foucault's (1979a) work on 'governmentality' details the emergence of 'the population' as the new target of government which ushered in social welfare policies and new forms of control aiming less at sporadic and spectacular interventions, and more at fine and continuous surveillance and modification. In this light, the Abortion Act can be seen as part of a shift in political rationality in the 1950s and 1960s, with reforming legislation reconstructing modes of control.

The Abortion Act undoubtedly served in one way to lessen a particular modality of direct state control over abortion, by taking certain terminations out of the ambit of control of the criminal courts.[42] However, in the same process, indirect (medical) control was greatly enhanced and power was extended over the woman's 'private' sphere of action. Through the Abortion Act, the doctors, as 'parallel judges', are officially accorded the power to judge the woman and then to decide whether she should have the possibility of an abortion, or whether she should be denied relief and made to face the 'punishment' of being forced to continue with an unwanted pregnancy. As will be explored in the following chapter, within the regulations introduced by the Abortion Act, women are decriminalised in order to be pathologised,[43] to be made subject to the judgment not of the judiciary but of the 'parallel judges' of the medical profession. The partial decriminalisation of abortion corresponded with a finer deployment of power by way of a colonisation of existing lines of medical control and a legitimation, entrenchment and extension of those lines. Further, there is an attempt to make use of these lines, by way of the notification procedure and the control of premises, to monitor the incidence of abortion.[44]

If the Abortion Act is seen as representing not a lessening of control, but rather a shift in the modalities of control towards a more refined means of deploying power, the kind of freedom which women can exercise under it becomes more problematic, and in need of further analysis. This task will be taken up in Chapter 4.

3
'Tarts and Tired Housewives':
The Abortion Act and the
Regulation of Femininity

I believe that we must attempt to study the myriad of bodies which are constituted as peripheral subjects as a result of power (Foucault, 1980b, p. 98).

There are women who suffer from illnesses, which . . . will . . . make [them] less able to bear the burdens of motherhood . . . There is the case of the woman who is in prison, serving a long term commencing between the beginning of the pregnancy and the time at which she will give birth. Obviously that woman is inadequate to be a mother of a child. There is the persistent offender, or the shop-lifter, and there is the mother who has in the past been found guilty of neglecting or ill-treatment of her existing children. These are some of the cases I have in mind. There is the drug taker or the alcoholic. I am sure the right reverend Prelate (the Bishop of Exeter) would not suggest that such a mother is a fit person to be in charge of children. There is the woman who already has a large family, perhaps six or seven children . . . There is the question of the woman who loses her husband during pregnancy and has to go out to work, and obviously cannot bear the strain of doing a full day's work, and looking after a child. There is the woman whose husband is a drunkard or a ne'er-do-well, or is in prison serving a long term, and she has to go to work. These are the cases I have in mind (Lord Silkin, introducing his own 1966 Bill to the House of Lords, in Hindell and Simms, 1971, p. 150).

INTRODUCTION

In the previous chapter, I argued that it is a mistake to view the 1967 Abortion Act as a wholly permissive piece of legislation which envisaged a lessening of control over women's sexuality and fertility. The Abortion Act was revealed as motivated, *inter alia*, by the state's desire to take control of a situation of widespread illegality and to 'manage' the problem of unwanted pregnancy more efficiently. In this sense the

Abortion Act stood as an official recognition that abortion should be removed from the ambit of repressive criminal prohibition and relocated in the sphere of medical control. The modality of control adopted reflects certain assumptions of the nature of the deviance and deviants to be regulated. Within this shift, I suggested, women seeking termination were decriminalised in order to be pathologised. In this chapter, my concern will be to 'flesh out' the subject who is to be regulated through legislation dealing with abortion, to analyse how she has been constructed within law and how this construction serves to legitimate and perpetuate a certain model of control. This will serve to emphasise that, whilst it is useful to locate the Abortion Act within the general movement towards 'governmentality' identified by Foucault, it cannot be adequately understood without consideration of gender, as clearly gendered constructions of the subject to be regulated (the woman seeking abortion) underpin the model of reform adopted.

Foucault has written that the individual is both an effect of power and an element of its articulation.

The individual is not to be conceived as a sort of elementary nucleus, a primitive atom, a multiple and inert material on which power comes to fasten or against which it happens to strike, and in so doing subdues or crushes individuals. In fact, it is already one of the prime effects of power that certain bodies, certain gestures, certain discourses, certain desires, come to be identified and constituted as individuals. The individual, that is, is not the *vis-à-vis* of power; it is, I believe, one of its prime effects. The individual is an effect of power, and at the same time, or precisely to the extent of which it is that effect, it is the element of its articulation. The individual which power has constituted is at the same time its vehicle (1980b, p. 98).

The various discourses around the problem of unwanted pregnancy (of which the law is one) have operated to construct a particular female subjectivity for the woman seeking termination which stands both as an instance of power (the production of a 'true' account of her nature), and as a site for its exercise. Such a construction of her nature becomes justification for particular modes of control. This subjectivity is dynamic – the construction of the woman who would seek to terminate a pregnancy has not remained constant. Here, I will argue that the Abortion Act is clearly predicated upon a particular understanding of the nature of the woman seeking to terminate a pregnancy. It is one frozen moment in the development of this subjectivity, and one which continues to have important and enduring effects today.

In analysing the way that the female subject is constructed in law, I concentrate on the parliamentary debates leading to the introduction of the 1967 Act. At the very least, parliamentary debates seem to be in some way indicative of the predominant social discourses around the concept of woman which form the context within which the Abortion Act was conceived. More ambitiously, the statements made by MPs in this context seem to provide particularly important and powerful 'telling instances' of these discourses (Fitzpatrick, 1987, p. 120). In this more ambitious sense, it seems to me that Parliament provides a particularly significant arena for debate and not merely because of the inevitable relationship between the debates and the formulation of statute. What is especially significant about parliamentary debates is that speakers are inevitably very aware that what they say (especially on a topic of popular interest such as abortion) will be recorded, read and possibly reported in the media. As such, there is every incentive to speak to the spirit of the times, to try to tap into and to give voice to a perceived popular morality. Parliamentary speeches represent more than the feelings of the individual speaker: the more effectively a political discourse manages to capture broad-based social assumptions, the more it will carry its audience and the more effective it will be.[1]

It seems clear that not all of those active in the debates shared the vision of those women seeking abortion as somehow deviant and aberrant, which I will discuss below. Madeleine Simms was a founding member of the Abortion Law Reform Association (ALRA), which spearheaded the campaign for the decriminalisation of abortion. In 1971, in a book co-authored with Keith Hindell, she notes that the reformers did consider the situation of the ordinary woman who simply did not want to give birth, and that one wing of the reform movement did feel there was a need for abortion for all on request. They acknowledged, however, that politically this idea was far too radical to gain public acceptance and parliamentary approval. It was obvious throughout the reform campaign that they would only be able to carry the country with them if they concentrated on the hard cases (1971, p. 25).[2] It seems to me that this gap between private opinions and political (public) discourse makes the public discourse *more* rather than less significant. Even when the reformers believed in the right of all women to choose abortion, and that unwanted pregnancy was not merely a problem faced by marginal women on the fringes of society, they recognised that the most effective way to achieve a partial decriminalisation of abortion was through the exploitation of these stereotypes which played upon popular constructions of the kind of woman seeking abortion. Again, there is every incentive to speak to the spirit of the times.

In this chapter, I begin by drawing out the way that the pregnant woman seeking abortion is constructed within these debates by bringing together dispersed comments of MPs to present a more unified account of the general assumptions made about the 'type' of woman whom the legislation must address: what kind of woman would seek to terminate a pregnancy? I then examine how these constructions and the assumptions upon which they are predicated are reflected in the text of the Abortion Act itself.

IMAGES OF THE ABORTING WOMAN

From my reading of the parliamentary debates which preceded the passing of the Abortion Act of 1967, three major strands of narrative emerge, purporting to describe the 'type' of woman who would want an abortion. The accounts view this woman as peripheral: a marginal and deviant figure who stands against a wider norm of women who neither need nor desire abortion. The accounts which are given in Parliament reflect a strategic deployment of knowledge on the part of both the proponents and opponents of decriminalisation and, on a broader level, reflect images of women that were (and to a greater or lesser degree still are) predominant in other social discourses. The typifications adopted are extreme – they are predicated partially on stereotypes, and partially on real and concrete examples which continually recur within the debates as leitmotifs to become generalised as representing the reality of the woman who seeks abortion.

Two important constructions of woman used within the debates may be broadly (though not always consistently) identified with the reformer/opponent split. Whilst the reformers represented the woman who would seek to terminate a pregnancy as an emotionally weak, unstable (even suicidal) victim of her desperate social circumstances, the conservatives viewed her as a selfish, irrational child. This schema is inevitably a simplification and imposes a unity and coherence which is doubtless lacking, but none the less it is useful in understanding and highlighting the way that women are represented in the debates. In view of a growing recognition of feminist writers that it is important to analyse how the female legal subject is constituted in classed and raced as well as gendered terms (Smart, 1992b, p. 10), this distinction might productively be analysed in terms of class. In this sense the poor, working-class woman fits the model of the unstable and desperate 'multi-child mother'[3] or 'tired housewife' (Ferris, 1966, pp. 10–11) who will have to resort to a cheap and dangerous abortion in the backstreets should legal relief be denied her. On the other hand, the rich, educated, middle-class (working) woman is open to accusations of selfishness for choosing to have a career rather than to raise a child and choosing abortion when she can afford to have a child.

Here I will outline three images of femininity that were presented in the debates: the woman as minor, as victim and as mother. In the following section, I will go on to address how these assumptions have been incorporated into the 1967 Act.

Woman as Minor

The conceptualisation of women as minors is often to be found in the narrative of the opponents of abortion (although normally the central place in their accounts would be ceded to the foetus). Here, the woman is constructed as a minor in terms of immaturity or underdevelopment with regard to matters of responsibility, morality and even to her very femininity or 'womanliness'. Her decision to abort is trivialised and denied rational grounding, being perceived as mere selfishness: she will abort 'according to her wishes or whims',[4] for example, in order to avoid the inconvenience of having to postpone a holiday. She is immoral for being sexually active for reasons other than procreation; she is irresponsible for not having used contraception, and now for refusing to pay the price for her carelessness; she is unnatural and 'unwomanly' because she rejects the natural outcome of sexual intercourse for women: maternity. There is a hint that one day she will come to realise the error of her ways and want children, yet may be unable to have them as a result of the abortion.[5]

Jill Knight (Con., Edgbaston), still active in Parliament and one of the leading opponents of reform, plays heavily on the idea of the woman as selfish and irresponsible within the debates leading to the 1967 Act.[6] She reveals an image of women seeking abortion as selfish, treating 'Babies . . . like bad teeth to be jerked out just because they cause suffering . . . simply because it may be inconvenient for a year or so to its mother.'[7] She later adds that 'A mother might want an abortion so that a planned holiday is not postponed or other arrangements interfered with.'[8] The ability and willingness of the woman to make a serious decision regarding abortion, considering all factors and all parties is dismissed. Rather (like a child) she will make a snap decision for her own convenience. The task of the law is thus perceived essentially as one of responsibilisation – if the woman seeks to evade the consequences of her carelessness, the law should stand as a barrier:

> People must be helped to be responsible, not encouraged to be irresponsible . . . Does anyone think that the problem of the 15-year-old mother can be solved by taking the easy way out? . . . here is the case of a perfectly healthy baby being sacrificed for the mother's convenience . . . For goodness sake, let us bring up our daughters with love and care enough not to get pregnant and not let them degenerate into free-for-alls with the sleazy comfort of knowing, 'She can always go and have it out.'[9]

By forcing her to continue with the pregnancy, the law will seek to ensure that the pregnant woman will be more responsible in the future (an application of the old adage that she has made her bed, and now must lie in it). As another MP comments, again with regard to whether abortion should be allowed to a 15-year-old girl, 'one needs to think twice before one removes all the consequences of folly from people'.[10]

The woman who seeks abortion is also seen as morally immature, and hence undeserving of help. Simon Mahon (Lab., Bootle) asks who is to be given priority in terms of treatment: is it the 'feckless girl who has an unwanted pregnancy from time to time' or the 'decent married woman who is awaiting investigation or treatment for sterility'?[11] The use of this rhetorical trick which opposes the 'feckless girl' to the 'decent married woman' serves to emphasise that the girl is not only feckless but is also indecent and unworthy of respect. Such juxtapositions form a recurrent theme in anti-choice discourse and in more recent years, as Smart has noted, have been compounded by a growing recognition of the problem of infertility (1989, p. 148). This is perfectly illustrated by the comments of Professor Jeffcoate (an implacable opponent of the Abortion Act, and subsequent President of the Royal College of Obstetricians and Gynaecologists). Speaking after the decriminalisation of abortion he asked, 'Is it right that the promiscuous girl, who has not troubled to practise contraception should have priority over the decent married woman who has been waiting perhaps twelve months for admission for investigation of sterility?' (in Kitzinger, 1978, p. 366).

Several participants in the parliamentary debates give voice to an implicit assumption that it is morally wrong for women to make a distinction between sex and procreation, that is, women should not indulge in sex if pregnancy is not desired. William Deedes (Con., Ashford) makes these sentiments clear in expressing his concern that 'science and its little pill will enable so-called civilised countries to treat sex more and more as a sport and less and less as a sacrament in love, a divine instrument of procreation'.[12] Perhaps the single most telling quotation here comes from David Steel himself, defending a clause to allow abortion in cases of rape,[13] which was eventually dropped after debate in Parliament, for reasons which were discussed in Chapter 2 (pp. 27–8), and will be further developed below (pp. 44–5). He states,

> Most honourable Members would agree that to have a woman continue with a pregnancy which she did not wish to conceive, or in respect of which she was incapable of expressing her wish to conceive, is a practice which we deplore, but the difficulty is to find an acceptable wording which will enable termination to be carried out following sexual offences of this kind but which does not allow an open gate for the pretence of sexual offences.[14]

What is startling here is Steel's correlation of 'a pregnancy which she did not wish to conceive' with conception following rape. Steel fails to imagine that the vast majority of requests for abortion will be for pregnancies that the woman did not wish to conceive. In using this argument to justify abortion in cases of rape, he implicitly equates consensual intercourse with desired conception. Wanting sex equals wanting pregnancy equals wanting motherhood.

Woman as Victim

The second narrative account strongly present in the parliamentary debates is that of woman as a victim of poverty and harsh social circumstances. This construction is typically that of the reforming forces, where the woman and her social situation enjoy a far more central place. The reformers here seek to capitalise on the public sympathy for women facing unwanted pregnancy. Newspapers, magazines and books had reported horror stories of backstreet and self-induced abortions and, as David Steel tells the House of Commons, in the years preceding the introduction of the Abortion Act, an average of thirty women per year were dying at the hands of criminal abortionists.[15] Further, the well-publicised thalidomide cases had contributed to public sympathy for the woman carrying a disabled foetus.

The image of the woman seeking abortion here draws her as 'not only on the fringe, but [as] literally, physically inadequate' (Greenwood and Young, 1976, p. 76). She is presented as distraught, out of her mind with the worry of pregnancy, possibly because she is young and unmarried, but normally because she already has too many children. She is desperate, and should the doctor not be able to help her, her potential actions are unpredictable (suicide is discussed).[16] Her husband is either absent or an alcoholic, her housing situation is intolerable. She is at the end of her tether simply trying to hold the whole situation together. As Madeleine Simms, of the Abortion Law Reform Association (ALRA), later wrote 'It was chiefly for the worn out mother of many children with an ill or illiterate or feckless or brutal or drunken or otherwise inadequate husband that we were fighting' (1985, p. 81).

Lord Silkin was one of the most eloquent exponents of this narrative, and he had many opportunities to develop it during the passage of his Bill through the House of Lords.[17] The following letter, which he read to the House of Lords during the second reading of his own Bill, provides a typical and tragic illustration of the woman to be helped as she was envisaged by the reformist forces:

> Dear Lord Silkin, I am married to a complete drunk who is out of work more than he is in. I have four children and now at 40 I am pregnant again; I was just beginning to get on my feet, and get some of the things we needed. I've been working for the last three years, and cannot bear the thought of that terrible struggle to make ends meet

again. I've tried all other methods that I've been told about, without success, so as a last resort I appeal to you – please help me if you possibly can (cited in Hindell and Simms, 1971, p. 80).

The same kind of image is also repeatedly drawn in the House of Commons, where one MP speaks of 'the mothers with large families and the burdens of large families very often with low incomes'.[18] Another describes the illegal abortions he has known:

I have represented abortionists, both medical and lay. I have, therefore, met the 30s. abortion with Higginson's syringe and a soapy solution undertaken in a kitchen by a grey-faced woman on a distracted multi-child mother, often the wife of a drunken husband. I have also come across the more expensive back-bedroom abortion by the hasty medical man whose patient returns to a distant town, there to lie in terror and blood and without medical attention.[19]

Even Bernard Braine (Con., Castle Point), a vocal opponent of the Bill, accepts this image of the woman presented by the reformers:

The hope of the sponsors of the Bill is to change the law so that many abortions which take place at the moment illegally – either in the backstreets or, self-induced by some poor unfortunate woman, driven to desperation – shall be brought into the framework of legality.[20]

The woman who wishes to terminate her pregnancy is portrayed as someone who is not completely in control of her actions and who may be driven to madness if relief is denied to her. David Owen states:

Such a woman is in total misery, and could be precipitated into a depression deep and lasting. What happens to that woman when she gets depressed? She is incapable of looking after those children so she retires into a shell of herself and loses all feeling, all her drive and affection.[21]

Here again, we see worries for the health of the woman related back to concern for the well-being of the family (see pp. 20–1 above). A more extreme example is the tragic story related by Lena Jeger MP which I mentioned in Chapter 2: an 'honest young woman' with five children, recently deserted by her husband, was refused an abortion because 'she did not seem quite depressed enough'. The woman was forced to continue the pregnancy, and her depression following the birth of her sixth baby was so extreme, that she killed the baby by throwing it on the floor. The woman was now in Holloway prison, the children in care.[22] Lord Strange notes that 'nearly every woman in this condition [of unwanted pregnancy] would be in a state bordering on suicide'.[23] The woman's irrationality is sometimes conceptually linked to her pregnant condition. As David Owen states, for example, 'The reproductive cycle of women is intimately linked with her psyche.'[24] This pathologises women, playing on the notion of female behaviour as dominated and controlled by biology.[25]

This image of the desperate woman is emphasised by contrasting it with the cool impassive figure of the doctor. The doctor represents a calm, responsible, rational and reassuring figure – everything that the woman is not. He is without doubt a male figure[26] who is perceived as the epitome of maturity, common sense,[27] responsibility and professionalism. He is a 'highly skilled and dedicated',[28] 'sensitive, sympathetic'[29] member of a 'high and proud profession'[30] which acts 'with its own ethical and medical standards'[31] displaying 'skill, judgment and knowledge'.[32]

Woman as Mother

The image of the woman as mother is appropriated for the cause of both reformists and conservatives alike. It is not until the 1990 debates that (some) MPs feel able to challenge the inevitability of maternity for all women.[33] For the conservatives in 1966–7, the woman who rejects maternity is seen to reject the very essence of womanhood. Kevin McNamara (Lab., Hull N.) provides a strong account of woman's maternal instinct:

> How can a woman's capacity to be a mother be measured before she has a child? Fecklessness, a bad background, being a bad manager, these are nothing to do with love, that unidentifiable bond, no matter how strange or difficult the circumstances, which links a mother to her child and makes her cherish it.[34]

This implicit assumption of woman as mother is further reflected in the consideration of her existing responsibilities to children and family (and an apparent inability to see her outside of this role of wife and mother). Jill Knight informs us that 'if it comes to a choice between the mother's life or the baby's, the mother is very much more important'. This is not, according to Knight, because the woman is more important in her own right, but rather because 'She has ties and responsibilities to her husband and other children.'[35]

The reformists seek to capitalise on the idea of maternity as the female norm. Madeleine Simms (ALRA) argued that it was precisely the woman with a fully developed 'maternal instinct' who might require an abortion. She pointed out that most women wished to have not more than two or three babies and were appalled if they found they were having more children than they believed they could adequately care for. Should they accidentally become pregnant, she argued, they would then seek an abortion because of their feelings of responsibility to their husband and family, and because of their maternal instinct towards their existing children (1985, p. 81). Likewise, another prominent reformer, Alice Jenkins, wrote that 'the principal beneficiary under a new law would be the decent mother of a family who has as many children as she can cope with' (1960, p. 47). In the House of Lords, Joan Vickers reinforced these ideas and summed up sentiments which are often expressed or implicit in statements of other parliamentarians when she noted, 'I think that most women desire motherhood. It is natural for a woman to want to have a child . . . It is only in extreme cases that a woman wants to terminate her pregnancy.'[36] In defending the need for a social clause (to allow abortion where the woman's social and economic circumstances are deemed inadequate) within the Act, Roy Jenkins (Lab., Birmingham, Stechford, then Home Secretary) argued that without the presence of such a clause, 'many women who are far from anxious to escape the responsibilities of motherhood, but rather wish to discharge their existing ones more effectively, would be denied relief'.[37] Dunwoody asserts in similar vein that

in many cases where we have over-large families the mother is so burdened down physically and emotionally with the continual bearing of children that it becomes quite impossible for her to fulfil her real function, her worthwhile function as a mother, of holding together the family unit, so that all too often the family breaks apart, and it is for this reason that we have all too many problem families in many parts of the country.[38]

Dr Michael Winstanley (Lib., Cheadle, Steel's medical adviser for the Bill) makes the related argument that women should be allowed to abort disabled foetuses, because the woman who is forced to give birth to a disabled child will seldom allow herself to become pregnant again.[39] Implicit here is an understanding of the role of law as being to protect and entrench motherhood, to encourage women to adopt the maternal role.

THE ABORTION ACT: A MORE SUITABLE MODEL OF CONTROL

In his closing speech before the final vote was taken, David Steel asserted that the duly amended Abortion Act (or as it was then termed the Medical Termination of Pregnancy Bill) is what a 'reasonable man would regard as a reasonable statement of the law'.[40] This impression of reasonable compromise pervades much of what has been subsequently written on the Act. The Act is often depicted as a complex balancing act between two competing sets of rights: the right to life of the foetus versus the right to choose (or right of self-determination) of the woman. However, if the law aims to protect and entrench any *rights* it is not those of the woman (nor indeed those of the foetus) but rather those of the doctor. Indeed, the statute was specifically constructed in such a way that women would not be accorded any substantive rights under it. Further, if the law can be described as achieving any sort of compromise, it is one of a reconciliation of the competing narrative accounts of the kind of woman who would seek abortion which I have outlined above. Law has incorporated and entrenched certain aspects of these narratives, in working with certain assumptions about women's maternal role, and the essential irresponsibility and sexual immorality of the woman who would seek to terminate a pregnancy. In its embodiment and entrenchment of these assumptions, the law itself (re)creates the peripheral, deviant subject which it will then seek to discipline and regulate. Equally it simultaneously reinforces the image of the good woman who does not seek to terminate her pregnancy and who provides the norm against which such deviance is to be measured.

Maternity as the Normal Role for Women

As was seen above, the law regarding abortion functions in terms of a blanket ban (sections 58 and 59, Offences Against the Person Act 1861) which renders abortion illegal. The Abortion Act offers a defence against this statute where two doctors deem that the circumstances of the individual woman fall within the general categories which are laid out within its section 1. The decision to abort is not seen as an intrinsically acceptable one, as a choice which any woman could face at some time in her life. Rather, it is an option which may be justified only in certain cases by the individual circumstances (or inadequacies) of individual women, in the opinion of two doctors. Conceptually then, abortion stands as the exception to the norm of maternity. No woman can reject motherhood. The only women who should be allowed to terminate pregnancies are those who can do so without rejecting maternity/familial norms *per se*, in other words those who have reasons to reject this one particular pregnancy without rejecting motherhood as their destiny in general. In this sense, women who are carrying the 'wrong sort' of foetus, who have obligations to meet to existing children, or whose living conditions are at present inadequate for a child will be allowed by doctors to terminate a pregnancy. Likewise, it was felt that where the particular pregnancy was thrust upon the woman through rape or incest, the doctor should be free to authorise termination (although, as will be seen below, a specific clause to this effect was felt to be unnecessary).

In this way, for example, section 1(1)(b) of the Act provides that abortion can be allowed where 'there is a substantial risk that if the child were born it would suffer from such physical or mental abnormalities as to be seriously handicapped'. Whilst clearly displaying eugenicist considerations,[41] this clause can also be interpreted with regard to the status of the woman. It was justified in part on the grounds that to force a woman to carry an abnormal child to term will discourage her from future pregnancy[42] and, as Dr Winstanley points out, 'In every case the duty of the medical practitioners should be, wherever possible to encourage aid and support the mother towards term with the pregnancy.'[43] The disabled baby or child is not seen as being as desirable as a 'normal' one and does not feature in the romanticised family ideal. As Dr Winstanley says of the woman who has a higher than normal chance of giving birth to a disabled baby: 'this mother does not know whether she will get a baby which will make her very happy or one which will make her very sad'.[44] Thus, the woman can reject this (abnormal) pregnancy without rejecting the whole institution of motherhood itself.

The woman's role as mother is again emphasised where section 1(1)(a) of the Abortion Act allows abortion where the continuance of a pregnancy 'would involve . . . injury to the physical or mental health of . . . any existing children of her family'. The woman is allowed to reject pregnancy in order to fulfil her existing responsibility as a mother more effectively. Here again she is seen to reject one particular pregnancy, rather than motherhood itself. Indeed, she may reject this particular pregnancy precisely in order to be a better mother to those children already in her family. This idea is still more clearly embodied in the wording of Steel's original Medical Termination of Pregnancy Bill which stated as a separate head for abortion: 'that the pregnant woman's capacity as a mother will be severely overstrained by the care of a child or of another child as the case may be' (clause 1(1)(c). It is perhaps worthy of note that the version which is eventually incorporated into the Abortion Act only allows termination on this ground where the woman already has children, where the original version included it equally where the child would be a woman's first. This may be seen to reflect the image of the overstrained 'multi-child mother' who wishes to terminate one pregnancy in order to care better for her existing family.

The assumption of maternity as the female norm is reflected both in terms of the very structure of the law and in specific provisions which allow abortion in cases where the continuance of a pregnancy would involve injury to the health of any existing children of the woman's family. The need for intervention is felt to be justified not merely on the basis of a woman's own health and well-being, but also by that of her family: 'in the name of the responsibility they owed to the health of their children, the solidity of the family institution and the safeguarding of society' (Foucault, 1979b, p. 147).

Female Irresponsibility and Untrustworthiness

Section 1(1) of the Abortion Act provides that

> Subject to the provisions of this section, a person shall not be guilty of an offence under the law relating to abortion when a pregnancy is terminated by a registered medical practitioner if two registered medical practitioners are of the opinion, formed in good faith . . . [that various conditions are fulfilled].

The female subject conceived of within the Abortion Act is clearly treated as someone who cannot take decisions for herself. Rather responsibility is handed over to the reassuringly mature and responsible (male) figure of the doctor. Thus, the legislation here assumes that the doctor will be better equipped to judge what is best for the woman, even though he may never have met her before and may have neither knowledge of, nor interest in, her concrete situation. The entrenchment of such a construction in law fits precisely with the images of woman deployed in the debates. If the woman is distraught and irrational, then she is an unsuitable party to take such an important decision. Indeed she inevitably and inherently lacks the necessary emotional *distance* to make such a choice in a considered way. Equally, if she is selfish and self-centred, intellectually and morally immature, considering only her own needs, and giving no weight to other factors (such as the claims of the foetus) in her snap decisions, she is again incapable of making such an important choice. She is thus in need of the normalising control of the doctor to impose either calm and rationality or moral deliberation and consideration of the interests of others.

Here, it is worth returning to the proposed rape clause, included in Steel's original Bill and notable by its absence in British statute law. A separate heading (section 1(1)(d)) allowed termination in the case of rape, with s.1(2)(4) providing 'A termination of pregnancy performed on the ground of rape shall require the certificate of a registered medical practitioner consulted by the patient freshly after the alleged assault that there was the medical evidence of sexual assault upon her.'

Arguments for allowing abortion in the case of rape were dismissed for a combination of reasons, some of which have already been discussed (see p. 42). First, despite widespread agreement that a woman who had been raped should be allowed to terminate any resulting pregnancy, it was felt that she would already have access to abortion under the law as it stood.[45] Secondly, as was noted in Chapter 2, medical bodies opposed the inclusion of a clause which explicitly decriminalised abortion in case of rape, as they felt that this would lead women to assert a right to termination in that circumstance. Thirdly, it was argued that the woman could not be trusted to tell the truth about whether she has been raped. As one MP noted, 'We also know that a great many charges of rape are made which are quite unfounded and which are made for quite different motives.'[46] One academic commentator explained the decision not to include a specific rape clause: were it to be included, 'women would have a stronger inducement to allege that an unwanted or embarrassing pregnancy had been imposed by rape'. He goes on:

> This crime always poses problems of definition. The differences between rape and determined 'masculine' seduction can be fine, and the presence or absence of consent can sometimes be impossible to find conclusively. Further, a woman may provoke her own rape by finally withholding consent from a man who is unable to control the passion she has deliberately aroused. At present, charges of rape are occasionally found where a woman wishes to protect her reputation, for example, where she is unmarried, but the prospect of having the pregnancy terminated, without anyone having to be prosecuted or convicted, would be an attraction which some women might find hard to resist (Dickens, 1966, p. 139).

Were it somehow possible for the verification of the occurrence of rape to fall within the competence of doctors, however, this might well have proved sufficient for the rape/incest clause to have survived to be included in the text of the Abortion Act: 'if there were a way in which doctors could decide whether or not a lady had been raped, I would be content to allow the provision on rape to go in', said one MP.[47]

Consideration of women's untrustworthiness in evidencing one's own rape for the purposes of requesting abortion, finds an interesting parallel in the requirement that the judge is obliged to warn the jury that it is unsafe to convict on the uncorroborated testimony of the rape victim, where the only evidence in a rape trial is her testimony.[48] Sheila Duncan argues that, despite the many justifications for this warning,

> At the root of them in respect of rape is the notion that the complainant in sexual matters may be falsely accusing the defendant as a result of a refusal to admit consent and accept responsibility for the sexual events which have occurred with the defendant (1994, p. 16).

Her conclusion, that '[t]he female Other is constructed as inherently untrustworthy', would seem to be equally applicable here.

Female Sexuality

The Abortion Act contains a strong moral element, distinguishing between categories of deserving and undeserving 'victims' of unwanted pregnancy. The former are allowed abortions, the latter denied them. This distinction works on the one hand with regard to whether or not intercourse was wanted and, on the other, with regard to whether the woman has a legitimate reason for changing her mind and rejecting this particular pregnancy (because of foetal disability).

Although, unlike many other western European statutes, the 1967 Act does not explicitly foresee abortion for cases of pregnancy resulting from rape or incest (for the reasons noted above), there are still lengthy discussions of this matter in Parliament which are informative with regard to perceptions of female sexuality. There was practically unanimous agreement that women should be allowed abortion in case of rape, although the clause which specifically authorised it within the Abortion Act was deleted for the reasons discussed above. Here then the woman who did not desire sex and hence did not make a distinction between sex and procreation should be allowed by doctors to terminate her pregnancy.

It has been argued above that the provision with regard to foetal disability (section 1(1)(b)) is strongly influenced both by eugenic considerations, and the construction of woman as mother. This clause also, I would argue, bears some relation to constructions of women's sexuality, as it serves to provide a 'get-out clause' for 'good' women who want to become pregnant (and thus do not commit the sin of making the fatal distinction between sex and procreation), but through no fault of their own happen to be carrying a foetus 'of the wrong sort'. The form adopted by the legislation refuses to legitimate a disassociation of sex and procreation. Avoidance of procreation remains something which can only be justified by the inadequacies of a particular woman or a problem with a specific pregnancy.

CONCLUSIONS

At the end of this catalogue of all the various kinds of medical conditions or adverse situations where abortion may be the best course, it may be asked if the reformers considered the woman who simply did not want to give birth to the embryonic child inside her . . . it is an injustice to the well-adjusted, healthy woman that she cannot get the same relief from a pregnancy as her inadequate or overstrained, or unmarried, or rubella-infected, or incestuous sisters. One wing of the reform movement in fact did feel there was a need for abortion for all on request. They acknowledged, however, that politically this idea was far too radical to gain public acceptance and parliamentary approval (Hindell and Simms, 1971, pp. 24–5).

Deviance, like beauty, lies in the eye of the beholder. As Quinney has written:

> crime is a definition of human conduct that becomes part of the social world . . . Criminal definitions in their official formulations . . . are the most powerful means of social control used to control actions which conflict with the interest of those who create these criminal definitions (in Lacey et al., 1990, p. v).

However, law does more than draw lines between acceptable and unacceptable behaviour, in order to define deviance. Law also constructs deviants: it acts not on a pre-existing external, knowable individual, but itself (re)creates this individual, drawing upon and entrenching certain social assumptions and stereotypes. The woman seeking to terminate a pregnancy achieves a particular subjectivity within the 1967 Act. She is identified as a peripheral subject, distinguishable from 'normal' women, characterised by certain qualities and inadequacies. In this sense, I have argued that the Abortion Act is predicated upon certain ideas of maternity as the female norm, female irresponsibility and emotional instability and implicit assumptions about appropriate female sexual morality. It is thus the woman's own nature which serves as a basis for legitimating the particular modality of normalising medical control adopted within the 1967 Act.

Women seeking abortion, more than any other, are 'hysterized', medicalised 'in the name of the responsibility they owed to the health of their children, the solidity of the family institution, and the safeguarding of society' (Foucault, 1979b, p. 147). Inherent female pathology is seen as exacerbated by pregnancy. This reconstruction of 'woman' combined with a gradual redefinition of birth as a medical event, meant that medical control was the obvious 'solution'. Foucault writes of

> a threefold process whereby the feminine body was analyzed [sic] – qualified and disqualified – as being thoroughly saturated with sexuality; whereby it was integrated into the sphere of medical practices, by reason of a pathology intrinsic to it; whereby, finally, it was placed in organic communication with the social body (whose regulated fecundity it was supposed to ensure), the family space (of which it had to be a substantial and functional element), and the life of children (which it produced and had to guarantee, by virtue of a biologico-moral responsibility lasting through the entire period of the children's education): the Mother, with her negative image of 'nervous woman,' constituted the most visible form of this hysterization (1979b, pp. 146–7).

With the construction of the woman seeking termination drawn in this way, medical control becomes the obvious solution. There can be no doubt that it is imperative to get such a woman into the safe hands of her GP, so that he can take control and 'manage' the problem in the best interests of the woman herself, her family and the broader society. 'If we can manage to get a girl such as that into the hands of the medical profession, the Bill is succeeding in its objective', argues David Steel.[49]

It is not only the woman seeking abortion who is constructed in the 1967 Act, however. The subjectivity created here must be read alongside an implicit assumption of the 'normal' woman. The aborting woman is simultaneously the paradigmatic example and the antithesis of this female norm. In one sense she is its natural conclusion, standing as an extreme example of female instability and irrationality. In her attempt to deny maternity, the natural (and desired) destiny of the good woman, however, she is also its dark side or alter ego. In these senses, the female norm of the 'good woman' is simultaneously (re)constructed and enforced by the creation of her deviant sister.

4
Abortion, Reproduction and the Deployment of Medical Power

One must distinguish between the purely technical activities of treatment and the social interaction and manipulation surrounding those acts . . . The former is clearly founded on medical science, that special knowledge of the profession which justifies its autonomy; the latter is not (Friedson, 1970, p. 342).

Of course there is room for variation in opinion. All we can say is that we have to rely on the ethics of the medical profession to act in good faith. I accept that, just as there are bad Members of Parliament and clergymen, so there are bad doctors (David Steel).[1]

INTRODUCTION

Women's experiences at the hands of doctors have formed the subject of a good deal of feminist scholarship. This is not surprising given that it has become increasingly apparent that broader social constructions of gender rely heavily on medical discourses. In the late nineteenth century, the deployment of medical knowledge was integral to the attempts made to keep women in the home, through claims that studying outside it would damage their reproductive capacities (Ehrenreich and English, 1978; Thomson, 1995). Medical knowledges have been seen to constitute women as *psychologically* and *socially* vulnerable and therefore in need of close medical surveillance, advice and guidance (Scully, 1980, p. 14; Turner, 1987, p. 102; see generally Ehrenreich and English, 1978; Showalter, 1987) and *biologically* as natural patients, at the mercy of their bodies or hormones (Turner, 1987, p. 109; see also Ehrenreich and English, 1978). Medical texts have been seen to characterise women by irrationality, sexual passivity, and a desire for maternity (Scully and Bart, 1973; Merchant, 1980; Easlea, 1981; Martin, 1987) and various historical studies have demonstrated how doctors have acted to ensure female compliance with these constructions through such draconian measures as ovariectomies (Scully, 1980) or committal to psychiatric institutions (Smart, 1992c, p. 38).[2]

Although the claims and methods of the medical science of more recent years seem (by and large)[3] far less dramatic, at times evidence

49

of the same pattern of medical enforcement of appropriate female behaviour is still clearly visible. Furthermore, women use health services more frequently than men and thus, it has been argued, are more subject to a routine, daily medical control (Gardner, 1981, pp. 130–1; Roberts, 1985; Pfeffer, 1985; Davis, 1988a). Barrett and Roberts' study of GPs and female patients, found that GPs and hospital specialists would often relate to women in terms of non-medical, social criteria in order to reinforce women's traditional social role:

> In consultation after consultation the GP smooths away the surface anxiety and adjusts the woman to the limitations of a life totally located in a home from which the children have moved away. In this respect the institution of medicine legitimates and endorses the status quo in relation to the position of women, and in so doing it fulfils an ideological function as an agency of disguised social control. We found that frequently doctors would use the authority of their medico-moral language to offer not neutral, clinical advice but a set of prescriptions based on the conventional wisdom of their own social milieu (1978, p. 42).

The 'Medicalisation' of Daily Life

Work on the experience of women in this area accords with a more general recognition that over the last two centuries medical power has greatly increased its sphere of influence. For writers such as Eliot Friedson, the high status of the medical profession and the faith invested in its members' abilities to perform miracles have resulted in other social problems being inappropriately defined as illness. Friedson contends that as a result of the widening of medical jurisdiction, more social resources have become directed towards illness, and as a consequence, the medical profession's power and influence have increased markedly in the twentieth century, with little scope to question its activities or use of resources (1970).

Medicine enjoys a very privileged position within modern society with a particularly strong claim of access to 'truth'. In a movement away from a narrow disease model of ill-health, the medical profession is now capable of claiming jurisdiction far beyond that which it once enjoyed and far beyond what would accrue purely on the basis of a technical competence, training and knowledge. Modern society has witnessed a shift from the centrality of religious knowledges to the new-found pre-eminence of scientific rationality as the fundamental way of ordering and making sense of the world. In the case of understanding the human organism, medical science is now central.[4] The medical profession has taken over a large part of the function traditionally linked to the clergy as the guardians of social reality with a claim to identify abnormality, deviance and social disorder (Friedson, 1970; Zola, 1977; Donzelot, 1979; Foucault, 1989b).

For Foucault, the body is the ultimate site of political and ideological control, surveillance and regulation – what he describes as disciplinary power (1991). State apparatuses such as medicine, the educational system, psychiatry and law define the limits of behaviour and record activities, punishing those bodies which violate the established boundaries, and thus render bodies productive and politically and economically useful. For Foucault, the medical encounter is a supreme example of surveillance, whereby the doctor investigates and questions while the patient acquiesces, with little knowledge of why the procedures are carried out. What is particularly useful in Foucault's work is his attempt to balance study of the individual subject and the broader population. For Foucault was also concerned with what he called 'bio-power', the State's interest in governing and controlling populations. Again, medicine has an important role to play here in developing and supporting public health measures (mass screening, fitness tests, health education campaigns), carrying these through at the level of the individual.

The operation of power in the medical relationship is still more pronounced than in other expert/non-expert relationships (for example, lawyer and client): in the medical case, the patient herself becomes the very object of study, with the doctor the one who has the claim to understand her and to be able to explain her illness. Moreover, the basis of the authority of the doctor – to overcome suffering and even death – cannot be matched by other professionals. In this sense, the closest analogy might be to the power which was traditionally enjoyed by priests. Doctors are seen to hold powers over bodily health similar to the powers of the clergy over the soul: they are 'a therapeutic clergy' or 'priests of the body' (Foucault, 1989b, p. 32). Doctors' credibility depends on their ability to make successful claims about the scientific value of their work and the way in which their medical knowledge is grounded in precise, accurate and reliable scientific information. The power of the doctor is to categorise and classify the patient within the medical framework (healthy/ill, normal/abnormal) and thus to claim the ability to understand, to treat and to cure. Any challenge to the power basis in the doctor–patient relationship must therefore begin with a process of demystification. One step towards this is the recognition of medical discourse not as an abstract logical system, but as a specific cultural form (Turner, 1987; Foucault, 1989a, 1989b). This reveals one further, important insight: since these forms of rationality reside on a base of human practice and human history – since they have been *made*, they can be unmade (Raulet, 1983, p. 206).

Women and Medical Power

While doctors may have taken on the role of 'therapeutic clergy' for the whole of the population, their work is seen as doubly necessary with regard to female patients, who are characterised by an inherent pathology. This rests on a particular ideology of the nature of woman, her role and needs. It represents a medical relationship overlaid by gender assumptions. Reproduction is the most important area where doctors operate control over women's lives. Birth, an event long controlled by women with help from friends, older women and midwives, has gradually fallen under a hegemonic medical control. Today, 98 per cent of births in Britain take place in hospital and the number of births performed by caesarian section continues to increase (Bridgeman, 1993c). Whatever benefits the medicalisation of reproduction may have brought in the way of safety (and these are not undisputed),[5] it has also led to considerable erosion of women's autonomy. As reproduction has become more and more technologised, reproductive knowledge has become increasingly privatised, available only to the medically trained. This has provided the rationale for all sorts of reproductive decisions traditionally made by women (regarding pregnancy, contraception, infertility and abortion) to be made instead by – or at best in conjunction with – doctors. Moreover, those doctors who try to provide a more woman-centred service and leave more choice to women as to how they wish to give birth, can face extreme hostility from their colleagues, as was clearly illustrated by the Wendy Savage case.[6]

The medicalisation of reproduction has received further legitimation from the recognition of a foetus as a patient in its own right and a perceived need to protect it. This has been entrenched by the development of techniques making it possible to see and to monitor the foetus *in utero*. Whilst the figure of the woman fades into the background as the mere 'maternal environment' or 'grainy blur' at the edge of the image (Petchesky, 1987; Hartouni, 1991), the foetus itself comes to enjoy an increasingly central place as a separate candidate for medical attention. Despite their benefits for individual women, the new technologies (ultrasound, amniocentesis, *in vitro* fertilisation, electronic foetal monitoring, routine caesarian deliveries and *in utero* foetal therapies) also have the effect of carving out more time and space for the obstetrical management of pregnancy (Petchesky, 1987, p. 64; Wells, 1993). Moreover, increasingly the major threat to foetal well-being is seen to be the behaviour of the pregnant woman.[7] The idea that the doctor is the best representative of the foetus's interests receives further legitimation from medical technology which provides him with ever more knowledge about previously invisible processes within the woman's body. This also has implications for the regulation of abortion, in terms of entrenching the role of the doctor as the only one capable of representing the interests of the foetus (against those of the pregnant woman).

In previous chapters I have argued that the Abortion Act represents a shift from a model of law based on prohibition to one which seeks to manage and regulate abortion by locating power in the hands of the medical profession. In this sense, I have explored how the Abortion Act has attempted to entrench a particular site of control over women. In this chapter, first I will attempt to sketch out how this operates in practice: how is power deployed at the level of a request for a termination? Secondly, I will assess the role of law in encouraging, facilitating and limiting medical power in this context. The empirical evidence which I draw upon in discussion of women's experiences of abortion services is inevitably anecdotal and is often rather dated. This poses some problems for its relevance today, given that it is inconceivable that medical practice and opinions will not have been subject to some change over the past years. Given the contemporary lack of interest in conducting this kind of research, it is impossible to map any trends in this process. The present chapter must thus content itself with making claims for some of the ways in which power has been (and may continue to be) deployed in the abortion interview, and with mapping the role of law in this process.

MEDICAL CONTROL OF ABORTION

At the outset I would like to make two distinctions. First, there will clearly be a difference between the experiences of women seeking access to state-funded terminations and those who opt for abortions in the private sector (including the abortion charities, such as the British Pregnancy Advisory Service). In Britain, GPs operate as gatekeepers to other health services and NHS terminations are obtainable only if a woman's GP will agree to refer her to a second (hospital) doctor who must agree to perform the termination.[8] Women who choose this course face much more uncertainty regarding the kind of response they will receive, as there is no way of knowing the views of either GP or consultant in advance, and there is certainly no guarantee of sympathetic treatment. If women attend a specialist abortion clinic in the private sector, they are obviously extremely unlikely to encounter healthcare professionals who have strong feelings against abortion, and they are therefore less likely to meet with hostility. As the latter option is normally available only to those women who have the necessary £300 or so to pay for the termination, this inevitably introduces an element of class into the analysis, with the experiences of poorer women being more likely to be negative.[9] 'Women who know their way around the system are also likely to fare better, which would go some way to explaining some of the problems encountered by ethnic minority women in accessing abortion services (see Daud, 1993). Secondly, it is also important to distinguish between different categories of medical professionals, notably nurses, GPs and gynaecologists/obstetricians. There is some evidence that there may be significant differences of opinion regarding abortion between these groups (Hordern, 1971, p. 30; Homans, 1985; Simms, 1985; Farrant, 1985)[10] and it would be strange if this had no impact on their professional practice.

In this chapter I will distinguish between four different levels of control: *technical* control of the actual performance of abortion operations, *decisional* control over which women should be permitted to terminate their pregnancies, and *paternalistic* and *normalising* control which may be exercised over women who request termination (regardless of whether they are granted access to it). This is an analytical distinction, designed to clarify the way that power operates at this level. Some of these 'types' of power have received more attention than others: in Britain the feminist call for abortion on demand has focused on decisional control, typically (although not invariably) assuming a medical retention of technical control.

Technical Control over the Performance of Abortions

No law expressly prohibits any unregistered or unqualified person from practising most types of medicine and surgery, unless such a person deliberately represents him or herself as being a registered practitioner, or as having medical qualifications. Along with the treatment of venereal disease,[11] abortion is one of the few specified exceptions to this. Although the technology involved in terminating a pregnancy can be very simple, under section 1 of the Abortion Act, abortion can only be legal 'when a pregnancy is terminated by a registered medical practitioner'. In a rather creative decision of the House of Lords, this has been interpreted as meaning nothing more than that a doctor must remain in charge and accept responsibility throughout the termination. Where parts of the procedure can, in accordance with good medical practice, be performed by auxiliary staff, the operation would still fall within the terms of section 1 of the Act, and such staff would be protected from prosecution.[12] The medical technical monopoly is more easily justified in some cases than in others. The most common form of early abortion – vacuum aspiration – is an easy and quick process with a very low rate of side-effects.[13] Here, it is by no means self-evident that such terminations could not be performed just as safely by trained lay personnel, nurses or midwives. In practice, terminations by prostaglandins (PG) have for some time been performed by nurses rather than doctors (see pp. 96–8) although the requirement that the doctor retains a supervisory role still applies.

The issue of technical control has been thrown sharply into relief by the decision to license the drug RU486 for the provision of chemical abortions in Britain.[14] As will be seen in Chapter 7, despite the fact that RU486/PG abortions have been marketed as easier and needing less control than conventional terminations, the procedure for the administration of RU486/PG has been seen as leading to an *increase* in the level of medical supervision necessary. It is especially relevant to recall here that the performance of abortions is (in practice) a monopoly of certain – and not all – doctors. Although the proposal of the Royal College of Obstetricians and Gynaecologists (RCOG) that terminations should only be performed and authorised by or under the supervision of a consultant gynaecologist[15] was not incorporated into the Abortion Act, the law does provide that abortions must be performed in licensed medical premises (such as hospitals or clinics).[16] This has greatly restricted the ability of some doctors – in particular GPs – to perform terminations. As will be seen in Chapter 7, this is particularly relevant to the provision of RU486/PG terminations, where the GP might otherwise administer either one or both of the stages of treatment.

A particular instance of *de facto* resistance to this technical control of abortion by doctors has been the emergence of small groups performing very early abortions by menstrual extraction in the US.[17] In a climate of fear that rights to abortion might be drastically restricted there,[18] a self-help guide to abortion by this means, *A Book of Women's Choices* (Chalker and Downey, 1992), was published. Menstrual extraction performed in small self-help groups would seem to be the most radical means of rejecting the technical level of medical control over pregnancy (and obviously the other levels of control discussed below would fall with it). Here there is no 'expert' in the group – all the women are at once practitioner and patient. There is no hierarchy and no privatised knowledge which is available to one but not all. However, menstrual extraction has clear limitations. First, it is useful only in the very early stages of pregnancy, often before a woman would even know with any certainty that she were pregnant (although pregnancy tests are increasingly sensitive). Secondly, outside of the limits of the Abortion Act, menstrual extraction is clearly an offence under s.58 of the Offences Against the Person Act. Indeed, its legality is dubious even when performed *within* those limits. Tunkel (1979) discusses the case of Dr Goldthorp, who performed menstrual extraction within 10–18 days of a missed period. The DPP asserted that this was illegal whether or not performed within the terms of the Abortion Act which protected the doctor only when a 'pregnancy is terminated'. This wording was understood to exclude 'speculative' operations.[19] Subsequently the Law Officers (the Attorney General and Solicitor General) expressed the opinion that such a procedure would be legal if (and only if) performed in accordance with the terms of the Abortion Act. No reasons were given for this.[20] Thirdly, it is to be assumed that many women would not wish to use this method, which implies an intimacy with one's own body and the bodies of other women that might be unwelcome. Furthermore, it involves challenging a still strong taboo around menstruation. Finally, whatever the claims made by exponents of the method as to its safety, they also note that it is riskier when the groups are less experienced in its use (Chalker and Downey, 1992, p. 129).

While doctors hold the monopoly of the right to perform abortions, they also benefit from a clearly specified right *not* to participate in the provision of abortion services for reasons of conscientious objection, under s.4 of the Abortion Act.[21] This distinguishes abortion from almost all other treatments. One important result of the right of conscientious objection is the extent of regional variation as to the possibility of obtaining an abortion on the NHS. In 1995 (the last year for which figures are available), of 156,539 terminations performed on resident women in England and Wales, only 67 per cent were funded by the NHS,[22] whilst in Scotland, 99 per cent of the demand for abortion is met by the NHS.[23] Moreover, there is a tremendous degree of regional variation within England and Wales. For example, in North Tyneside, 95 per cent of women have their terminations funded by the NHS, compared with only 43 per cent in Solihull. Thus, two women, in identical situations with the same reasons for seeking termination, but living in different parts of the country, are likely to receive different answers to their requests for an NHS termination.

The situation regarding NHS funding, whilst still unsatisfactory, has recently shown some change for the better. In 1990, the National Health Service and Community Care Act radically altered the administrative structure for the provision of services. The 1990 Act created an 'internal market' in the NHS whereby District Health Authorities and GP fundholding practices can buy services from DHA-managed units, NHS trusts or private clinics. In terms of the provision of abortion services, the result of this seems to have been their increased provision on the NHS. Table 4.1 sets out the number of terminations which have been performed on resident women in England and Wales over the last ten years for which figures are available, showing whether these were funded by the NHS.[24] As can be seen, the number of terminations paid for by the NHS seemed for some years to have settled at around, or just under, the 50 per cent mark. From 1992 onwards, however, the percentage of terminations which are NHS funded has steadily increased from 57 per cent in 1992 to 63 per cent in 1993 to 71 per cent in 1995. The most likely explanation for this trend would seem to be the desire of both the providers and purchasers to keep resources within the NHS. In addition, it may be that providers tend to accept that there is a need for NHS abortion services; consultant gynaecologists who were formerly reluctant to terminate pregnancies have become more willing when such activity increases departmental income (Paintin, 1993, p. 1).

Table 4.1 NHS funding of abortions for resident women in England and Wales. (NHS agency patients are NHS patients treated in the non-NHS sector.)

	Total number of abortions	NHS	NHS agency	Non-NHS	Percentage of NHS-funded abortions (%)
1986	147,619	67,451	6,819	73,349	50
1987	156,191	69,442	8,041	78,708	50
1988	168,298	69,103	9,357	89,838	47
1989	170,463	70,722	9,200	90,541	47
1990	173,900	73,517	9,582	90,801	48
1991	167,376	75,172	9,197	83,007	50
1992	160,501	79,543	11,982	68,976	57
1993	157,846	84,071	14,835	58,940	63
1994	156,539	85,243	19,551	51,745	67
1995	154,298	84,464	24,365	45,469	71

Source: Office of Population Censuses and Surveys, 1993 Abortion Statistics, HMSO AB Series, no. 20 (London: HMSO, 1995) and Office for National Statistics, Monitor, AB 96/5.

Despite the fact that these figures show clear improvement, recent research has shown that a combination of moral judgement and informal means-testing is widely used by GPs and health authorities to restrict the number of abortions performed on the NHS (Abortion Law Reform Association, 1997). A survey conducted by the Abortion Law Reform Association (ALRA) found that some health authorities were limiting approval for NHS abortion to their own list of specific criteria and that some were deliberately rationing their abortion service by setting a target considerably below the known local need. Furthermore, ALRA found that decisions regarding NHS funding for abortions are sometimes based on moral judgements rather than health need and the availability of termination of pregnancy in NHS hospitals is directly related to the willingness of key consultant gynaecologists to perform such operations (ALRA, 1997).

Since April 1996, abortion services have been included on the schedule of services and treatments liable to be purchased by GP fundholding practices. This obviously raises an additional problem with regard to conscientious objection: what of GP fundholders who will not be prepared to purchase such services? In response to this concern, the Department of Health has made provision for conscientious objectors to be able to opt out of paying for these services.[25] According to its guidelines, where one GP in a practice has an objection to the purchase of abortion services, he should notify a colleague who can then take responsibility for making the necessary contractual arrangements on his behalf. Where *all* the fundholders have an objection, then the practice must notify the relevant regional office of the Health Authority which will retain responsibility for purchasing terminations for the practice. GP fundholders are also told that they should inform patients of the practice's purchasing intentions, possibly by way of leaflets.[26]

Some GP fundholding practices have already opted out of the purchase of termination services.[27] What remains unclear is how the regulations are to be enforced when such initiative is not forthcoming on the part of the fundholding practice. In so far as I have been able to discover, no action has been taken against any fundholding practices which have failed to make such arrangements and the Department of Health has not indicated that it will be taking any steps to monitor whether all fundholding practices are purchasing termination services.[28] Moreover, reviewing decisions regarding resource allocation has always been notoriously difficult (Newdick, 1995) and given that one of the stated aims of the 1990 reforms was that of a more accurate assessment of prioritisation of need at the local level, there would seem to be certain problems inherent in central administration retaining this kind of control. It is unclear, for example, how the Department of Health might respond to a fundholding practice who argued that they are refusing to purchase termination services not for reasons of conscientious objection, but merely because they view abortion as a lower priority than the purchase of certain drugs or other treatments.

Decisional Control over Access to Abortions

Women have no positive legal right to an abortion. Rather they may *request* termination, and it is the medical professionals who must decide whether their request is founded with regard to the various criteria laid out in the Abortion Act. Where the doctor is not a conscientious objector, his personal position on abortion *should* in legal terms be irrelevant. However, in practice this is far from the case. The views of doctors regarding abortion will, naturally enough, run the whole gamut of those opinions present in the wider British society from very liberal (favouring abortion on demand of the woman) to very restrictive (regarding abortion as unacceptable in any circumstances). The crucial difference here is that no other member of society is legally granted the right to impose his views over those of the pregnant woman.

Although it is impossible to arrive at any clear idea of the frequency of such refusals, there is no doubt that even women whose situations would seem to fall clearly within the conditions foreseen in the law are refused abortions. For example, Denise Winn cites the case of a 22-year-old divorcee with two children, who had suffered a miscarriage five months previously and was pregnant again after her ex-husband forced her to have sex while he was drunk. She was refused an abortion by an NHS consultant (1988, p. 10). The wording of the Abortion Act is deliberately vague, allowing a very liberal or very restrictive interpretation by those empowered to interpret it and to grant or refuse abortion. As was seen in Chapter 3, the Act was carefully worded so as to leave full discretion possible with the doctor rather than granting formal rights to women. In Britain, many medical practitioners have taken a very liberal interpretation of the Act and the result is that most women are able to obtain a termination, if not on the NHS, then in the private sector. In the absence of a positive right to abortion, however, this may require some initiative on the woman's part in order to find a sympathetic doctor where her own GP does not agree with her decision. It will also require the funds to pay for the termination herself where necessary. As was noted above, this is obviously likely to mean greater problems for certain categories of women. Seema Daud asserts that illegal abortion is still prevalent within minority ethnic communities, with cultural abortifacients being imported from 'back home'. These include bamboo sticks, or twigs of irritant plants (1993, p. 151). Young women may also face problems. They are more likely to be intimidated by their doctors and less likely to have the independent funds, self-assurance and knowledge necessary to go elsewhere, should their requests be refused.

The tremendous discretion left to doctors under the Abortion Act means that if a woman approaches her GP seeking to terminate a pregnancy, it is normally impossible for her to predict how her request will be received. The doctor may be supportive and helpful. Alternatively, he may be moralising and judgemental. As was seen above, the GP has a right under the terms of s.4 of the Abortion Act not to participate in the provision of abortion on grounds of conscientious objection. Whether he has a duty to refer the woman to a colleague with a different view of the matter is debatable (see below pp. 162–3).[29] What makes this especially problematic is that there is no way for a woman to know her GP's views on abortion before approaching him. A proposal that the Abortion Act's conscientious objectors should be registered on a list which would be available to women, was rejected in 1990 on the grounds that it might lead to discrimination. The suggested amendment to the Human Fertilisation and Embryology Act was sponsored by Labour's then frontbench spokesperson on women, the late Jo Richardson (Barking), a stalwart campaigner for abortion law reform. She argued that the reform was essential to cut down on delays in the NHS:

> One of the problems is that doctors who have a conscientious objection to abortion tell women they are not entitled to abortions, when in fact they are. If a public register of doctors were available, women would not approach unsympathetic doctors and, as a result, get their abortions more quickly.[30]

The problem of delay has been highlighted with regard to RU486 terminations which depend on a speedy referral (see Chapter 7). Women may be unable to choose this method of termination because their requests for abortion take so long to be processed. A study by the Royal College of Obstetricians and Gynaecologists found that in 1981, 16 per cent of all terminations were carried out after twelve weeks, and that 2.3 per cent occurred after 19 weeks (Alberman and Dennis, 1984).[31] One thing which emerged clearly from the report was the delay between referral by the first doctor and the actual operation. Of those women aborting at 13–14 weeks, 25.6 per cent had been referred by the ninth week, as had 16.8 per cent of those aborting at 15–16 weeks. Even more worrying was the fact that over 20 per cent of the women having their terminations between 20 and 23 weeks had been referred at twelve weeks, and 7 per cent had been referred at nine weeks. By 1995, much progress seemed to have been made on this front, with 89 per cent of terminations carried out before twelve weeks, and almost half of these occurring before nine weeks. A Birth Control Trust report provides one particularly clear example of how delay can build up in the NHS.

> A separated woman, aged 27, went to her GP when her period was one week late. He told her she was too early and to return in four to five weeks. The pregnancy test took ten days by which time she was around twelve weeks pregnant. Her GP then referred her to a consultant but the appointment was delayed because the consultant was on holiday. She was 15 weeks pregnant before she was seen. The consultant agreed to perform the abortion and told her he would admit her for the operation when possible. She waited for the appointment but nothing happened. After a while she phoned the hospital and was told that the doctor was away again. She told the hospital of her concern over the lateness of the pregnancy and was told she was now too late and they could not perform the abortion. By the time she found alternative help she was at least 21 weeks pregnant (Francome, 1986, p. 55).

According to Francome, some of the women whom he interviewed for his study of abortion practice believed that doctors can sometimes deliberately create delay in the hope that women will continue with their pregnancies:

> I went to my doctor and at first he said I wasn't pregnant. For a month I felt unwell and when I went back to him he said I was three and a half months and that I was too late for an abortion. I believe he said I wasn't pregnant on purpose (Francome, 1986, p. 55).

Decisional control makes it all the more easy for unsympathetic GPs to attempt to impede or hinder women seeking termination. A doctor cited in another study illustrates the fact that speedy treatment is allied to a sympathetic attitude. He said:

> They're entitled to the benefit of the law. I've given up moral judgement. If it's for a reason like they have a heavy mortgage etc I forget to write sometimes. I say 'Too late, love, sorry. It's the hospital appointment system. You'll have to have the baby' (Cossey, 1982, p. 9).

Similarly, Dawn Primarolo (Lab., Bristol S) told the House of Commons about

> a young woman who went to see her doctor when she was two weeks pregnant. She did not know that her doctor was an anti-abortionist. The doctor was a man and he did not declare his conscience. By the time that young woman finally managed to get through the bureaucracy and to have the abortion that she had sought at two weeks, she was 22 weeks pregnant.[32]

The situation regarding delay is also greatly influenced by the views of senior obstetricians and gynaecologists and their level of commitment (or hostility) towards the provision of abortion services. Another Birth Control Trust report concludes that the areas which have been most successful in avoiding delay are those with interested and sympathetic gynaecologists (1987, p. 41). A survey conducted regarding abortion provision in Wessex Regional Health Authority found that twelve of its 32 NHS consultants had conscientious objections to abortion, and these consultants were directly responsible for the delays suffered by some Wessex women in obtaining abortion who, refused an NHS operation, turned to the private sector. Some districts in the Wessex RHA were served by only two consultants and if both had a major objection to abortion then NHS abortions were very difficult to obtain in that district (Cossey, 1982, p. 9).

In cases of refusal, women must go to a private clinic or to one of the abortion charities and thus lose the possibility of NHS funding (which is normally dependent on a GP referral). Government-collected statistics, which are based on terminations reported to them, do not show how many women are refused terminations. Francome cites a survey in Wessex in 1978, which showed that 16 per cent of patients at the BPAS clinic had been refused NHS terminations. However, he contends that women's decisions to 'go private' are not entirely a result of refusal but also reflect an unwillingness to face bureaucracy, delay and the uncertainty of how the doctor will decide (1986, p. 53). A survey of patients attending a London Pregnancy Advisory Service showed that three-quarters of the respondents to a questionnaire, although not dissatisfied with the private care they had received, would have preferred NHS treatment had it been available (*Abortion Review*, Winter 1993).

The doctor is not legally entitled to allow abortion to any woman who asks for it without more ado – the one reported prosecution of a qualified doctor acting with the second opinion foreseen in the 1967 Act was of a doctor who took just such a view of the law.[33] Thus the law reinforces the element of decisional control, even should the individual doctor concerned seek to reject it. However, it is clear that not every doctor would wish to do so. MacIntyre, in her analysis of the views publically expressed by the medical profession in the months leading up to the Abortion Act, found near unanimity, even in the Medical Woman's Federation, that the decision should be made by the doctor although the pregnant woman would have the right to 'state her case' (1973, p. 131).[34] This control is seen as essential with regard to abortion for, as I argued in Chapter 3, the very nature of the woman who would seek to terminate her pregnancy would make her an unsuitable person to exercise self-determination.

An interesting illustration of the problem inherent in a law that demands that doctors act as gatekeepers, controlling access to abortion, is the case of London GP, Trisha Greenhalgh. Greenhalgh was approached by a pregnant woman of 38, who was married, with a large house and a nanny for her three children. She requested termination as pregnancy would interfere with her holiday plans. After counselling, Dr Greenhalgh felt unable to sign the referral form, but asked another GP at the practice, who did so. Dr Greenhalgh wrote

> I am a feminist. I have marched and lobbied in support of a woman's right to choose, and I would do so again. But I am not a rubber stamp. I am a thinking and feeling professional and I must live with the clinical and ethical decisions I make (1992, p. 371).

A letter responding to Greenhalgh's article argued that

doctors would not need to be confronted with difficult decisions of this type if the British law was amended to match the law in most developed countries . . . [which] allows women free choice of abortion during the first 12 weeks of pregnancy, and a reason does not have to be stated (Campbell, 1992, p. 589).

At present, even when a doctor feels that the decision of whether or not to terminate should rightly belong to the woman, he may not feel at liberty to repudiate all control of the situation. Indeed, legally speaking, he is not entitled to do so. Greenhalgh, although stating a commitment to women's right to choose, did not feel able to allow the woman absolute freedom of choice in the face of a law which still states the decision to be that of the doctor. The role foreseen for the doctor is not simply to 'rubber stamp'.

In leaving the decision to doctors, law leaves a free rein to the individual doctor's prejudice or opinion. In the exercise of the doctor's discretion, the age, ethnic origin, class background, or marital status of a woman may be deemed important (Aitken Swan, 1977; MacIntyre, 1977). Moreover, there is some grounds for believing that the criteria used by doctors to decide who should have access to NHS abortions vary tremendously. MacIntyre notes that, when examining statements made by the medical profession at the time of the introduction of the 1967 Act, she was struck by the different rationales for decisions to refuse or to authorise terminations and how far these were on the periphery of medical knowledge. One doctor suggested that termination should be avoided for middle-class women because they frequently consciously or unconsciously desire the pregnancy and, if they go to term, cement relationships with their own mothers. Another, however, considered an unwanted pregnancy worse for a middle-class woman than for a lower-class woman, whether married or not. He would therefore be more likely to allow a termination to the former even in the presence of less strong medical indications. MacIntyre also found that students are deemed to have more of an interest and investment in their occupational careers than those already in the labour force in manual or white-collar jobs, and are thus more likely to be awarded abortions. She concludes:

There appears to be an extremely wide variation in the factors likely to influence different doctors. What is clear is that idiosyncratic moral views or definitions of social and psychological reality are put into practice by doctors, and that this can have enormous implications both for individual women and society as a whole (MacIntyre, 1973, p. 132).

It also seems clear that historically it has been easier for certain groups of women to obtain abortions. According to Oakley, it is unmarried women with no children whose request for abortion is most likely to be unsympathetically interpreted; as a group they are most likely to have private rather than NHS abortions (Oakley, 1981, p. 92; see also MacIntyre, 1977; McDonnell, 1984). However, a study of more recent statistics seems to provide no basis for this assertion. Single women accounted for around 65 per cent of all lawful terminations performed in England and Wales in 1993 and 66 per cent of those terminations performed in the non-NHS sector. There is no way of knowing what number of women decide to go through with a pregnancy having been refused a termination by their GP as the OPCS collects no statistics on refusals. It does seem, however, that it may be easier for women who have passed what is seen as the normal child-bearing age to obtain abortion. An article in *The Times* reported that one in three pregnant women over the age of 40 is *automatically* offered an abortion by their doctor.[35] Doctors may be more willing to offer termination in the case of foetal handicap. Indeed, Morgan (1990) has asserted that at the time of pre-natal testing for defects in the foetus, women are often asked for an *undertaking* to terminate should it prove to be affected.[36] Another report in *The Times* expressed the fear that doctors are putting pressure on women to have abortions in certain cases of foetal abnormality.[37]

The doctors' decisional control also makes it more difficult for a woman to resist the hostility or moralising lecture that she may encounter: she is very much a captive audience. Such evidence as exists of doctors availing themselves of the opportunity to air their views on the morals of the woman who has approached them to request a termination is largely anecdotal, and its occurrence is thus impossible to quantify. However, reports of such scenarios occur with such frequency in what studies there are of women's experiences of abortion as to demand very serious attention (see, especially, Francke, 1980; Cossey, 1982; Neustatter and Newson, 1986; Winn, 1988; Davies, 1991). The following are some examples of the kind of negative experiences women seeking abortion have had:

> The worst part was going to my doctor, who was very insensitive and cruel. My doctor refused flatly to grant a termination but offered a second opinion by another doctor. The second was a lady who still did her best to make me feel like a monster for wanting an abortion (Davies, 1991, pp. 69–70).

> [The gynaecologist] was horrid. He treated me like a piece of meat and then really told me off. He said he would only consider abortion at all because I had been depressed. I had to be grateful he would even condescend to see me. I felt so ashamed but, also, angry. That

behaviour made me the more determined to go ahead (Winn, 1988, p. 50).

He was determined I was going to have the baby. He said ' . . . then someone else who can't have babies can have your child'. It was a shock. My mum was upset and she's got heart trouble, and she said 'Don't I have any say in it?' and he said 'No' . . . so we changed doctors (14-year-old girl, in Cossey, 1982, p. i).

Their moralising and obvious hostility . . . put me on the defensive. I'd used contraception responsibly for seven years . . . Although I had expected some resentment and a few nasty comments from anti-abortion staff, this sort of scaring tactic was hard to believe (Cossey, 1982, p. 14).

Some of the above examples might, of course, be characterised as instances of medical malpractice. The point is, however, that the current regulation of abortion leaves the woman with very little ability to resist such treatment – she is dependent on the goodwill of the doctor to secure access to a termination. Moreover, she seems to have little recourse against a hostile doctor. The fact that many GPs do not act in this way does not provide any justification of a system which leaves women at the mercy of those who do. Whilst decisional control rests with the doctor, the woman seeking termination has the choice between risking submitting to this treatment, or seeking a termination in the private sector. Obviously the possibility of taking the latter option depends on the woman's financial situation and her knowledge of the existence of such services. Whether or not an individual doctor grants access to abortion is based on his perception of the situation – the only limitation being that his opinion must be formed in good faith: there is no requirement that the opinion must be reasonable and judges are reluctant to supervise how the doctors will exercise this control (see Chapter 5).

Paternalistic Control

Many GPs adopt a very sympathetic attitude towards women who approach them with unwanted pregnancy. However, one should not assume that by this fact alone, power is not being deployed over women. In a work which focused on how a patient's initial presentation of complaints was diagnosed and treated in the course of consultation, Kathy Davis argues that the process is carried out not strictly on the basis of medical and scientific criteria, but is also tied up with the constitution of an asymmetrical gender relationship (1988a, 1988b). She speaks of the Janus-like quality of interviews, with GPs often being sympathetic and kind, but still making moral judgements or failing to take women's problems seriously: 'it was precisely the intimate, pleasant quality of the medical encounter itself that made issues like power and control continue to seem like something else' (1988a, p. 48). Davis developed the concept of *paternalistic control* in order to understand the way in which power was being deployed in these encounters. She defines paternalism as

> limiting the freedom of another person by means of well-meant regulations. In this way, benevolent intentions are combined with relations of power. The person in authority may restrict and coerce, but only for the good of the other . . . Paternalism . . . implies a relationship of asymmetry. The original model for a paternalistic relationship is that of parent and child (1988b, pp. 23–4, references omitted).

In abortion, where the legal regulation is *overtly* paternalistic, explicitly according the doctor the power to decide in the woman's best interests, this kind of power is especially significant. Moreover, as was seen in Chapter 2, the woman seeking abortion is powerfully constructed as someone in need of this kind of control. The benevolent doctor's function might here be seen as apostolic: to guide the woman to the correct decision, one which will be objectively discernible to the trained doctor with access to medical knowledge. The doctor thus is better equipped than the woman herself to determine what constitutes her best interests. Even where the doctor is sympathetic and kind towards the pregnant woman, he or she may equally deploy power over her, influencing her course of action, rather than facilitating her arrival at her own decision.

This interpretation of the medical relationship fully concords with the role of the doctor as foreseen in the parliamentary debates which, as was seen above, was that of someone who would be able to reassure and support the woman, and encourage her to go ahead with the pregnancy (pp. 24–7). Paternalistic control may involve influencing a woman to continue (or equally to terminate) a pregnancy. Equally, it may be failing to tell her about some of the alternatives open to her – the doctor has considerable power over the 'agenda' of what will be talked about in the medical interview. The doctors in MacIntyre's study varied as to which options they would discuss with a woman. Some said they would present all women with all the possible alternatives (including abortion); some said they would mention the possibility of abortion only after ascertaining that the woman was not intending to marry, while others said that they would not discuss termination at all unless the woman herself raised the subject. One doctor told MacIntyre, 'She must bring up the subject of termination – I won't. I think if they'd like a termination they will bring the subject up – I don't want to put ideas into their heads' (MacIntyre, 1977, p. 75).

Further, doctors may put pressure on women, telling younger women that they must inform their parents (MacIntyre, 1977, p. 80; Cossey, 1982, p. i), or attempting to persuade a reluctant woman to tell her partner. Several of the doctors in MacIntyre's study said that they favoured marriage as the best 'solution' to an unwanted pregnancy. One of them told her,

> The majority of girls, those I've known since they were children, I manage to persuade them to get married. Girls from outside town, those I haven't seen previously – they're more difficult to persuade. Occasionally, girls do come in demanding termination but most can be talked out of it (1977, pp. 75–6).

Another had quite opposite views: 'If they say, "I'm getting married in September anyway" I ask if they *really* were intending to – I'm enough of a rebel to say, "Don't get married if it's just because of the pregnancy"' (MacIntyre, 1977, p. 76, emphasis in original).

Given the lack of current empirical research on this point, it is difficult to say to what extent doctors do influence the woman's decision to terminate (or not to terminate) a pregnancy. Suffice it to say here that the current legal regulation leaves women in a particularly weak position to counteract the exercise of such influence.

Normalising Control in the Medical Interview

> In order to be able to offer each of our patients a course of treatment perfectly adapted to his illness and to himself, we try to obtain a complete, objective idea of his case; we gather together in a file of his own all the information we have about him (Sournia, 1962, in Foucault, 1989b, p. xv).

There is also, I would assert, a fourth important deployment of power in the request for a termination of pregnancy, which goes beyond these three levels – this is the element of a normalising control exercised over women in the process of their request for an abortion. This 'type' of control is, of those described here, the least tangible and the most difficult to define coherently. Normalisation is the combination and generalisation of 'panoptic techniques': a process of insertion, distribution, surveillance and observation, which subsumes other forms of power (Foucault, 1991). Through constant observation, all those subject to control are individualised, and a body of knowledge about them is built up, with examinations producing dossiers and records containing observations about each individual: 'Not only has power now introduced individuality in the field of observation, but power fixes that objective individuality in the field of writing. A vast, meticulous documentary apparatus becomes an essential component of the growth of power' (1991, p. 190).

Details of the woman's abortion will be recorded in her medical records and also registered on notification forms which must be forwarded to the Chief Medical Officer (or the Secretary of State for Scotland). These reports enable the authorities to fix a web of objective codification, as more knowledge leads to more specification. This accumulation of documentation regarding individual women in a systematic ordering makes 'possible the measurement of overall phenomena, the description of groups, the characterization of collective facts, the calculation of gaps between individuals, their distribution in a given population' (Foucault, 1991, p. 190).

In the field of abortion, this is seen in the yearly publication of statistics which provide a wide range of information about women who have terminated pregnancies in the preceding year. Thus we know reasonably accurately how many women of a child-bearing age will terminate their pregnancies in any given year, where they live, their marital status, age, how many children exist in their family, the grounds for performing the termination and so on.

A woman may succeed in obtaining an abortion referral from her GP, and have her pregnancy terminated, yet to achieve this she must still undergo a certain interviewing process. The strategy of the deployment of power which I want to capture here is the control exercised in the process of the medical interviews preceding an abortion, firstly the initial interview with one's GP preceding referral (or refusal of the same) and secondly, that with the obstetrician/gynaecologist. Here, there is the requirement that the woman open herself to the medical gaze and reveal quite intimate details of her personal life in order to justify her request and convince the doctor, as it is the doctor's interpretation of her life experiences which will be valid and recognised for all official purposes. The very way that the law is phrased seeks to make every aspect of the woman's life and 'actual or reasonably foreseeable environment' relevant to her application. Indeed, it imposes the medical surveillance and control as a duty (see below pp. 83–7).

A 1978 book entitled *Unwanted Pregnancy: Accident or Illness*, written by two doctors, provides a particularly interesting insight into how abortion interviews might serve as sites in a network of normalising power. The book provides a study of various women seeking abortion, with the aim of increasing the abortion counsellor's understanding of the 'illness' (sic) underlying these women's requests for terminations (Tunnadine and Green, 1978, p. 15).[38] The doctors' information comes from a discussion group with other doctors, each of whom would present to the group an account of each woman who approached them with a request for abortion. They present 42 case studies selected from 147 women considered in their study. Here I will discuss just the first case by way of illustration of their approach.

The relevant facts of the first case (as they present them) are as follows: the patient, 'Angeline', was 26 and married with three children. At her first appointment, she said that she had become pregnant as the result of an accident, and had decided with her husband that she would have an abortion. Her doctor told her that she should make the decision for herself, but that he would make an appointment with a gynaecologist for her, and see her regularly in the meantime. At the next appointment, she came with her children. The third appointment was missed, and the fourth time she came without making an appointment. Angeline had left home at 19, because of a bad relationship with her mother. She had recently seen her mother in the High Street, yet they had turned away from each other without speaking. She experienced a sexual coolness between the births of her first and second children, and had also complained at this time of a lack of energy. During the second pregnancy, she had rectal pain and, after the birth of her second child, the husband sent her to the doctor because of dyspareunia. Lack of finance forced the couple to move to a smaller house, Angeline conceived again and, towards the end of the pregnancy, she had a series of minor haemorrhages. After delivery the placenta was reported to be perfectly normal (Tunnadine and Green, 1978, pp. 10–12). From these facts, the doctors draw the following conclusions:

> It could be seen from the above that there are signs that Angeline was someone who had shown, at least over the last few years, an *inability to cope with her sexual life and her pregnancies*. She had *never really matured* and yet Angeline's GP attempted to get her to make her own decision. She had to decide what to do despite the evidence that she was *not a responsible or full-value woman* (1978, p. 12, my emphasis).

Her GP was criticised for having allowed Angeline to take the decision regarding her abortion for herself.

Obviously it is necessary to bear in mind that this study is around twenty years old and the opinions of the doctors might not have been typical even in the late 1970s. What is interesting for our purposes is the *process* they describe. In that sense, I find two things are particularly striking about this case study. The first is the extent of the detail which the examining doctor is able to report from the woman's life. Although Angeline's GP was criticised for his failure to really get to know her situation, he is still able to relate details of the couple's finances (why they had to move to a smaller house) and sex life. He even knows when Angeline last saw her mother, and what the circumstances and outcome of the meeting were. All of this is seen as necessary and relevant in her request for abortion and yet is still deemed insufficient detail by the study. If this is considered an inadequate knowledge of the woman's life, one can only wonder what degree of minute detail Tunnadine and Green would feel is necessary. I am reminded of Foucault's quotation from Sournia which I cited above: 'we gather together in a file of his own all the information we have about him. We "observe" him in the same way that we observe the stars or a laboratory experiment' (in Foucault, 1989b, p. xv).

The woman is only required to be passive in terms of decision making. However, as Douzinas and McVeigh point out (with regard to the medical interview in general), 'the patient is required to speak and to explain her relationship with the world (sexual, social, business etc) . . . the medical object becomes the speaking subject, the orator of the personal experience or relation of health' (1992, p. 20).

The second thing which particularly impressed me about this study is that the authors feel able to draw very radical conclusions from such information as they do have. The bad rapport between Angeline and her mother no doubt seemed particularly important to them, given the strong significance which they attach to the maternal relationship (1978, pp. 181 and 183). The 'inability to cope with her sexual life and her pregnancies' is presumably inferred from the sexual coolness between the births of two of her children. Perhaps it is also this that leads them to assert that Angeline is not a 'full-value woman'. The conclusion of irresponsibility is possibly based upon the fact that she had difficulty in keeping her appointments. The obvious alternative interpretation that, as Angeline has three children to care for, she does not enjoy complete freedom with her own time, is not considered. The doctors here explore the details of Angeline's life to produce an authorised account of her reality, albeit one that may have precious little to do with her lived experience of it. Their account, moreover, has the stamp of medical 'truth'. I argued above that the power of the doctor is tied to his ability to understand, to classify and then, on this basis, to treat. After a close surveillance, Angeline is located within a conceptual framework, her problems identified and explained, her sickness understood, the correct treatment decided. In the normal course of events, the examining doctor will then go on (if the woman is referred for abortion) to register the abortion, with explanation for the contraindications which justify her referral. It is thus the doctor's version of events which are officially recorded in state archives and in the woman's medical records.

What is especially relevant about Tunnadine and Green's book is the light which it sheds on the medical method: the woman's life is put under the spotlight, her problem is located within a medical frame of reference, and the medical professional can thus claim the power to understand and to cure. This same process, I would argue, is present even in the approach of the far more progressive Dr Greenhalgh (discussed above, pp. 62–3). Greenhalgh talks in depth to the woman seeking abortion, assesses her situation and then decides that a referral is unjustified. Despite her own liberal views on abortion, and the fact that she has marched in favour of a woman's right to choose, she cannot recommend a referral in this case. Her perception of her role is that of a 'thinking and feeling professional', rather than a 'rubber stamp'. The value judgements may be different, the process is the same.

Several of the women in Sally MacIntyre's study were surprised and somewhat disconcerted by the amount of questions which their GPs asked regarding their pasts. As one woman concisely put it, '[w]hat does it matter what form of contraception we was using – it didna' work, did it?' (1977, p. 81). MacIntyre comments:

> Information about events and relationships in the past provided GPs with the major evidence by which they could typify the women and understand their circumstances. This could be resented by women wishing a simpler form of diagnosis and management, e.g. who wished confirmation of pregnancy and access to further services. Some saw questions about the past as prurient curiosity that had to be tolerated in order to obtain the required services, and as irrelevant to the management of their pregnancies (1977, p. 81).

Other women have spoken about these interviews as painful and unpleasant:

> He kept asking questions about my boyfriend . . . very embarrassing questions which I wouldn't answer . . . he made my mum cry (Cossey, 1982, p. i).

> I took great exception to being told off in a very condescending, humiliating manner. He wanted to know how long I'd known the man and asked what kind of relationship we'd have after this. I told him it was none of his business. He treated me like a stupid little girl. I was almost in tears and I was furious that he should have made me feel like this (Cossey, 1982, p. 14).

> I didn't like her. She was trying to blame me for everything. She said I was wasting other people's money and the bed (15-year-old girl describing hospital doctor, Cossey, 1982, p. i).

Part of the distress expressed by these women may be due to a reaction against having the doctor's definition of their lived realities imposed upon them.

Uncertainty as to how one's request will be received by doctors means that women may feel the need to convince doctors that they are justified in seeking abortion and thus are unable to really talk through their reasons for abortion in a way that may be helpful for them, or to voice any uncertainty or ambivalence about choosing abortion. In this sense, they are forced to collude with the doctor's interpretation of their circumstances. This belies the idea that the GP's role is that of counsellor. The woman's awareness that the final decision rests with the doctor greatly detracts from any possibility of his acting effectively in this way (Berer, 1993a), even where this is how the GP views his role. Two of the women interviewed by Denise Winn expressed this very clearly:

> I felt I had to express guilt to get a letter for an abortion, so the decision was made. I felt I couldn't have expressed reservations (1988, p. 51).

> I told the doctor that I was only 22, did shift-work, had no home and everything was chaotic. I think I was saying all that because I was basically going to ask for an abortion. So I was putting forward the negatives (1988, p. 47).

The doctor may act on the image of the woman's reality which he has constructed in order to try to influence her in a certain way. Here the category of normalising power begins to merge with that of paternalistic power. The abortion operation may also offer the opportunity to pressurise women into having further surgery. Wendy Savage relates the story of a West Indian single parent, whose gynaecologist refused to perform an abortion unless she consented to sterilisation concurrently. Whilst accepting that this is anecdotal, Savage argues that there is abundant published evidence that some doctors continue to press their ideas on women with regard to sterilisation. As some evidence for this, she points out that the rate of sterilisation at the time of abortion has always been higher in the NHS than the non-NHS sector (1982, pp. 294–5). Other doctors are explicit in encouraging women to continue with their pregnancies, when they feel this to be the right option: 'The GP was very rude. He basically said: "my wife had her first child at 19, so what's the problem?" I was living with a junkie at the time, in a squat in Bath.'[39]

I do not want to overstate the existence of what I have classified here as 'normalising' control. While this is built into the very structure of the medical interview, its extent will vary from interview to interview. One factor which may minimise the woman's experience of this type of control might be simply that, given the current pressures on the GP in terms of the time he can spend with his patients, he will not have a great deal of time to investigate the woman's situation fully before making his decision as to referral.

Normalising control is significant not just in terms of the women who seek abortion but in terms of reinforcing constructions of all women. The popular perceptions of the woman seeking abortion (women as mothers, women as immature, immoral and irrational) which underpin the Abortion Act are equally present here and the point which I made at the end of Chapter 3 applies equally strongly: the woman seeking abortion is at once the antithesis and logical conclusion of all women see p. 48.

CONCLUSION

I have argued that the relationship between a doctor and a woman approaching him for a pregnancy termination is pervaded with power. The patient approaches the doctor as a lay person to an expert, (s)he is the object of knowledge which the doctor must locate within a medical framework, to understand, to classify and to treat. This perceived need for medical control is reinforced when the patient is a woman, and even more so when she is a woman seeking abortion. With regard to abortion, this control operates first at the level of a *technical* control of the means of avoiding reproduction, secondly at the level of *decisional* control – policing who should (and who should not) be allowed the possibility of an abortion, thirdly at the level of *paternalistic* control (where the benevolent doctor still enforces her views through 'persuasion'), and lastly at the level of a *normalising* control exercised in the medical interview over women seeking abortion. Secondly, I have reviewed how the law is implicated in structuring the use of medical power in this instance.

If we accept with Foucault that a claim to knowledge is always already an assertion of power, then it seems that as new and more complex techniques and medical knowledges are developed, this will inevitably enhance and enforce the medical control over women's lives. The maintenance of absolute control over technical medical procedures is essential for the survival of modern medical power over abortion and other medical services. There is no guarantee that the removal of decisional control can by itself solve the problems posed by other forms of control. Davis's study shows paternalistic control as prevalent in doctor–(female) patient interaction regarding other medical matters (1988a). It is questionable, then, how easily the process of separating out the various strands of control, which I have here attempted on an analytical level, will be possible in practice.

State and law cannot be seen as neutral in this matter, with women's negative experience in access to abortion stemming from the hostility of individual medical practitioners. Where an appearance of official 'neutrality' does exist on the part of the government, it takes the form of a distancing from decisions regarding abortion, an abdication of responsibility to the medical profession and this can only serve to support the existing status quo and the power imbalance which characterises it. Moreover, as has been seen, state intervention goes further than this: the law actively imposes the control of the woman as the doctor's responsibility. A doctor fulfilling the role foreseen for him by statute will exercise *all* those forms of control described above. Medical professionals are legally obliged to take technical and decisional control and this will be enforced in the courts (see Chapter 5). Moreover, as has been seen in previous chapters, one very explicitly stated purpose of introducing the Abortion Act was to allow doctors to exercise paternalistic control more effectively, that is, to reassure women and to encourage women to continue with their pregnancies. Finally, in terms of normalising control, the rules laid out in the Abortion Act make it clear that the doctor must take responsibility for defining and understanding the woman's reality in order to determine whether access to abortion should be accorded to her. This must be an individualised judgement based on a close analysis of her circumstances. Those doctors who attempt to minimise these operations of power – those who view their role as one of helping the woman to make her own choice, for example – do so by attempting to step outside of this role.

5
The Judicial Protection of Medical Discretion

> Not only would it be a bold and brave judge who would seek to interfere with the discretion of doctors acting under the [Abortion] Act, but I think he would really be a foolish judge who would attempt to do any such thing, unless possibly, there is clear bad faith and an obvious attempt to perpetrate a criminal offence. Even then, of course, the question is whether that is a matter which should be left to the Director of Public Prosecutions and the Attorney-General (Sir George Baker P).

> I do not mean to say that the law fades into the background or that the institutions of justice tend to disappear, but rather that the law operates more and more as a norm, and that the judicial institution is increasingly incorporated into a continuum of apparatuses (medical, administrative, and so on) whose functions are for the most part regulatory (Foucault, 1979b, p. 144).

INTRODUCTION

As has already been seen, the medical control of reproduction is a matter which has provoked a great deal of concern and an ever-expanding literature from feminist commentators. The role of the courts in protecting and entrenching such control has not gone unregarded. In particular, the growth of the body of medical knowledge regarding the development of the foetus has already led to important social restraints on the autonomy of pregnant women, and concern has been expressed regarding the possible consequences of importing such knowledges into law. The dangers of this have been graphically illustrated in the US courts. In several cases, pregnant women have been charged with criminal offences such as supplying drugs to minors as a result of substance abuse during pregnancy. In a recent case, a Wisconsin mother who had drunk alcohol throughout her pregnancy and who eventually gave birth to a child suffering from foetal alcohol syndrome was charged with attempted murder. Assistant District Attorney Joan Korb was quoted as saying, 'hopefully, we'll start holding women accountable for the harm they do to their unborn child'.[1]

Whilst British courts have not witnessed such dramatic developments, the potential for similar actions clearly exists. In an article in the *Modern Law Review*, British academic Jane Fortin has argued that it is only right that law should take account of such matters for, 'In most circumstances, the unborn child is much more likely to be harmed, not by a third party but by his [sic] own mother' (1988a, p. 75).[2] The courts have so far refused to make the foetus a ward of court in order to protect it against the activities of the woman who is carrying it,[3] but they have been prepared to take account of a woman's conduct during pregnancy, when considering the need to make a care order following the baby's birth.[4] Moreover, as will be seen below, the High Court has also made it clear that the female patient's autonomy can be overridden in certain circumstances in the interests of a viable foetus.

The aim of this chapter will be to discuss the case law dealing with various aspects of the regulation of abortion and, in particular, to develop an argument which has already been made in previous chapters regarding the medicalisation of the law in this area. Judicial deference for medical opinion will be clearly marked. However, in the case law dealing with abortion, this may have had quite different results for considerations of women's bodily autonomy than in other areas of concern. In order to put the cases dealing with abortion in a broader context, I will first briefly sketch two cases where medical discretion and female autonomy have come into clear conflict before going on to examine in more detail some of the issues which the courts have faced with regard to the regulation of access to abortion services.

FEMALE AUTONOMY IN CONFLICT WITH MEDICAL DISCRETION

Re S (Refusal of Medical Treatment)[5]
S was admitted into hospital with the foetus in a position of transverse lie with an elbow protruding through the cervix. Doctors attempted to persuade her to have a caesarian section but, backed by her husband, she refused on religious grounds. The doctors applied to the courts for a declaration that they could lawfully perform the operation even in the absence of S's consent, the consultant surgeon testifying that it was a question of 'minutes rather than hours' and that this was a 'life and death situation'. He maintained that S's baby could not be born alive in the absence of a caesarian operation and that S herself was in imminent danger of a rupture of the uterus.

The position in English law is that a caesarian section (like any operation) is saved from constituting an assault only by the patient's consent to it, and a mentally competent adult patient has every right to withhold that consent. This case seemed to be complicated, however, by a statement made *obiter* by Donaldson MR in an earlier decision, *Re*

T, where he specified the only possible qualification to this principle might be, 'a case in which the choice may lead to the death of a viable foetus'.[6] President of the Family Division, Sir Stephen Brown granted the declaration as sought and the caesarian was performed. S's baby died shortly afterwards and her own condition was reported to be critical following the operation. In his reasoning Sir Stephen seems to go no further than noting that this point seemed to have been left open in *Re T*, judging the caesarian to be in the best *medical* interests, and stating (probably incorrectly) that an injunction would be accorded under US jurisprudence.[7] As Derek Morgan quite rightly points out this should have been no more than the starting point for his deliberations (1992, p. 1448). It seems relatively clear, however, that the only possible legal basis for the decision can be the (medically determined) interests of the foetus.

Re S provoked a storm of discussion and protest[8] and the ethical committee of the Royal College of Obstetricians and Gynaecologists have since decided that the life of the foetus should *not* give doctors grounds for overriding a woman's explicit refusal to undergo a caesarian section.[9] Notwithstanding this, several further court orders have been granted authorising caesarian sections in similar circumstances.[10] The case has been reported as the first time in English law that the rights of the unborn child have taken precedence over the rights of the pregnant woman to determine her treatment[11] and as establishing that a competent woman's absolute right to decide treatment could be overridden where the operation might save the child's life and would do the mother no harm.[12] As Morgan wryly adds in his commentary on this case, if a non-consensual caesarian section can be described as doing the mother no harm then it is difficult to imagine how other possible interventions to the benefit of the foetus could be refused (1992, p. 1448).

Re W[13]

Another controversial area and point of potential conflict between female autonomy and medical control is that of the ability of young women to give or withhold consent to medical treatment. In the case of *Re W*, the doctors of an anorexic 17-year-old, who had expressed her wish to refuse medical treatment, were granted permission to force-feed her. Jo Bridgeman mounts a strong critique of this judgment as 'taking a paternalistic approach, based on the assumption that treatment recommended by the medical profession must always be in the patient's best interests' (1993a, p. 69). For Bridgeman, this case highlights an illogical distinction in the law regarding the medical treatment of minors: whereas children are often now allowed to override parental wishes in *consenting* to medical procedures, they cannot override parental wishes in *refusing* to consent to them.[14] Within the context of judicial respect for medical opinion, this distinction becomes easier to understand: in the first case the child is agreeing with the medical opinion, in the second she seeks to oppose it. The latter requires parental support, the former not. This reveals the courts as biased towards upholding the decision of the medical professionals involved.

Whilst a general concern with the excessive space allowed to medical discretion is clearly evident in academic commentary (see especially Kennedy, 1988; Montgomery, 1989), it is feminist writers who have done most work in this area. In these cases of conflict between woman and doctor, the judicial respect for medical discretion and prioritisation of medical opinion in defining a woman's best interests has facilitated a significant encroachment into female bodily autonomy. Moreover, whilst these legal precedents remain exceptional, it is impossible to know what practical day-to-day effect they have in weighting the power balance in the doctor–patient relationship still more heavily against the patient. The two decisions discussed above must surely seriously compromise the consent requirement for medical treatment. What real meaning can a patient's consent to a procedure have, if she believes that if she withholds the consent, the doctor can secure a court order to authorise treatment without it?

THE MEDICAL CONTROL OF ABORTION

The medical control of abortion cannot be understood outside of the context of these other cases of judicial support for medical discretion. Yet for abortion, the existing case law has a very different flavour. In the two cases discussed above, a woman's claim of bodily autonomy has come into conflict with her medically defined 'best interests'. In the cases dealing with abortion which I will discuss below, however, the woman normally approaches the court desiring the same verdict as her doctor. Thus, in these cases, the same judicial prioritisation of medical opinion and reluctance to interfere with good medical practice has had far more positive results for women regarding the possibility to exercise some reproductive autonomy. Where problems may still occur for women, however, is when law is called upon not to protect the medical relationship from *outside* challenge, but to protect the woman *within* it.

First, I will address five series of cases involving the regulation of abortion which have been faced by the English courts: prosecutions for the unlawful procurement of miscarriage under s.58 of the Offences Against the Person Act 1861, before and after 1967; applications for injunctions to restrain an intended abortion; the legality of abortions by medical induction; and cases of abortion where consent is problematic (where the pregnant woman is a minor or has learning disabilities). Finally, I will address the case of non-consensual abortion.

Prosecutions under s.58 of the Offences Against the Person Act: prior to the 1967 Act

Even prior to the introduction of the 1967 Abortion Act, there were relatively few prosecutions for illegal abortion. As was noted in Chapter 2, despite estimates of 10,000 to 100,000 illegal abortions per year, in 1966 there were 62 prosecutions, only 28 of which resulted in convictions entailing prison sentences. Further, very few of these prosecutions were of registered medical practitioners. Prosecutions both before and after the introduction of the Abortion Act seem to be based on two criteria: whether the abortionist is a qualified doctor, and if so whether he is operating within the bounds of good medical practice.

R v. *Bourne*[15]

Until 1967 the provision of legal abortion in Britain was governed by the decision in *R* v. *Bourne* and this still forms the basis for what abortions are performed in Northern Ireland, where the Abortion Act does not apply.[16] In this case, a girl of 14 was pregnant as the result of being raped by a group of soldiers. Alec Bourne, a surgeon of good reputation, openly performed an abortion in a London hospital without charging any fee. He was charged under s.58 of the Offences Against the Person Act 1861 with unlawfully procuring a miscarriage. Bourne's major problem in defending his actions was that the Offences Against the Person Act provided no specific defence against this crime. However, the judge, Macnaghten J, directed that the word 'unlawfully' implied that there must also be certain circumstances in which abortion might be considered lawful. He advised the jury that the scope of lawful abortion should be equated with the scope of lawful child destruction under the Infant Life (Preservation) Act. Thus, the jury were directed that in order for Bourne to be convicted, the prosecution must prove beyond reasonable doubt that the operation was not performed 'in good faith for the purpose only of preserving the life of the mother'. Here Macnaghten J established a wide definition of life which was to form the basis of the performance of legal abortions for the next thirty years:

> if the doctor is of the opinion, on reasonable grounds and with adequate knowledge, that the probable consequences of the continuance of the pregnancy will be to make the woman a physical or mental wreck, the jury are quite entitled to take the view that the doctor, who, in those circumstances, and in that honest belief, operates, is operating for the purpose of preserving the life of the woman.[17]

The judge's interpretation of statute comes close to a recommendation made by the Criminal Law Commissioners in 1846 that the law should be amended so that abortion should not be an offence when performed in good faith for the purposes of saving the life of the mother.[18] Given that the drafters of the 1861 Act had refused to amend the law in line with this suggestion, the judge's interpretation of the statute seems even more creative.

According to his 1962 autobiography, Bourne had actually made the decision to bring such a case to court three years earlier when, to his anger, his house surgeon had walked out during a termination performed on a girl of a similar age. He himself informed the police of the operation, and it seems highly probable that he would never have been prosecuted were he not to have done so. His acquittal rests squarely on the fact that he is a qualified doctor. This is noteworthy in that, at this time, no such distinction existed in law as to the professional status of the abortionist. In his summing up, however, the judge pointedly and repeatedly distinguished between the act of the backstreet abortionist and an operation openly performed by a qualified surgeon. He contrasted the case in hand with another which had come before the court earlier in the month. In that case:

a woman without any medical skill or any medical qualifications did what is alleged against Mr. Bourne here . . . She did it for money. £2 5s. was her fee, and she came from a distance to a place in London to do it . . . She came, she used her instrument, and, within an interval of time measured not by minutes but by seconds, the victim of her malpractice was dead on the floor. She was paid the rest of her fee and she went away. That is the class of case that usually comes before the court. The case here is very different. A man of the highest skill, openly, in one of our great hospitals, performs the operation . . . as an act of charity, without fee or reward, and unquestionably believing that he was doing the right thing, and that he ought, in the performance of his duty as a member of a profession devoted to the alleviation of human suffering, to do it.[19]

Indeed, it was the norm in such cases to distinguish between 'respectable', qualified medical providers of abortion acting within the bounds of good medical practice and unscrupulous, unqualified backstreet abortionists, operating for profit. Again, in the later case of *R v. Bergmann and Ferguson*,[20] a sharp distinction was made between unqualified people performing such operations and those lawfully engaged in the practice of medicine. Drs Bergmann and Ferguson were subsequently acquitted.

It seems, however, that this stark distinction between the altruistic medical practitioner and callous and greedy backstreet abortionist is far from representing the reality. It belies the fact that a great many qualified medical practitioners were actually making large sums of money from performing abortions (see Chapter 2) and that at least some backstreet abortionists were motivated more by compassion and a desire to help a woman in trouble than by any financial motive. Sometimes these abortionists were women who had first terminated a pregnancy for a friend in trouble and frequently they charged very low amounts for their services. In 1963, Moya Woodside interviewed 44 women who were in Holloway prison for the performance of abortions in the early 1960s. She found that although most knew abortion to be illegal, they did not feel it to be wrong. They asserted that they had acted out of 'compassion and feminine solidarity' for women facing unwanted pregnancies and denied that financial gain was their chief motivation (1963, p. 100).

According to Andrew Grubb (1990, p. 152), *Bourne* marks the first (albeit primitive) regulation of abortion. Three factors are especially significant in the form of this regulation: first, the judge notes that only the medical profession can lawfully perform abortions; secondly, a doctor should act only when he has consulted some other member of the profession of high standing; thirdly, the judge distinguishes between paid and unpaid abortionists. As Grubb rightly points out, the bases for such requirements are not easily found in the existing law of the time, but they provide the first judicial confirmation of the ascendancy of the medical profession over any rivals it might have had in earlier times, whilst sketching some safeguards against possible abuse by doctors. This case clearly signals the lines which will be followed by the British courts in treating abortion as a medical procedure. Particularly important to note is that judicial confirmation of greater access to abortion is integrally related to the tightening of an exclusionary medical monopoly over it.

R v. Newton and Stungo[21]

Ms Smith was referred to Dr Newton by a psychiatrist, Dr Stungo, who deemed that, given her suicidal state, her pregnancy should be terminated. Dr Newton saw Ms Smith at 2.30, told her to think about it and come back at 5.30. When she returned, still requesting an abortion, he administered utus paste by way of uterine injection and sent her off to her hotel in a taxi. He charged Ms Smith a total of £75 for the operation, accepting the sum in cash in advance. He admitted that the fee was high, but explained that he had done this on purpose 'to discourage her from having anything done'. Ms Smith became ill the same evening and was vomiting continuously the following morning when Dr Newton examined her. Her condition continued to deteriorate and on the third day he claimed that he decided to send her to hospital, but that she declined. She was finally admitted to hospital the following day. The prosecution claimed that the delay in sending Ms Smith into hospital showed gross negligence or an intention to conceal for as long as possible the fact that he had terminated her pregnancy. In the letter requesting her admission to hospital, Dr Newton stated the reason for admission as 'incomplete abortion' but made no reference to the fact that it was he who had treated Ms Smith. Further, according to the registrar at the hospital, when Dr Newton phoned to check on Ms Smith's condition he explicitly denied that he himself had performed the abortion.

The respective verdicts delivered for the two defendants are instructive. Dr Stungo, who had acted in accordance with regular medical practice, and whose good faith was demonstrated by the low fee (of three guineas) which he had charged, was acquitted of being an accessory before the fact of procurement of miscarriage under s.58 of the Offences Against the Person Act 1861. Dr Newton, however, was found guilty both under this section, and also of manslaughter by unlawfully using an instrument to procure a miscarriage. He was sentenced to consecutive terms of two and three years' imprisonment respectively. Dr Newton had not acted in accordance with good medical procedure. He had operated in his consulting rooms, without admitting Ms Smith to hospital and without anyone else being present. He delayed in admitting her to hospital and then lied about the fact that it was he who had terminated the pregnancy. Finally, he had charged an unusually large amount for performing the operation. The expert witness for the prosecution testified that where a patient was three months pregnant, the normal medical practice would be to keep her in hospital for five to seven days. He refused to recognise Dr Newton's actions as proper: indeed everything pointed to the fact that he was carrying out the operation clandestinely for profit.

If Dr Newton had charged a lower fee and had carried out the operation more openly, it is highly unlikely that he would have been convicted. Harvard, writing of this case, argues:

> in practice it is often found that a doctor who terminates pregnancy unlawfully will make certain departures from accepted medical practice in order to conceal the matter. Such is the integrity of the medical profession that abortions carried out under the accepted medical procedure are rarely, if ever, questioned, at any rate since the decision in *Bourne* (1958, p. 607).

He goes on to conclude that this case confirmed that the accepted medical indications for terminating pregnancy will be recognised as constituting the defence of necessity. Provided that the operation was carried out in good faith for the purposes of preserving the life or health of the woman, it seemed that doctors should have nothing to fear.[22]

Prosecutions under s.58 OAPA: after the 1967 Abortion Act

If there were few prosecutions of doctors before the Abortion Act, understandably there have been still fewer following its introduction. In fact, there has been just one reported conviction of a doctor operating with the necessary second opinion foreseen in the Abortion Act. One might have foreseen the possibility of more prosecutions – the Act explicitly refuses complete freedom of action to doctors, but rather allows them to perform abortions in the presence of specified indications. However, the only requirement for the doctor in attesting to the condition of such conditions is that he reached his decision in good faith. There is no requirement that the assessment be a reasonable one. As Hoggett foresaw in the months before the Abortion Act came into force, 'the availability of abortion will rather be governed by medical ethics than by legal requirement' (1968, p. 257). Later, Denning MR, in a judgment which is explicitly hostile towards the liberal provision of abortion, confirms this in asserting the impossibility of controlling the doctor's decision beyond the requirement for good faith. He states that the only limitations on abortion imposed by the Abortion Act are the requirement of a certificate signed by two doctors, that the abortion must be done in hospital or other licensed premises, and that it must be done by a registered medical practitioner.[23]

Furthermore, the courts have exercised only a minimum of supervision as to what constitutes good faith. In a frequently cited comment from the judgment in *Paton* v. *BPAS*, Baker P notes that 'not only would it be a bold and brave judge who would seek to interfere with the discretion of doctors acting under the [Abortion] Act, but I think he would really be a foolish judge who would attempt to do any such thing'.[24]

The 'discretion of doctors' is here interpreted very widely by the judge, as anything which does not include 'bad faith and an obvious attempt to perpetrate a criminal offence'. Even then, according to Baker P, it is possible that this matter may still be best left to higher judicial authority. Given this judicial reluctance to convict doctors, it is worth examining in some detail the only reported conviction of a registered doctor operating within the 1967 Act.

R v. *Smith*[25]

A woman of 19, who wanted an abortion, was sent to Dr Smith, a general practitioner with a specialised practice in the termination of pregnancies. Dr Smith neither examined her internally nor enquired about her medical history but agreed to perform the operation on the payment of a fee of £150 a week or so later. Their appointment lasted just 15 minutes, and he made no suggestion of the need for a second opinion or further enquiries. Eight days later, Dr Smith performed the abortion at a nursing home. The woman did not see any other doctor in the meantime, nor were any enquiries or investigations made about her. Further, there was some doubt as to whether the operation was carried out in accordance with good medical practice. In particular, she claimed that her anaesthetic was administered by a man who was later identified as a porter at the nursing home. Dr Smith was subsequently charged and convicted of illegally procuring a miscarriage under s.58 of the Offences Against the Person Act 1861. It was held that he was not protected by the defence offered under the Abortion Act, as he cannot have been acting in good faith when he operated, having allowed himself no opportunity to form a bona fide opinion as to the balance of risks between termination and continuation of pregnancy. The Court of Appeal upheld the judgment.

The case is interesting for the light which it throws on the very liberal judicial interpretation of the limitations imposed on the medical profession by the 1967 Act. Scarman LJ summarises the operation of the Abortion Act in the following way:

> The Act, though it renders lawful abortions that before its enactment would have been unlawful, does not depart from the basic principle of the common law as declared in *R* v. *Bourne*, namely that the legality of an abortion depends on the opinion of the doctor. It has introduced the safeguard of two opinions: but, if they are formed in good faith by the time the operation is undertaken, the abortion is lawful. Thus a great social responsibility is firmly placed by the law on the shoulders of the medical profession (at 381).

However, this does not delegate total responsibility to the medical profession:

> If a case is brought to trial which calls in question the bona fides of a doctor, the jury, not the medical profession, must decide the issue . . . By leaving the ultimate question to the jury, the law retains its ability to protect society from an abuse of the Act (at 381).

Again, however, the only requirement is one of good faith.

The issue of the case became, according to Scarman LJ, to determine whether or not Dr Smith had abused the trust placed in him by the Act of Parliament (383). The judge in first instance had explained that the defendant took the view that if any girl wanted her pregnancy terminated, that of itself was, if not entirely sufficient, a very powerful indication of the risk of injury to her mental health if the pregnancy continued being greater than if the pregnancy was terminated. The verdict of the court reveals that to authorise abortion for no more reason than a woman's desire to have one was indeed an abuse. It seems from the judgments delivered in *R* v. *Smith*, that if Dr Smith had examined the woman then there would have been no possibility for the judges to 'second-guess' his opinion. His failure here was that, objectively, there was no possible way in which his opinion could have been formed in good faith based on an assessment of the case in hand, as there was no possibility that a real assessment had been made. Rather he was prepared to provide a termination for any woman who had the money to pay for it. Other actions of Dr Smith's also indicated a failure to act in accordance with good medical practice: the doubt as to who applied the anaesthetic, the fact that their appointment was so short, his failure to inform the woman of the need for a second opinion and the size of his fee.

Significantly, the doctor's failure to act in good faith is evidenced by the fact that he did not act within the bounds of good medical practice. This standard is not met here because of his failure to exercise the level of control foreseen in law. Dr Smith advised the woman that she might have an abortion without any medical investigation or discussion of her social circumstances. His defence was that if any girl wanted her pregnancy terminated, that of itself was a very powerful indication of the risk of injury to her mental health. There is no suggestion that there was any danger to the woman's health; however, Dr Smith's actions are an abdication of the role which Parliament had foreseen for him. Indeed, given the role of the doctor as envisaged in the parliamentary debates as discussed in Chapters 2 and 3 (see especially pp. 26–7, 40), it is hardly surprising that the conduct of Dr Smith failed to impress. Another doctor gave evidence to the court:

> one would want to know as much as one could about the patient's general background and so on . . . Then there is the girl's own history, her past medical history, has there been mental illness in the family, one would expect to check that.

As Scarman LJ summarises, 'He made it clear that in his opinion careful enquiries on a number of matters would be needed before an opinion could be formed' (382).

Thus, at least as it was seen in 1971, the discretion granted to doctors under the 1967 Act has one very important limit: it does not include a discretion to abdicate control and allow abortions indiscriminately, simply on the basis that a pregnant woman wants and is able to pay for one. If doctors do operate in this manner in practice, they are expected to be able to justify their decisions in some other way. Some level of control is demanded and will be enforced by the law. This is emphasised in the 1976 Regulations issued by the Minister of Health, which require the doctors to base their opinions on the woman's individual circumstances and to state whether they were formed after seeing the patient.[26]

Notification Forms and the 'Statistical Argument'

It is unlikely that the British courts will see a similar prosecution to the one described above as it seems now to be widely accepted that some doctors are very liberal in their interpretation of the Abortion Act. In 1982, in an effort to tighten up the rules for legal abortion, the Department of Health and Social Security changed the abortion notification forms. The new forms made no reference to environmental (or non-medical) grounds for termination of pregnancy.[27] Rather, they demanded to know the main *medical* condition justifying abortion.[28] Pro-choice doctors responded by answering with 'pregnancy' as the grounds justifying intervention. No prosecutions have been brought in these cases. Indeed such a prosecution would be extremely difficult as, under section 1 of the Abortion Act, an abortion is justified where there is risk to the woman, greater than if the pregnancy were terminated. It is generally agreed that where abortion is performed early in the pregnancy, statistically speaking, it poses less of a risk to the woman than carrying the pregnancy to term. A successful prosecution of a doctor in these circumstances would need to show that the doctor on trial did not honestly believe these statistics to be valid, and so had failed to act in good faith. Thus, it would seem that abortions (at least where performed in the first trimester) can be freely available from a doctor who is prepared to accept the statistical argument. However, this does not relieve doctors of their duty to make a comparison between the risks to the particular woman of continuing or terminating a given pregnancy: as was seen above, the 1967 Act requires the doctor to make an individualised decision.

What the courts have done in these cases is to actively protect and entrench the monopoly of doctors, whilst policing those marginal cases which did not fall within the bounds of good medical practice. This accords with a long tradition of leaving the regulation and control of medical practice largely to the medical profession itself. As has been seen above, the courts act only in the most exceptional cases and this serves to sanction and legitimate the 'ordinary' cases in which they do not intervene. Further, they confirm the legitimacy of day-to-day medical practice by adopting medical standards ('normal medical practice' or 'good medical practice') and punishing only those who deviate from them. Thus, in the interaction between the two systems (legal and medical), doctors can be held criminally liable when they deviate from what are thus essentially standards developed within the medical profession.[29] Judges constantly reiterate and reinforce the naturalness and correctness of the medical control of abortion and the autonomy of medical practice. This seems neatly to illustrate an argument made by Peter Fitzpatrick (1997, p. 91):

By intervening occasionally and to correct excess, law confirms the normal run of administration as the unexceptional, as 'the nature of things'. In their relation, there are indefinable but inevitable limits to what law can do about administration. The supervising judge will ultimately recognise and respect the bounds or the integrity of administrative expertise.

And, as Grubb concludes, 'There can be little doubt that the English judiciary has no desire to challenge, except in the most exceptional circumstances, the medical decision-making power conferred upon doctors by the Abortion Act 1967' (1990, p. 156). The judicial recognition of the authority of these 'parallel judges' of the medical profession has meant that doctors who decide to take a liberal interpretation of the Abortion Act are unchecked, and women's access to legal abortion is thus facilitated.

Injunctions to Restrain Abortion

Judicial reluctance to step within the area of discretion carved out for medicine can also be seen in cases where injunctions to prevent a proposed abortion have been requested. The granting of such an injunction has never been reported in Britain, nor in any other common law jurisdiction, with the one notable exception of the Canadian case of *Tremblay* v. *Daigle*. Here, the judge at first instance granted the woman's sexual partner an injunction to prevent her proposed abortion, commenting:

> The child conceived but not yet born, regardless of the term that is given to his civil status, constitutes a reality which must be taken into consideration. It is not an inanimate object, nor anyone's property, but a living human entity, distinct from that of the mother that carries it, which two human beings have given existence to, which they procreated, and which, at first blush, is entitled to life and to the protection of those who conceived it.[30]

This case has since been overturned and is hence bad law. British men have failed in two well-publicised similar attempts to secure similar injunctions. The Society for the Protection of the Unborn Child (SPUC) has also attempted to restrain a proposed termination of pregnancy pending the provision of certain information to the pregnant woman concerned.

Paton v. *Trustees of British Pregnancy Advisory Service*[31]
Mrs Paton obtained the two necessary certificates from registered medical practitioners which would enable her to have her pregnancy lawfully terminated under section 1(1)(a) of the Abortion Act. She did

not consult her husband, nor was he consulted by the authorising doctors. Mr Paton opposed the foreseen abortion, arguing that he had a right to have a say in the destiny of his child. He applied to the court for an injunction restraining his wife from causing or permitting an abortion to be carried out on her without his consent. The court refused the injunction on the basis that a husband had no right, enforceable either at law or in equity, to stop his wife having, or a registered medical practitioner performing, a legal abortion. The court refused to supervise the discretion of a doctor acting under the Abortion Act where there was no clear indication of bad faith.

Paton clearly illustrates the judicial attitude to the position of doctors acting within the 1967 Act. The role of medicalisation in depoliticising the judges' decision is also very clear. The judges here explicitly deny the relevance of moral values stating an aim of applying the law, 'free of emotion or predilection'.[32] The first question addressed by the court was whether the plaintiff had any right which was enforceable at law. The foetus was held to be incapable of having any rights of its own until it was born and had a separate existence from its mother (989). To have succeeded, the action must therefore have rested on the rights of the father. As the illegitimate father can have no rights at all (other than those which he is explicitly accorded by statute), the claim would have had to have rested on his rights as a husband (990), but the court will not seek to enforce or restrain by injunction matrimonial obligations. Therefore, Baker P concluded that the husband cannot by injunction prevent his wife from having a lawful abortion within the terms of the Abortion Act. He dismissed the plaintiff's claim that if the doctors did not hold their views in good faith (which would be an issue triable by jury following *R* v. *Smith,* see above), then the plaintiff might recover an injunction. Baker P held that it was unnecessary to decide this 'academic question' because it did not arise in this case: 'My own view is that it would be quite impossible for the courts in any event to supervise the operation of the 1967 Act. The great social responsibility is firmly placed by the law, on the shoulders of the medical profession' (991).

He concluded that it was not and could not be suggested that the certificate was given by the doctors in other than good faith and that that was an end to the matter in law (991). He ended his consideration of English law with the now famous words (which are cited more fully above): 'not only would it be a bold and brave judge . . . who would seek to interfere with the discretion of doctors acting under the 1967 Act, but I think he would really be a foolish judge . . . ' (992).

The husband's action thus failed in the face of the broad discretion accorded to doctors working within the terms of the Abortion Act and the refusal of the judges to police within this discretion. *Paton* was the first occasion that the courts were faced with making such a decision and it was by no means self-evident that they would have found in such a way.[33] Furthermore, the case was taken all the way to the European Court of Human Rights, and so the decision is supported by the very highest authority.[34] It is not surprising, therefore, that few similar actions have been brought.

C v. *S*[35]

The case of *C* v. *S* involved an application by Robert Carver, president of the Oxford University Pro-Life group, on his own behalf and as next friend of the 'child en ventre sa mère', for an injunction to restrain his pregnant ex-girlfriend from terminating her pregnancy. Carver conceded that he had no *locus standi* based on a claim of biological paternity (this much was clear from *Paton*).[36] However, he argued that he had a sufficient personal interest to do so as the proposed termination would be a crime concerning the life of his child. Further he argued that the foetus was a proper party to the proceedings since it was the subject of a threatened crime. Carver argued that the issue to be decided could be distinguished from that in *Paton*, given the gestational age of the foetus (between 18 and 21 weeks). This, he argued, meant that it was 'capable of being born alive' and the act of aborting it would thus constitute the offence of child destruction under section 1(b) of the Infant Life (Preservation) Act 1929. Carver defined 'capable of being born alive' in terms of the ability to demonstrate real and discernible signs of life, namely a primitive circulation and movement of the limbs.

The judge at first instance refused to grant an injunction, holding that the foetus had no right to be a party and that Carver had failed to establish that an offence under the 1929 Act would be committed if the termination was carried out. Carver appealed to the Court of Appeal which dismissed the action, holding that although a foetus of between 18 and 21 weeks of gestation could be said to demonstrate real and discernible signs of life, the medical evidence was such that it would not be 'capable of being born alive' within s.1(1) of the 1929 Act. The foetus would be incapable of breathing either naturally or with the aid of a ventilator and 'capable of being born alive' was held to include some capacity for independent survival. Given that lung development does not occur until around 24 weeks of gestational development, capacity for life could not be presumed before that point. The House of Lords upheld the decision by refusing leave to appeal.[37]

Thus the issue in *C* v. *S* is essentially a medical one, and the task of the judges is to sift through medical evidence provided in the affidavits of 'medical men, all of high reputation and great experience' (1235) to arrive at the correct definition of 'capable of being born alive'. Here the judge must take into account the 'rapid, extensive and truly remarkable developments in medical science, not least in the field of obstetrics' (1238). One interesting aspect of *C* v. *S* is that, despite the very clear authority of *Paton*, Carver still thought that there was a possibility to obtain an injunction by challenging the received legal construction, i.e. the rebuttable presumption that viability is presumed to occur at 28 weeks, contained in the Infant Life (Preservation) Act 1929, with the argument that it has been overtaken by medical technology and the production of expert medical witnesses to testify to this effect. The judge is then forced to step on to essentially medical territory, in weighing up different medical criteria for viability and choosing from amongst them. In so doing, he does indeed find the limit of 28 weeks to be too high, but he fails to accept the criteria (and the still lower time limit) proposed by Carver. The judge also weighs up the different medical definitions against pre-existing case law on the matter, and thus retains final authority for the law.[38] He adds

> It is not necessary for me, nor would I want, to try to decide on affidavit evidence in a somewhat limited sphere the answer, which baffles men and women with great scientific expertise, to a very profound question. I would, however, say that I am not greatly attracted to the very limited definition relied on by [the expert medical witness for the plaintiff] and I do not accept it as a realistic one (1240).

Paton and *C* v. *S* show the same reluctance on the behalf of the judiciary to supervise the doctors or to second-guess their decisions (other than in clear cases of bad faith or bad medical practice) as was seen in the other cases discussed above. As Sir Roger Ormrod, then a judge of the Court of Appeal and a qualified doctor, stated in 1976, 'Abortion has become generally available, if not yet quite on demand, but subject only to the attitude of the surgeon concerned or of the clinic to which the woman is referred' (in Grubb, 1990, p. 154).

SPUC and the Patient's Right to Informed Consent
On 4 August 1996, Professor Phillip Bennett, a leading researcher in the field of obstetrics, gave an interview describing some of the cases facing him in his work which he found ethically difficult.[39] One such case involved a woman (here referred to as 'A'), pregnant with twins, who had asked Professor Bennett to terminate one twin. This particular story was picked up by other papers and provoked a storm of interest and protest. The fact that the abortion requested involved one of a pair of twins was seen by many to make it qualitatively different from other terminations. Eventually, however, discussion in the media broadened to consider the provision of abortion services in general.

On 6 August, it was reported that the Society for the Protection of the Unborn Child (SPUC) had approached Queen Charlotte's Hospital, where Professor Bennett worked and A was being treated, wishing to offer a substantial sum of money (put forward by its members) to enable her to carry on with her pregnancy. The hospital responded that it was unable to promise to pass the offers on, saying that this was a matter of 'clinical judgement'. It was claimed that the offer of such a large sum of money would unduly influence A's decision.

SPUC responded by applying to the High Court on a variety of grounds including an order for *certiorari* to quash the decision to refuse to pass on their offer to A; an order for mandamus for the transmission of such information; a declaration that the policy of the Area Health Authority was unlawful; an interlocutory injunction to prevent the termination of the pregnancy until such information as was directed by the Court was transmitted to the woman, and, finally, discovery of hospital records. At 4.32 p.m. on 6 August, an injunction restraining the respondents from terminating the woman's pregnancy was granted until 10 a.m. the following morning. Notice was served on the respondents setting out the terms of the injunction and advising them that they were entitled to appear in court the following day to respond to the matters raised. Early that evening, however, it was reported that the abortion had in fact already taken place. Accordingly, the following day, SPUC withdrew its application.

Over the two days, when press interest was at its highest, various further pieces of information regarding A were reported. She was described as a single mother of limited means who already had one child and felt that she could not afford two more. A was defended as a tragic victim of circumstance, pushed to make an impossible decision:

> Abortion is always a difficult and painful act for those concerned: as a single mother in 'socially straitened circumstances' who already has one child, she clearly believes she cannot call on support, either financial or emotional, in our fragmented, individualistic culture. It is this dimension of the story that should really concern us, rather than letting one tragic case be used as an argument for re-examining the existing law.[40]

The press later reported that A was not in 'socially straitened circumstances', but was actually the wife of a wealthy and successful businessman. It seems that Professor Bennett, attempting to mitigate the worst effects of his potential breach of confidentiality, had made some attempts to disguise A's identity. This revelation seemed to provoke a shift in the discussion regarding A's situation as public perception of her situation slid between the popular constructions of women in this kind of situation. This served to renew discussion in the media regarding whether abortion services are too easily obtained.

This shift was heightened by comparison with another story which hit the press on 11 August 1996. Mandy Allwood, a woman who had conceived eight foetuses as a result of super-ovulation drugs, was announcing her intention to keep all of them despite medical advice to the contrary.[41] The *News of the World*, who broke her story, headlined with 'I'm going to have **all** my 8 babies'. The story continued on page 2 with the title, 'I won't choose which ones should live and which ones should die'. Mandy Allwood was constructed in this piece as selflessly maternal, prepared to take risks for her children and matter of fact about the danger posed to her health. However, she too was soon to be attacked, with other papers revealing that her lover was a 'ladies man', that their living arrangements were 'odd'. Successive revelations detail her conditional discharge for failing to surrender to bail on a fraud charge, an abortion three years before, the failure of her marriage and the failings of her relationship with her lover, Paul Hudson. Lynda Lee-Potter for the *Mail* went the furthest, summing the situation up as 'a grizzly and seedy fable of lust, greed, selfishness, dysfunctional families and living for the moment'. Allwood, she said, was 'scheming' and had behaved with 'wanton selfishness', possibly trying deliberately for a multiple pregnancy, in the hope of selling the story. The *Independent* headlined its report of the case under the title 'How to sell your baby in 8 easy steps'.

Both of these stories show the same ability of the press to manipulate facts to produce interesting copy which will sell papers. Both play on the same constructions of femininity as were seen in Chapter 3. A and Mandy Allwood are initially reified as the good mother. A was portrayed (at least by some newspapers) as making an impossible decision in order to care more effectively for her existing children. Allwood was shown in the *News of the World* as risking her own life as a result of her refusal to make such a choice. Both women quickly fall from grace when this image of selflessness is challenged. A loses support when it is discovered that financially there is no reason why she could not have had both twins. Allwood is constructed as grasping and interested only in the money she will get for her story. The polarity of these representations evidenced in the denigration of the two women do not seem to have moved on at all in the last thirty years of legal abortion.

Selective reduction of multiple pregnancy is not new to medical practice. For pregnancies resulting from *in vitro* fertilisation, it has been common to implant a number of embryos in the womb and to selectively reduce the resulting foetuses when it becomes clear how many have successfully implanted. From the lawyer's perspective, since 1990, the legality of selective reduction has been relatively clear. Parliament evinced a clear intention that selective reductions should be covered by the Abortion Act (both in the sense that they must be performed in accordance with its terms and also in the sense that those who performed them would have a valid defence within it) and introduced explicit wording into that statute to that effect.[42]

Confusion had resulted from the fact that the Offences Against the Person Act creates the offence of 'procurement of miscarriage' whilst the Abortion Act protects against 'termination of pregnancy'. It was argued that the doctor who selectively reduces a pregnancy does procure a miscarriage (which refers to one foetus) but does not terminate a pregnancy as, after the medical intervention, the woman is still pregnant with a singleton. Still more confusing was the issue of whether a doctor could properly be said to have provoked a miscarriage at all given the nature of the intervention which would normally involve killing the foetus *in utero*, but not causing it to be expelled until the birth of its live sibling (see Keown, 1987; Price, 1988). Some commentators have argued that the present wording is still technically inadequate. However, it is inconceivable that a court would fly in the face of such clear parliamentary intention, to find a doctor who had performed a selective reduction in good faith in accordance with the formalities foreseen in the Abortion Act to have acted unlawfully.[43]

In terms of the *ethics* of selective reduction, it seems difficult to pinpoint any factor which distinguishes selective reduction from termination of a singleton. There have been two attempts to make such a distinction. The first argument put forward is that of the psychological consequences for the remaining twin.[44] However, it seems unlikely that this argument, which is reliant on some form of *in utero* bonding, would be persuasive to many in the absence of a significant body of evidence. The second factor which was more widely advanced was the notion of something deeply morally offensive in the actual process of making an arbitrary choice between the two foetuses. 'It's like *Sophie's Choice*', a friend suggested to me. Again, however, this argument strikes me as rather unconvincing. The horror in the decision facing Sophie (who must choose which of her two children will go with her into the concentration camp and which will be gassed immediately) surely rests in large part on the fact that this is a choice between two known and loved individuals, two children with developed personalities with whom she has established relationships.

The representation of Mandy Allwood's story in the *News of the World* would certainly suggest that it was this factor that the journalists for that paper believed to be significant in the juxtaposition of the two stories: 'Proud dad Paul said: "When I realised how delighted Mandy was with our babies. I became happy too. I was immediately against 'reduction'. Which one would you choose first? It's too horrific to contemplate."' Allwood concurred, 'I won't choose which ones should live and which ones should die . . . I love children.'[45]

Following *Paton* v. *BPAS* and *C* v. *S*, it is clear that SPUC would have had no possibility of obtaining an injunction to prevent the termination of A's pregnancy. The basis of SPUC's action was an attempt to force the respondents to convey their offer of financial help to A in order that she might reconsider her decision to terminate one twin. Counsel for SPUC raised four grounds in support of the application all of which assert A's right to receive information regarding her treatment: the Abortion Act itself, a common law right to freedom of information, the Equality Directive, and the implied contractual relationship between citizens and the NHS.[46] It is important to note that none of these grounds are specific to a case involving selective reduction.

SPUC's application was very quickly drawn up and some of the arguments used within it bear clear witness to this fact being both tenuous and underdeveloped.[47] Two of the arguments put forward on behalf of SPUC are worthy of some consideration, however. First, it was argued that the decision to terminate a pregnancy must be an informed one based on factual circumstances (including consideration of 'actual or reasonably foreseeable circumstances' as per s.1(2) of the Abortion Act). The certifying doctors must make this decision in good faith. Where factual circumstances change by reason of the acts of third parties and such acts would be likely to have a bearing on the termination decision, it was argued, the previous decision to terminate would be invalid and the woman would be entitled to be informed of such developments and to reconsider her decision. In the light of this, SPUC argued, the responsibility of the medical practitioner is to reconsider the termination in the light of statutory guidelines and the refusal to transmit information was *Wednesbury* unreasonable, i.e. it was a decision that no reasonable Health Authority could have made.[48]

Secondly, SPUC argued that the woman had the right to be informed of their offer under a common law right to freedom of information. This right, they argued, also included the right to *receive* information. In support of this, they cited *AG* v. *Guardian Newspapers*[49] and *Derbyshire County Council* v. *Times Newspapers Ltd*[50] as stating the English common law position to be the same as that expressed in article 10 of the European Covenant of Human Rights and article 19 of the International Protocol on Civil and Political Rights respectively, and *Leander* v. *Sweden*[51] which states that there is an implied obligation that freedom of expression includes freedom to *receive* information. It is by no means clear, however, that any of this imposes any *duties* on a reluctant third party to impart information.

SPUC's claim did seem to have some merit on the face of the facts as they were known. Here we had the case of a woman requesting a termination because she could not afford to care for two children. Surely a payment of £80,000 would be a material factor for her to take into account in making her decision? Does she not have a right to receive such information? Could it be reasonable to refuse to pass on such an offer? The hospital's claim that the cash sum would 'unduly influence' her decision seemed both paternalistic and unconvincing, ignoring the fact that A's original decision (as it was thought at the time) was equally the result of economic factors: her decision to terminate one twin was already 'unduly influenced' by financial considerations.

Notwithstanding the above, it seems inconceivable that had this case been considered fully by the High Court, SPUC's injunction would have been granted. Despite the rhetoric of the Patient's Charter (which SPUC intended to cite)[52] and the common law right to *receive* information which they intended to deduce, the High Court would not have been able to ignore a clear chain of authority from our highest courts detailing the specific obligations of doctors with regard to the provision of information. And this chain of authority quite clearly states that precisely what information a patient needs to make an informed choice remains a matter for the discretion of her medical practitioner (with the proviso that the doctor must act in accordance with a practice accepted as proper by a responsible body of medical opinion).[53] Thus, were the woman's doctors to have made the argument that the termination was in her best interests and that this information was not, in their clinical judgement, useful to her in making this decision, it seems likely that the court would not have contradicted this. Moreover, as has been seen above, the courts have shown themselves to be consistently reluctant to second-guess clinical discretion in cases relating to abortion. The Abortion Act is most explicit in that it is the doctor who must consider the woman's actual or reasonably foreseeable circumstances and make a decision as to appropriateness of termination. It contains no provision that he or she has a duty to pass on information. Moreover, the courts have imposed the most minimal of conditions regarding what will be necessary to meet the requirement that the decision was taken in 'good faith'.[54]

If SPUC had succeeded in restraining this termination pending the disclosure of certain information to the woman, it would have set a very dangerous precedent. The idea that it is the anti-choice groups who should dictate what information should be given to women considering abortion cannot fail to alarm. The spectre is raised of the kinds of measures deployed in the United States where, in some states, women have been subject to dissuasive counselling or forced to watch anti-choice material before deciding on termination in the name of the right to make an informed choice. However, this spectre seems one which is unlikely to haunt British women given the courts' protection of a broad space for medical discretion and refusal to second-guess decisions made within it.

Terminations by Medical Induction

Royal College of Nursing of the United Kingdom v. *Department of Health and Social Security*[55]
The Department of Health and Social Security (DHSS) sent out a circular to regional and area medical officers and district nursing officers, dealing with abortions by medical induction.[56] In it they advised that it was not necessary for a doctor personally to perform every action in the process, providing that he decided on and initiated the process and remained responsible for it throughout. The Royal College of Nurses (RCN), seeking to test the law, requested a declaration from the courts that the advice given in the Department's letter and annexes was unlawful in that nurses were not registered medical practitioners, and that the defence in section 1(1) of the Abortion Act, applying only when 'pregnancy is terminated by a registered medical practitioner', was therefore not available to them.

Woolf J, ruling in the case at first instance, decided in favour of the DHSS, arguing that section 1(1) should not be interpreted narrowly. The RCN appealed to the Court of Appeal who overturned the decision. In turn, the DHSS appealed to the House of Lords which (by a majority verdict of three to two) reversed the Court of Appeal's decision. Their Lordships held that the 1967 Act must be construed in the light of the fact that it was intended to clarify the previously unsatisfactory law, to broaden the grounds on which abortions might lawfully be obtained and to ensure that they were carried out with proper skill in hygienic conditions in ordinary hospitals as part of ordinary medical care and in accordance with normal hospital practice. Thus, in the words of Diplock LJ:

> a registered medical practitioner . . . should accept responsibility for all stages of the treatment for the termination of the pregnancy. The particular method to be used should be decided by the doctor in charge of the treatment for termination of the pregnancy; he should carry out any physical acts, forming part of the treatment, that in accordance with accepted medical practice are done only by qualified medical practitioners, and should give specific instructions as to the carrying out of such parts of the treatment as in accordance with accepted medical practice are carried out by nurses or other members of the hospital staff without medical qualifications. To each of them, the doctor, or his substitute, should be available to be consulted or called on for assistance from beginning to end of the treatment (571).[57]

There is almost a circularity to the logic here: doctors are legally authorised to do what doctors normally do. This is a clear statement of the judicial preference for self-regulation by the medical profession and the development of standards for good medical practice to be determined within the profession. Accordingly, so long as a doctor prescribed the treatment for the termination, remained in charge and accepted responsibility throughout, and the treatment was carried out in accordance with his directions, the pregnancy was 'terminated by a registered medical practitioner' for the purposes of the 1967 Act, and any person taking part in the termination was entitled to the protection afforded by section 1(1).

This case is notable for several reasons. Perhaps its most striking feature is the extent to which those judges who found for the DHSS are prepared to stretch an interpretation of the terms of the Abortion Act in order to reach an acceptable decision. The decision which the House of Lords eventually comes to is the common-sense verdict and no doubt accords with 'the obvious intention of the Act',[58] yet it is one that is squared with the actual wording of the statute only with great difficulty. When the doctor's actual involvement in the termination is limited to the insertion of the catheter – an act preparatory to the administration of the prostaglandins which cause the uterus to contract and expel the foetus – it involves a rather creative interpretation to see the doctor as terminating the pregnancy rather than the nursing staff who do everything else. Explicitly underlying this decision is a refusal to interfere with 'good medical practice'.

Feminist theorist Elizabeth Kingdom welcomed the final verdict in the *RCN* case, arguing that had the House of Lords upheld the Court of Appeal's decision this would have been 'a setback to feminists' hopes that trained personnel other than registered medical practitioners might, in the future, lawfully terminate pregnancies' (1991, p. 53). However, whilst Kingdom is correct to state that this case does not represent a setback to such hopes, neither would it be right to see it as particularly advancing them.[59] The situation is now governed by the statement of Lord Diplock cited above. Whilst nurses are hereby authorised to carry out certain actions in this kind of termination, they can still do so only under the control of the doctor who retains the ultimate responsibility for the operation. This strict hierarchy of the relationship between doctor and nurses is thus reproduced in the legal assessment and the doctors' monopoly over the performance of abortions is reasserted. Especially telling here is Lord Keith's statement: 'I find it impossible to hold that the doctor's role is other than that of a principal; and I think he would be very surprised to hear that the nurse was the principal and he himself only an accessory' (575).

The doctor's control of the process is thus enforced: it is irrelevant if it is the nurse who physically performs the actions necessary to bring about termination, so long as the doctor remains in control and instructs. As Montgomery comments on this case:

> In order to justify the [DHSS's] position it was necessary to construe the actions of the nurses as being those of the doctors in the eyes of the law . . . their Lordships characterised the relationship between the two professionals as one in which the nurse is little more that the doctor's handmaiden (1992b, p. 145).

Kingdom raises a second interesting point with regard to this case: the fact that the catalyst which provoked it was a departmental circular.[60] This highlights a trend in the regulation of abortion for decisions to be made at the level of administrative or medical practice. Such decisions are less open to public scrutiny and challenge. As Kingdom notes, in the *RCN* case the use of administrative measures was consistent with improved abortion facilities. However, in other cases it may not be. Kingdom also cites the introduction of new notification forms which I discussed above (p. 86) and which were seen by pro-choice campaigners as a retrograde step (1991, p. 53).

The *RCN* case demonstrates again how the reluctance of law to interfere with medical discretion and good medical practice can benefit women by protecting the provision of abortion services. It also emphasises, however, how this goes hand in hand with an entrenchment of doctors' control over such services.

Abortion in the Absence of Consent: Minors and Women with Learning Disabilities

Abortion, like any medical procedure involving physical contact, is only saved from constituting a battery by way of the consent of the patient. In certain cases, this is problematic as the pregnant woman is not legally competent to consent, either because she is too young, because she is mentally incapacitated or (as will be considered in the following section) in an emergency situation where she is unconscious. In such cases, difficult ethical and legal issues arise as to who is in a position to make the decision on her behalf. Since the case of *Gillick* v. *West Norfolk and Wisbech Area Health Authority*,[61] the courts have adhered to the principle that where the care and upbringing of a child was at issue, the court must treat the welfare of the child as the paramount consideration. In practice, typically the courts find that the best interests of the child accord with the opinion of the medical professionals involved.

Re B[62]

L, a schoolgirl of 12, was cared for by her mother until she was 18 months old. Since then she had been brought up by her maternal grandparents, but was in regular contact with her mother, who now had two other children living with her. L became pregnant and, being informed of the pregnancy by her GP, the local authority initiated wardship proceedings and applied to have the pregnancy terminated. The Official Solicitor (who represented L), the maternal grandparents and the putative father of 16 all supported L, who was said to be 'of normal intelligence and understanding' and who had been 'constant' in her wish to have the abortion. Her mother, however, opposed the application, arguing that 'it is not right to take the baby's life'. Medical evidence was conflicting. Two obstetricians and gynaecologists said that L, who was small in build, was both physically immature and mentally inexperienced and although termination would be traumatic it was in her best interests. A different prognosis was offered by two obstetricians and gynaecologists on behalf of L's mother, who suggested that psychological effects might surface years after an abortion and there was also a risk of future premature births. In their view the risk of an abortion at this stage was higher than the risk of pregnancy. However, it seems that they were also clearly influenced by considerations other than the strictly medical, as they also argued that it was 'wrong to kill the baby simply because it is inconvenient to have'. Referring to *Gillick*, Hollis J rejected the view that 'it is wrong to kill the baby' as putting the interest of the foetus and not the ward of court as paramount. Having considered L's age, the wishes of all those concerned, the competing medical opinions and the view of the Official Solicitor, he asserted that it was clearly in L's best interests to have the pregnancy terminated since its continuance involved greater risk both to her mental and physical health.

One commentator described this case as an important landmark in the continuing erosion of parental rights, complaining that it is now the medical profession who has the power to define what is in the best interests of the child:

> Today, on medical matters, at least, parental rights seem relatively unimportant, and the medical profession apparently has the final say on any contested issue of the treatment of children . . . Is there any important respect in which a parent can hold out against medical orthodoxy when it comes to the treatment of a child and when the state has become involved?[63]

Here, the adoption of the girl's best interests (as determined by her own doctors) accorded with her own wishes and the *Gillick* test. The medicalisation of the issue favoured a verdict which accorded with considerations of the girl's autonomy.

The English courts have never yet had to decide on a case where a pregnant minor opposes an abortion, when this is desired by her parents and recommended by her doctor. However, it has been suggested that the law as decided by *Re W* (see above) could lead to abortions being carried out by doctors with the consent of parents, despite the refusal of 16- or 17-year-olds. Donaldson MR considered this possibility and stated (rather ominously) that although it might be possible as a matter of law, medical ethics would ensure that it was only the case if it were in the 'best interests' of the young woman (see Bridgeman, 1993a, p. 80).

Similarly, in cases involving women with learning disabilities, the courts have held that a medical adviser must consider what decisions should be reached in the patient's best interests.[64] Once again the doctor is located as the appropriate expert to take a decision which is not merely a (narrow) medical one, but one involving far-reaching social and ethical questions. This offers some protection to the girl or woman and seems to have ensured prioritisation of her interests over those of the foetus.

ABORTION IN THE ABSENCE OF CONSENT

In March 1993, Barbara Whiten, a 35-year-old woman, was in hospital for a hysterectomy to relieve a painful and chronic disease of the womb which she believed had left her unable to conceive. The operation was performed by a consultant gynaecologist and obstetrician, Reginald Dixon. During the operation, Mr Dixon noticed that Mrs Whiten's uterus was enlarged, one possible cause of this being pregnancy. He decided against delaying the removal of the womb so that a scan could be arranged in order to determine the cause of the swelling and (if due to pregnancy) to give Mrs Whiten the opportunity to decide whether or not she wished to go ahead with the operation. Rather, he removed ovaries and uterus and the next day informed her that she had been pregnant and that he had removed a healthy 11-week-old embryo, stating this to be 'the usual practice'. Mrs Whiten, who had been trying to conceive for some years, was horrified. She complained that she had had the possibility of making her own decision taken away from her.

In a letter to Mr and Mrs Whiten, Mr Dixon said that he felt an emergency termination was justified on the grounds of Mrs Whiten's age, desire for a hysterectomy and history of depression. In a second letter, he acknowledged that with hindsight he would have been better advised to have sewn up the abdomen and arranged a pregnancy scan. In this case, then, Mr Dixon has taken what, in retrospect, seems (also to him) to have been the wrong decision. Nevertheless, he has taken it in good faith and has acted within the grounds of what he considers to be 'usual practice'. This appears to be true. In the course of their investigations of Barbara Whiten's complaint, the police uncovered a second similar case. A woman called Jane Henson told detectives that a trainee gynaecologist acting under the supervision of Reginald Dixon ignored her concerns that she might be pregnant and removed her womb in December 1991. After the operation Mrs Henson was told that she had indeed been pregnant.[65]

After some activity on Mrs Whiten's behalf, the CPS eventually decided to prosecute Mr Dixon for unlawful procurement of miscarriage under section 58 of the Offences Against the Person Act 1861. It was accepted that he had acted without the necessary second signature foreseen in the Abortion Act. However, Mr Dixon argued that he had acted within the terms of section 1(4) of the Act which allows a registered medical practitioner to perform a termination without complying with certain formalities (including obtaining a second signature) where 'he is of the opinion, formed in good faith, that the termination is immediately necessary to save the life or to prevent grave permanent injury to the physical or mental health of the pregnant woman'.

Dixon was eventually acquitted of unlawful procurement of miscarriage by a decision of Nottingham Crown Court on 21 December 1995.[66] The court accepted that Mr Dixon had honestly believed this to be an emergency situation in that he believed that Mrs Whiten would not have been able to cope with an unwanted and unplanned pregnancy and that if she had had the baby there would have been a grave risk of permanent injury to her mental health. The legal outcome thus rests upon Mr Dixon's opinion that this was an emergency operation. What is relevant is not whether the situation *objectively* constituted an emergency, but *subjectively* whether Mr Dixon believed in good faith that it did so (there is no requirement of reasonableness).

The family solicitor told journalists that the Whitens had not yet had time to consider the possiblity of bringing an action in the civil courts. As was seen above, in discussion of *Re S* (see pp. 76–7), it is only the consent of the patient which prevents medical treatment from constituting a battery and, in Mrs Whiten's case, consent was clearly lacking. However, Mr Dixon has two possible defences. First, there is the defence of tacit consent. The standard form which patients sign before undergoing surgery authorises 'any procedure in addition to the investigation or treatment described on this form [which] will only be carried out if it is necessary and in [the patient's] best interests and can be justified for medical reasons'.[67] The doctor is only permitted to carry out further surgery without which the patient's life or health will be immediately at risk.

There is also a second possible defence: necessity. In emergency situations, the doctor is justified in taking any necessary action to save life and to proceed without consent, 'with any procedure which it would be unreasonable, as opposed to merely inconvenient, to postpone until consent could be sought' (Skegg, 1974, p. 518).[68] The crucial factor with regard to the success of both defences is whether the abortion was immediately necessary. Mr Dixon contends that it was, citing Mrs

Whiten's mental state, age, history of depression and desire for a hysterectomy.

Mrs Whiten might also consider suing Mr Dixon for negligence, the basis of her case being that in failing to wait and obtain her consent, he fell below the standard of care that she might have reasonably expected from a doctor in his position. Or, more precisely, he did not act 'in accordance with a practice accepted as proper by a responsible body of medical men skilled in that particular art'.[69] In practice, this means that Mr Dixon must produce other doctors who are prepared to testify to the effect that what he did was not outside the boundaries of what other medical professionals accept to be reasonable. Again the essential test becomes one determined within the medical profession, and if many (or even some) doctors are operating with similar standards (even if such standards seem unreasonable or unacceptable to the broader public) then Mr Dixon is not liable.

Barbara Whiten's story is an extreme and particularly tragic example of the effects of medical paternalism. Mr Dixon here felt able to make a decision for Mrs Whiten as to whether it was best for her to continue with her pregnancy. He may well be proved right in his contention that this falls within the bounds of what the courts will accept as 'usual practice'. The fact is that English law explicitly grants the authority to doctors to take important decisions regarding female reproduction – notably abortion – even when it is clear that these decisions are only rarely based on strictly medical criteria. Medical paternalism is not merely allowed by the law, with regard to abortion it is actively condoned and enforced. Such paternalism falls firmly within the bounds of 'good medical practice', and it is thus unlikely that the doctor will be subject to administrative or judicial reprisal (Mr Dixon has the support of his Health Authority and is not to be dismissed from his post).[70] The law seems far more reliable in protecting the medical relationship from outside challenge than it is in protecting female autonomy within it.[71]

CONCLUSION

The breadth of the discretion which the judiciary accords to doctors is as clearly apparent in the cases dealing with abortion, as it is in the cases of *Re S* and *Re W* which I discussed early on in this chapter. In the abortion cases, however, considerations of medical discretion have by and large not impinged on the possibility for women to exercise reproductive autonomy. On the contrary, judicial activity in this area has constituted a vital factor in the liberalisation of the provision of abortion services. This has been shown in a variety of cases. First, the safety from prosecution which doctors enjoy as a result of judicial respect for medical discretion has created a situation in which some doctors feel free to be increasingly liberal in the provision of abortion, even to the extent where those pro-choice doctors discussed above who specify 'pregnancy' as the reason for termination have not been prosecuted. Secondly, the court's complete refusal to supervise the doctors' decision, beyond ensuring the existence of good faith, was an extremely influential factor in establishing that women cannot be prevented from terminating a pregnancy by the opposition of their sexual partners. Thirdly, in the *RCN* case the courts let considerations of good medical practice dictate a very creative interpretation of statute, hence ensuring the possibility of legally providing abortions by medical induction. Finally, in cases where consent is problematic such as the case of *Re B*, L was allowed to terminate her pregnancy in accordance with her own wishes, despite the opposition of her mother.

The argument which I am making here is not an apologia (or still less a principled justification) for the benefits of the medical control of abortion. I argued earlier that such control rests on paternalism: a refusal to credit women with the necessary maturity, rationality and integrity to make our own reproductive decisions. It has also been clearly seen in previous chapters that such control has presented serious obstacles to the establishment of good provision of abortion services. What this analysis does reveal, however, is the peculiar difficulties of the situation which feminists face with regard to the medical control of abortion. The principled arguments against such control must be weighed against the practical and concrete benefits it has provided (and the security which it may continue to give) on the level of entrenching and extending women's access to abortion services. In the case of abortion, the judicial deference for medical opinion has been so beneficial for women because they approach the courts in conjunction with their doctor, desiring the same legal outcome. The benefits for them arise from the legal refusal to look within the doctor's area of discretion, and the doctor–patient relationship. Barbara Whiten's story reveals the limits of this in terms of protecting women's autonomy. It seems likely that, also in abortion cases, where the law has been effective at protecting the doctor–patient relationship from outside attacks, it is less useful at protecting female reproductive autonomy within it.

6
The Human Fertilisation and Embryology Act 1990: Winning the Battle but Losing the War?

> The outcome of voting on the abortion amendments to the government sponsored Embryology Bill was a massive defeat for the anti-abortionists, which poses a new stage in women's struggle for reproductive control. It decisively confirms the impact of the underlying trends in the position of women, and the political developments these make possible. Success in this most difficult abortion battle rested more than ever before on the tactical choices made by the Pro Choice movement. It is crucial that the left and the whole movement learns the lessons of these tactics and how the campaign was waged and won (Anne Kane, coordinator of the Stop the Amendment Campaign, 1990, p. 19).

> Political technologies advance by taking what is essentially a political problem, removing it from the realm of political discourse, and recasting it in the neutral language of science. Once this is accomplished the problems become technical ones for specialists to debate . . . Bio power spread under the banner of making people healthy and protecting them. When there was resistance or failure to achieve its stated aims, this was construed as further proof of the need to reinforce and extend the power of the experts . . . We are promised normalization and happiness through science and law. When they fail, this only justifies the need for more of the same (Dreyfus and Rabinow, 1982, p. 196).

> We need to establish a principle that is related to the best medical practices. We should not have to debate the matter year in, year out but should place our trust in medical practitioners and give them a legal framework within which they can operate and which the public can understand (Doran, 1990).[1]

INTRODUCTION

In 1990, after fierce and protracted debates both inside and outside Parliament, the Human Fertilisation and Embryology Act was voted on

104

to the statute books. The Act has three fundamental objectives: to provide a statutory framework for the control and supervision of research involving human embryos, to provide for the licensing of certain types of assisted conception, and to effect changes to the Abortion Act 1967. These changes are the first to be made to the Act since it came into effect, despite numerous previous attempts by way of Private Members' Bills, all of which failed.[2] As the reforms contained in the Human Fertilisation and Embryology Act were to be heard in Government time, however, filibustering was now impossible and it was inevitable that, after nearly 25 years, the 1967 Act would be put once again to the vote.

Although various additional amendments to the 1967 Act were suggested, the main point of contention in 1990 was the upper time limit on abortion. Pro-choice activists argued that the limit of viability read into the Act from the Infant Life Preservation Act 1929 should be maintained. Anti-choice activists demanded that this limit should be reduced to 18 weeks.[3] The eventual outcome of the voting was widely hailed as a gain for the pro-choice movement. The upper time limit was fixed at 24 weeks; however, this was not to apply in cases where the pregnant woman's life or health was seriously threatened by the pregnancy or birth, or when the foetus was seriously disabled. In this chapter, I look again at the reforms embodied in the Human Fertilisation and Embryology Act in order to ask how far they can be seen to represent gain, and how far they should be assessed as loss. My contention will be that whilst the reforms undoubtedly represent the most recent in a series of political victories for the pro-choice campaign, on a significant level, they also represent a defeat.

It is important not to be alarmist. The victories which have been won over the past 30 years are not negligible and repeated attempts at restricting the 1967 Act have all failed. The reforms introduced to the Act by way of section 37 of the Human Fertilisation and Embryology Act in 1990 did not introduce radical changes in respect of the practice which existed prior to its implementation and, if anything, have liberalised the operation of the Abortion Act. There even seems to have been, at the time of the Human Fertilisation and Embryology Act, an undertaking by the anti-choice forces in Parliament that if the possibility of voting on reforms of the 1967 Act was given, that they would 'go away for a while' and not introduce more bills aiming to restrict the Act (see below p. 108). Thus the immediate future of the provision of abortion services in Britain seemed doubly secure after 1990, the status quo assured.

However, whilst avoiding alarmism, one should also be careful not to succumb to complacency. In this chapter I analyse the broader assumptions and constructions which underlie this development. My contention is that although feminists have won an important series of legal battles, there may still be a danger of losing the wider war of definition of what is at stake in the issue of abortion (Science and Technology Sub Group, 1991, p. 147). This will develop the arguments made regarding medicalisation in the previous chapter. Feminist strategies have long aimed at directing attention to broader social issues, and to situate abortion in relation to issues of contraception, sex education, welfare benefits and general discussion over women's sexuality and position in society. Such broader concerns, however, are becoming increasingly marginalised even within pro-choice discourse. The mutually accepted framework of the abortion debate increasingly posits the issue as a narrow medical question, revolving exclusively around the status of the foetus and at what (medically determined) point its claim to protection becomes paramount. To accept an essentially medical framework for debate seems doubly dangerous given that, as has been seen, many of the problems faced by women seeking termination are related to medical control.

I will begin by looking briefly at the 1988 Alton Bill, a Private Members' Bill which received considerable public attention and which, despite its eventual failure, has been cited for its importance in establishing a new agenda for discussion of abortion (Steinberg, 1991) and thus provides a suitable starting point. I then move on to my main focus of attention, the Human Fertilisation and Embryology Act, with particular reference to section 37 (amendments to the Abortion Act). Here, the acceptance of a medical framework as the only legitimate structure for discussion of abortion is clearly marked. Likewise a construction of the issue in terms of protection of the (essentially separate) foetus seems to have been largely accepted (or at least inadequately challenged) within Parliament. I will also discuss briefly the provisions of section 3 (prohibitions in connection with embryos), for their significance in fostering a discourse of foetal protectionism which may yet have an impact on the provision of abortion.

THE ALTON BILL (1988)

The Alton Bill was introduced into Parliament in October 1987 by a Private Member, the Liberal MP for Mossley Hill (Liverpool), David Alton. It received its second reading in the House of Commons on 22 January 1988, where it was passed by a majority of 296 to 251. The main provision of the Bill was a reduction in the upper time limit for legal abortion to 18 weeks with exemptions of up to 28 weeks only where termination was necessary to save the life of the woman or where the child was likely to be born dead or with physical abnormalities so serious that its life could not be independently sustained. A further exemption for women under 18 years old who had suffered incest or rape was introduced at Committee stage. After vigorous campaigning by both anti-choice and pro-choice supporters, the Bill ran out of time at the Report Stage which follows Committee and failed without being put to the test of a final vote.

The Alton Bill forms the focal point of a fascinating series of essays published together in the book *Off-Centre: Feminism and Cultural Studies* (Franklin, Lury and Stacey, 1991). The contributors worked together as the 'Science and Technology Subgroup' (STSG) at the Centre for Contemporary Cultural Studies at Birmingham University and focused on the importance of science to recent debates about abortion in Britain. In a general conclusion to the essays, they assert that

> despite the fact that the Bill itself was legislatively unsuccessful, the terms in which abortion was to be considered had been forged in a way which left little opening for women's needs or interests or for exploring reproduction as a social, not just a technological, biological or individual issue (p. 215).

One member of the group, Deborah Steinberg (1991) argues that although the Alton Bill ultimately failed in that it did not pass into law, it was successful in several respects in shifting the terrain of the meaning of abortion. Amongst the legacies of the Alton campaign which she lists is the increasing degree of reliance on medical/scientific knowledges to define abortion and it is this which will form the major focus of my discussion concerning the Human Fertilisation and Embryology Act. According to these writers, the importance of the Alton Bill and its surrounding campaign should be seen in terms of the assumptions which it succeeded in establishing or further entrenching in the public consciousness. These assumptions were also fostered by the media coverage. Tess Randles contends that in the reporting of the progress of the Alton Bill, the media established a particular framework within which scientific knowledges were seen as structuring the debate. She argues that within the reporting of the Alton Debate, this consensual framework took the form of a 'medico-moral rhetoric' which drew upon a fusion of Christian dogma and state-of-the-art medical technological knowledges. This resulted in the establishment of a seemingly 'consensual' framework for debate which invited 'objective' decision making and 'rational' discussion (1991, p. 207).[4] The STSG conclude:

> the debate focused on fetal viability as the point of arbitration for abortion rights. This focus enhanced the already established role of medical expertise in the adjudications surrounding abortion in Britain. In addition, the enhanced role of medical expertise went hand-in-hand with the harnessing of abortion rights to the technological capacities of modern medicine and an unquestioning faith in scientific progress. Prenatal diagnosis, technological systems

for sustaining infants born prematurely and the technology which produces photo-images of fetuses were all invoked frequently during the Alton abortion controversy. In such circumstances, medical judgements and technical possibilities or limitations, not women's needs or lives, set the parameters of debate (1991, p. 214).

S.37, HUMAN FERTILISATION AND EMBRYOLOGY ACT

The most recent prolonged parliamentary discussions of abortion occurred in 1990, when certain reforms to the 1967 Act were introduced by way of section 37, Human Fertilisation and Embryology Act. Prior to this there had been no time limit in the Abortion Act itself, but an effective time limit on abortions had been read into it by way of the Infant Life (Preservation) Act 1929, which made it an offence to destroy a 'child capable of being born alive' whilst establishing a rebuttable presumption that a child would be held to be 'capable of being born alive' from 28 weeks of gestational development. In the Human Fertilisation and Embryology Act, the Abortion Act was specifically 'uncoupled' from the Infant Life (Preservation) Act, and a fixed limit of 24 weeks was inserted into the former, with exceptions made for cases of serious risk to the pregnant woman's life or health, or in the presence of serious foetal handicap.[5] These provisions did not greatly effect the operation of the 1967 Act – it had already become established medical practice to treat viability as occurring at around 24 weeks and thus not to provide terminations after this point (Hall, 1990; Murphy, 1991). If anything the provisions extended the circumstances in which abortion should be allowed, in allowing terminations up to birth in the case of serious foetal handicap. Murphy (1991) argues that in practice this is the only real change introduced by the reforms.

Following the introduction of the Human Fertilisation and Embryology Act, it seemed unlikely that there would be another challenge to the abortion law in the immediate future. There was rumoured to have been an understanding between the Government and anti-choice supporters within the House of Commons that if the former gave time for discussion of abortion and a re-evaluation of the working of the 1967 Act then the latter would 'disappear' for 'a decent interval' and cease their periodic attacks on the Act.[6]

All in all, the limited nature of the reforms introduced and the successful defence of the substance of the 1967 Act would seem to have been an emphatic victory for the pro-choice camp. The time limit introduced was that which had already been widely adopted and would potentially effect a very small number of women. In 1988 (the last year for which figures were available at the time of the debates), only 22 abortions had occurred after 24 weeks and under the specific exemptions in the new legislation, it seems likely that these would have been allowed in any case.[7] Anti-choice MPs were even committed to 'disappearing' for a while. However, a close analysis of the parliamentary debates and the actual form of the changes introduced present a more complex picture. In particular, I will argue that the debates display an unquestioning reliance on medical knowledges as the exclusive framework for approaching any question of abortion and an acceptance of the construction of the foetus as an essentially separate individual who must be protected from the pregnant woman. This construction is disturbing both with regard to future defence of the 1967 Act and in terms of how it might effectively block further progress towards liberalisation of the law.

Medicalisation

Deborah Steinberg's argument, that one legacy of the Alton Bill is the increasing reliance on scientific and medical knowledges, is wholly borne out by the Human Fertilisation and Embryology Act debates. First, the need for reform was introduced to the House of Commons as necessitated by 'developments in medical and scientific practice'. Virginia Bottomley (Con., SW Surrey), then Minister for Health, presented the need for reform as a narrow and technical matter – not a political issue, but a matter of updating the existing law in line with medical developments:

> The Government have . . . [the] role of advising Parliament of ways in which changes over time and the recent developments in medical and scientific practices may have affected the existing law in ways in which Parliament should take account. It is in that context that the Government have considered the question of abortion time limits.[8]

Secondly, there is an ongoing struggle within Parliament as to who could claim the medical 'high ground' and the support of the various medical bodies. Medical knowledge is accepted as the decisive factor in determining the need for change. In this sense, thirdly, there is extensive reliance on medical sources and knowledges by all participants in the debates to the exclusion of other factors.

Use of Medical Knowledges

Anti-choice campaigners make use of medical knowledges both in and out of Parliament and their literature increasingly relies on medically established facts to justify its claims. The following assertion taken from a LIFE leaflet, 'Abortion: A woman's right to choose?', is typical:

The unborn child is not part of [the woman's] body. He (or she) is a unique human being, genetically, physiologically, and organically distinct from both parents. Human life begins at conception – so from conception onwards the mother is carrying another human being. *Deny any of that and you deny the evidence of modern genetics and embryology.*

Anti-choice MPs make similar use of medical knowledges. They relate gruesome 'medical facts' of the reality of abortions, give medical accounts of the development of the foetus and cite letters from doctors and nurses who have been involved in performing abortions.[9] They base their main proposal for reform (a time limit of 18 rather than 24 weeks) on the grounds that a smaller reduction would be no fair reflection of 23 years of advancement in medical science[10] and that it is necessary to legislate for the future, which will no doubt bring technological advances to lower the gestational age at which the foetus can be considered as viable outside of the womb.[11] David Alton argues that the law needs to take account of the scientific advances since 1967:

Twenty-three years ago, let alone 61 years ago, there was no ultrasound scanning of the type that I have described, no electrocardiograms for a foetus, and no appreciation of the complete sensory development of the unborn child or knowledge that the unborn baby feels pain . . . Given those quantum leaps in our knowledge, it is absurd to leave our laws in the dark ages.[12]

Alton treats the medical as the decisive factor in discussion of abortion and, marginalising other concerns, sees reform as the inevitable result of medical 'progress'. It is interesting to note that the rhetoric which Alton adopts in Parliament is very different from the terms which he uses to discuss abortion in his 1988 book *What Kind of Country?* Here he opens the chapter which deals with abortion with a quotation from Mother Teresa of Calcutta: 'In destroying the child, we are destroying love, destroying the image of God in the world', and continues in a vein which gives moral and religious values priority over medical ones. From this it seems that Alton believes (correctly, no doubt) that in order to voice his opinions in Parliament and be effectively heard within the debates, the most effective discourse is the medical. Likewise, it is noteworthy that another anti-choice MP, the Reverend Martin Smyth (UUP, Belfast S), despite his vocation, makes use of medical, rather than religious or ethical, arguments within the debates.[13]

The defenders of the 1967 Act, who in 1966–7 had focused on social factors and in particular on the desperate situation of the woman facing an unwanted pregnancy, in 1990 chose primarily to work within this medical framework. The arguments used by pro-choice MPs fall into three categories: social, 'woman-centred' and medical. The social aspect, whilst not being completely ignored, has become increasingly marginal and appeared here only in the form of very occasional references to sex education, family planning facilities and the state of the National Health Service. The use of feminist arguments in the debates is also much more evident than was the case in 1966–7. However, it is confined to a small group of MPs.[14] Moreover, it seems that the efficacy of the arguments is doubtful given the ability of anti-choice activists to subvert them (Steinberg, 1991, pp. 181–2). David Alton, in particular, makes use of an explicitly feminist rhetoric both in the House of Commons and in his book:

> Men will often use their sexuality in a way that demonstrates a greater sense of machismo than it does responsibility towards their partners. At the heart of the debate about contraception . . . is the need to recognise that when love and a sense of responsibility is removed from sexual relations, there will always be a tragedy. Sometimes that can result in men trying to pressurise women into what people often perceive as the quick fix of an abortion.[15]

Overwhelmingly, however, the rhetoric and framework adopted is medical.

First, the defenders of the 1967 Act dispute the medical evidence of the anti-choicers. For example, David Steel attacks Anne Widdecombe for trying 'to set herself up as a medical authority, greater than others on the time limit that the House should accept'.[16] Likewise, Dawn Primarolo (Lab., Bristol S) argues, 'With, perhaps, a few exceptions, hon. Members are not medically qualified. They are not consultants and they are not the best people to make medical decisions. We should recognise that.'[17] Implicit here is the assertion of abortion as a purely medical matter and a corresponding claim as to who should be allowed to speak about it.

Further, pro-choice supporters make good use of medical knowledges and constructions to support their own arguments. Steel goes on later to cite an article in the *Lancet* which showed that 75 per cent of gynaecologists preferred a limit of 24 weeks. He argues:

> It would be a great mistake for the House to set aside the opinion of established medical bodies on the issue of setting a limit of 18 weeks . . . We are not entitled to cast aside all these opinions as though they did not matter, or to pluck out of the air a figure that we think might be better.[18]

Here, the choice which he presents is one of either accepting medical judgement or of complete arbitrariness.

The same medical framework was adopted in press coverage of the issue. The day before the voting took place the most consistently pro-choice of the broadsheets, the *Guardian*, ran an article which was described as 'an attempt to summarise the arguments'. It was entitled 'Most doctors opt for 24-week limit' and began 'There are few supporters for retaining the present 28-week limit, as the medical consensus is that babies are viable from 24 weeks, given the intensive care and technology of modern premature baby units.'[19] Thus the perceived framework within which the issue of abortion should be decided was essentially structured by medical knowledges.

The Adoption of a 24-Week Upper Limit

The actual voting on the upper time limit in Parliament was done 'pendulum' fashion, swinging between the extremes in order to allow all opinion to be canvassed. The new clause drafted by the Government envisaged a time limit of 24 weeks, and various amendments were tabled to challenge this. The order and results of the voting were as follows:

18 weeks:	165 (for)	375 (against)	Majority of 210 against
28 weeks:	141 (for)	382 (against)	Majority of 241 against
20 weeks:	189 (for)	358 (against)	Majority of 169 against
26 weeks:	156 (for)	372 (against)	Majority of 216 against
22 weeks:	255 (for)	301 (against)	Majority of 46 against
24 weeks:	335 (for)	129 (against)	Majority of 206 for

The time limit eventually accepted (by a majority of 206 votes) is that recommended by the Royal College of Obstetricians and Gynaecologists in a report which is often referred to in the parliamentary debates.[20] The limit adopted is that of 24 weeks, the point when the foetus is deemed to become 'viable' (capable of sustaining independent life outside the womb). It seems indisputable that this limit recommended itself on these grounds. The support for the lower limit of 22 weeks (defeated by only 46 votes) might be seen as a result of assertions that viability in some cases occurs below 24 weeks, with, in extreme cases, foetuses as of little as 22 weeks *in utero* development having survived. However, as Harriet Harman informed the House of Commons:

> The time limit of 24 weeks was not arrived at arbitrarily. When deciding on an abortion, doctors err on the side of caution and, in practice, a 24-week limit would mean something like a 22-week limit or even a 20-week limit . . . For the future, doctors believe that they can increase the chances of survival for babies after 24 weeks,

but because of the insufficiency of development, they do not expect to be able to keep babies born at 22 weeks alive in the foreseeable future.[21]

Here, then, viability takes on a force of its own, becoming accepted as the natural dividing line between those abortions which should (in some circumstances) be allowed by law, and those which should not. This construction completely obscures broader social issues. As McNeil writes, the adoption of viability as a dividing line

> shifts the focus of decision-making away from women who, in opting for or against abortion, make complex evaluations of their particular circumstances and of the social sustainability of new life. Such decisions have little to do with what medical science can sustain technologically. Saying that it is theoretically possible to plug a 24-week-old fetus into life support apparatuses is very different from saying that you personally will take primary responsibility for supporting – in every sense – a child through to adulthood (1991, p. 156).

The adoption of viability as the cut-off point for abortions has obvious attraction for pro-choice activists and has been put to effective political use in establishing a comparatively high upper limit. However, it also has limitations. The effect of the 1990 debates has been to entrench in the public – and parliamentary – consciousness that abortion is permissible prior to viability, but should be forbidden after this point. (It is important to remember here that prior to 1990 there was *no* such limit in the text of the 1967 Act, and that the notion of viability read into it by the Infant (Life) Preservation Act was developed for very different purposes than that of regulating legal abortion (see above, p. 15).) Nigel Cameron, editor of *Ethics and Medicine,* goes so far as to argue that the destruction of the disabled viable foetus is no longer a matter of abortion, but rather of euthanasia.[22] This is a notion which future campaigns may find hard to dislodge. Whilst the present state of medical science makes it impossible to sustain neo-natal life at much less than 24 weeks of gestational development for reasons of lung development, it is surely not inconceivable that this limit will be gradually pushed downwards. If this happens, pro-choice groups will face a particularly bitter struggle to try to separate out the legitimacy of abortion from the notion of viability. Even in the 1990 Commons Debates, anti-choice MPs in Parliament several times emphasised the need to 'legislate for the future' as

> medical techniques are advancing so rapidly that, long before 20 years is up, we shall regard a termination within 20 weeks as ludicrous . . .

> By that time, medical techniques will be so good that a foetus will be viable much earlier than that.[23]

> Medical science will continue to advance, and more and more babies born prematurely will survive. Surely we should legislate for the future and not for the past.[24]

> we should take decisions that bear a relationship to the present situation but, having regard to the advances in medical science, to the situation that is likely to develop in the next decade.[25]

Although various commentators have suggested that it is unlikely that it will ever become possible to sustain neonatal life much below the 24-week limit, due to limited lung development, this is still a point of concern.

A still more immediate cause for concern with increased medicalisation is that this can only further serve to entrench medical control of abortion. The more abortion becomes viewed as primarily (or exclusively) a medical phenomenon, the more it seems inevitable that it must fall into the sphere of authority of doctors to maintain both technical and decisional control over it. The medical control of abortion is very much accepted within the debates, with the majority of pro-choice MPs emphasising that this is a decision that should be made by the woman in conjunction with her doctor.[26] In the 1990 debates, two amendments which addressed the medical control of abortion were tabled. The first, tabled by Conservative MP Emma Nicholson (Devon W)[27] which sought to allow abortion on request for up to twelve weeks of pregnancy, was not selected to be put to the vote. The second, tabled by Harriet Harman (Lab., Peckham), sought to allow women to have abortions up to twelve weeks with the approval of only one doctor. Despite the fact that pro-choice MPs emphasised medical factors, arguing in terms of reducing the number of late abortions by facilitating procedures, eventually the amendment was defeated by 228 to 200 votes.[28]

Foetal Separation

> The fact that the unborn child is physically dependent on its mother prior to birth need not lead to the assumption that it has no relevant separate existence . . . (Fortin, 1988a, p. 82).

The other worrying trend highlighted during the 1990 debates is an acceptance of the foetus as a separate individual. This is no doubt closely linked with the medicalisation of the debates, for medical discourse itself increasingly reflects such assumptions (Arney, 1982; Martin, 1987; Petchesky, 1987). In recent years a number of feminist writers on both sides of the Atlantic have started to point with concern to the developing doctrine of 'foetal patienthood if not foetal personhood' (Petchesky, 1987, p. 64; see also Gallagher, 1987; Steinberg, 1991; Franklin, 1991; Hartouni, 1991)[29] – and concomitant 'fetalization' (Franklin, 1991) of the abortion debate. The fear expressed is that the development of technologies such as ultrasound, which have increasingly rendered the foetus visible to the outside world, have opened up a Pandora's Box of ills which may yet have very far-reaching consequences. The visual symbols produced by such techniques have a particularly powerful purchase in a society so oriented to the visual, and in the current context of continued battles and fierce political debates over abortion their political importance is not to be under-rated. Combined with an increasing medicalisation of the debate and even greater primacy accorded to medical knowledges, these developments have resulted in an entrenchment of the centrality of the foetus in discussion of abortion and the emergence of discourses of foetal protectionism and foetal rights.

The conceptualisation of the foetus as an individual, separate from the body of the pregnant woman dates back as far as the Old Testament, possibly even beyond.[30] What is novel is the increased possibility of relying on medical rather than religious knowledges to ground this construction. In 1989, the Society for the Protection of the Unborn Child (SPUC) spent £60,000 on producing half a million full-colour postcards showing a 'baby' (foetus) of 18 weeks' gestational development sucking its thumb, and colour leaflets 'showing the baby's humanity in words and pictures'. The latter were delivered to three million homes.[31] Although this campaigning tactic is not new, it is becoming increasingly effective due to the invention of techniques which allow the photographing of the foetus *in utero*. These images emphasise all that is baby-like about the foetus and, like a baby, it is shown as existing whole and separate from the body of the pregnant woman. The danger of such images is enhanced by their stamp of photographic 'fact' or 'truth': 'foetal imagery epitomizes the distortion inherent in all photographic images: their tendency to slice up reality into tiny bits wrenched out of real space and time' (Petchesky, 1987, p. 62). Petchesky argues that the appearance of the photographic image as a 'mechanical analogue of reality' without art or artifice, obscures the fact that the image is heavily constructed, or coded and grounded in a context of historical and cultural meaning (1987, p. 62). One form of such coding which she identifies is that the new foetal imaging techniques (such as ultrasound and *in utero* photography) have constructed the foetus as hanging in a void, like an astronaut dangling in space. Similarly, Barbara Katz Rothman has observed that 'The fetus in uterus has become a metaphor for "man" in space, floating free, attached only by the umbilical cord to the spaceship. But where is the mother in that metaphor? She has become empty space' (1986, p. 114).

The construction of the tiny yet intrepid 'space hero' hanging fearlessly in 'his' void is present in the 1990 debates. The use of the space imagery is striking in this comment taken from the debates:

> The stark and dreadful import of abortion is that what nature has successfully – in spite of all hazards – launched into the orbit of life, human hands seek deliberateiy to arrest and destroy in mid-trajectory. To make such a terrible intervention in the course of nature demands compellingly good reasons. The further the foetus has got off the ground, so to speak, the more vital it is that human intervention should be geared to assisting and upholding, not to arresting and destroying.[32]

Within the debates, two seemingly conflicting constructions of the foetus coexist – the image is of a 'little creature . . . a human being not yet born, yet with all the hope and expectation of life',[33] vulnerable yet intrepid, launched on a life journey and already embodying all the characteristics of a true individual.

What is worrying here is the failure of the pro-choice movement to actively counteract the construction of foetal separation, leaving the power of the visual image to be exploited by the anti-choice groups. This is emphasised by a strategy adopted by SPUC during the 1990 debates whereby each MP was sent a plastic replica of a foetus at 20 weeks' gestation. Although various MPs expressed their distaste at this strategy as 'obscene'[34] and 'a gross act of bad taste',[35] not one commented on what for me is the most worrying aspect of this tactic: that the foetus is represented in total abstraction from the body of the woman that carries it. It emphasises everything that is baby-like and vulnerable about a foetus and hides the essential difference from a baby: whilst the baby is separate and can be independent of its mother (if someone else cares for it), the foetus *is* not and *cannot* be so. The representation of the foetus as a free-floating and separate entity embodies a fundamental deceit, and one which has been inadequately contested.

Anti-choice MP Patrick Cormack (Con., Staffordshire S) commented:

> When I opened my parcel I found a legitimate and graphic piece of campaigning, because nobody disputes that is what a 20-week old foetus looks like. *If somebody had been able to produce medical evidence that this was a grotesque mock-up that was totally inaccurate and grossly misleading, it would have been the most obscene piece of campaigning that anyone could indulge in.* However nobody has suggested that. When I was in the Post Office yesterday an hon. Member came in, took his

parcel, opened it, and threw it in the bin. I could not help thinking that this is what happens to many foetuses.[36]

Worryingly, no one in the House of Commons challenged Cormack to suggest that in abstracting the foetus from the body of the woman, this 'graphic piece of campaigning' was indeed a 'grotesque mock-up' and 'totally inaccurate and grossly misleading' and, moreover, that it should not only be *medical* evidence that has the authority to challenge it. The failure to dispute this essential deceit in SPUC's representation of the issue reflects an implicit acceptance of the construction of abortion as revolving essentially around this free-floating foetus and what rights are to be attributed to it. Once the woman is abstracted from the equation in this way, then SPUC are already half-way to proving their central claim that there is a negligible difference between a foetus in the last stages of gestational development and a newborn baby.

Precisely such an assertion is made to the House of Commons by Anne Widdecome (Con., Maidstone):

At the moment, a child in an incubator can be kept alive, loved and cherished with all the resources of medical science being devoted to saving it, while a child of identical age and identical gestation in the womb has no rights and can be destroyed. There is something wrong with a law which allows that degree of inequity between *two individuals who are exactly the same except that we can see one and we cannot see the other* . . . we must bring about a situation in which there is at least equality. At present, we have a law which states that *a child who is seen is protected but that a child at an identical stage who is not seen is not protected.*[37]

Widdecombe's assertion that there is no difference between these two situations totally ignores the pregnant woman's role, her needs and her interests. In concentrating attention entirely on the foetus, the essential difference between the two situations (that one is occurring inside a woman's body) is hidden. Widdecombe is challenged by Emma Nicholson, a vocal pro-choice advocate. Nicholson makes no mention of the total absence of consideration of the pregnant woman in Widdecombe's argument. Rather, she notes:

The hon. Member for Maidstone (Miss Widdecombe) talked of identical babies whose only difference at 20 weeks was that one was visible and the other invisible to the naked eye. That is not true because the baby invisible to the naked eye may be hideously deformed and if born and brought to life, may face a future of unimaginable suffering. It may be visible to the naked eye through modern machinery and perhaps it can be kept alive, despite its wretched existence for many years.[38]

Having implicitly accepted the central importance of the foetus and the absence of any consideration of the pregnant woman, Nicholson adopts the terrain set out by Widdecombe and uses an essentially eugenicist argument against her, asserting that the essential difference in the foetus which we cannot see is that it may be disabled.

Steinberg argued that a eugenic dimension to the abortion debate would be a further legacy of the Alton Bill, with pro-choice MPs relying on the limitations of prenatal diagnostic technology in discovering foetal abnormality, in order to justify the continuing legality of 'late' abortions (1991, p. 187). It would obviously not be true to assert that the eugenicist rhetoric only appeared at the time of Alton, its presence also being clearly discernible in the 1966–7 debates (see pp. 43, 46). However, Steinberg is right to indicate an increased reliance on this kind of argumentation on the part of the pro-choice supporters post-1988. She points out that one of the problems caused by the adoption of eugenicist rhetoric is that it fails to challenge the central place accorded to the foetus, but rather implicitly supports and entrenches this premise. Women are seen as having the 'right' to 'late' abortions only on a special-case basis, where the status of the foetus so allows. Here, once again, the high moral ground is ceded to the anti-choice movement, with pro-choice supporters seen as pitted not only against the foetus, but also against the disabled. In his book, David Alton demands, 'What does it say about a society that snuffs out a life that is not deemed to have worth because of disease or disability? Ask the next disabled person you meet whether they are glad to be alive' (1988, p. 174). Such arguments have also been put forward with greater force by disabled feminists such as Jenny Morris (1991). Notwithstanding this critique, it is interesting to note the seeming success of this rhetoric in that, since 1990, women are legally allowed abortions without time limit in the presence of a serious foetal handicap.

In practice, medicalisation of the debates and the increasing importance of foetal separation are integrally related and mutually supporting. As medical knowledges become more important in the abortion debate, the issue of the (medically determined) status of foetal life becomes increasingly central. And as the status of foetal life becomes the prime concern, the place of medical knowledges and the authority of medical experts becomes ever more entrenched. This is the vicious circle which feminist campaigns must break. Moreover, as was argued in Chapter 4, developments in other areas of obstetrics and gynaecology have also contributed to the emergence of the foetus as a separate patient with the doctor perceived as the person best placed to represent its interests. This conceptualisation of the medical role equally serves to reinforce the notion of the doctor as the appropriate expert to also wield such authority in cases involving a request for abortion.

THE HUMAN FERTILISATION AND EMBRYOLOGY ACT, S.3 (PROHIBITIONS IN CONNECTION WITH EMBRYOS)

s.3(1) No person shall:
a) bring about the creation of an embryo, or
b) keep or use an embryo,
except in pursuance of a licence.

s.3(3) A licence cannot authorise
a) keeping or using an embryo after the appearance of the primitive streak.
. . .

Although it is impossible here to deal with the other provisions of the Human Fertilisation and Embryology Act 1990 in anything like the degree of detail which they deserve, it is important to include some mention of them here in so far as they may yet prove relevant to the abortion debate.[39] The Human Fertilisation and Embryology Act follows a report commissioned by the Government and headed by Mary Warnock, and is clearly informed by much of the analysis contained within it. Much of the moral argument regarding embryo research within the debates centred on 'personhood', the idea being that one particular point may be chosen at which we can say that someone becomes a 'person', and entitled to receive the respect owed to a person. The position which Warnock appears to have held, however, is that there is no absolute point at which a person appears and has moral status, but that a person emerges as a gradually present moral entity and one which becomes possessed of more and more rights as a juridical person. Indeed, Warnock has been criticised for her denial of the need to fix on one point at which personhood could be said to begin (Lockwood, 1985; Fortin, 1988a, p. 54). For Warnock, to make particular legal or political decisions, we have to select a point or a series of points. The solution she proposed with regard to embryo research was to choose a cut-off point of 14 days, with some limits as to what research could be done on embryos before that point.

The recommended cut-off point of 14 days took as its reference point the emergence of the primitive streak, which 'marks the beginning of individual development of the embryo' (Warnock, 1985, 11.22). Warnock notes that taking such a time limit had the added advantage of being consonant with the views of those who favoured the end of the implantation stage as a limit (1985, 11.22). The primitive streak appears as a heaping-up of cells at one end of the embryonic disc on the fourteenth or fifteenth day after fertilisation. Until this time, it is argued, the cells of the embryo are undifferentiated in terms of which will become the placenta and the embryo proper and this is also the latest stage at which identical twins can occur. As Jo Richardson (Lab., Barking) asserts in Parliament, '[the 14 day limit] is a well known chronological event and that is why the Warnock committee chose it. It is a particular stage in the development of a human being.'[40] The Human Fertilisation and Embryology Act follows Warnock's recommendation in taking the appearance of the primitive streak as the upper time limit on embryo research.

The explicit linking of abortion and embryo research by the inclusion of this section in a statute purporting to deal with human fertilisation and embryology shows how far abortion is accepted as revolving around the biological status of foetal life.[41] This assumption has been reflected and entrenched in the reporting of these issues in the media, with developments in the debates around abortion and embryo research consistently reported in the space of the same article. This can only have compounded the perceived connections between the two in the public consciousness. The *Guardian* reported the forthcoming parliamentary debates under the title, 'MPs to vote on two life issues'.[42] The problem faced in the two cases appears to be parallel: to choose one cut-off point after which the embryo/foetus is to be subject to a certain regime of protection. The solution adopted is also seen as parallel and resting upon a point of biological development (which may or may not be constructed in terms of a fixed period for reasons of legal clarity).[43] The comments of Kenneth Clarke (Con., Rushcliffe), then Secretary of State for Health, show how the debates have further compounded the understanding of the two issues as essentially linked:

> I was not instinctively attracted to the idea of debating the abortion law at the same time as discussing the introduction of law on embryo research. Even in the past month or two I have genuinely changed my mind, and today's debate has confirmed that. These subjects are so closely related that this is a suitable opportunity for the House to have a day at the end of which it can come to a conclusion, which should last a long time, on the time limits and future operation of the 1967 Act and its relationship with the Infant Life (Preservation) Act.[44]

The two matters are, however, in another sense quite different – one is dealing with the control of genetic and other medical research, the other with women who wish to end unwanted pregnancies. Such commonality as exists is provided by a focus on the status of the conceptus, with this narrow medical/biological issue seen as the determinate factor in both regulation of embryology and abortion. Consideration of any broader social factors and of women's needs is obscured in both cases.

One concern for feminists is that once the crucial question is defined as the status of the conceptus and the need to protect it from third parties (doctors or women), it may seem inconsistent to offer this protection at such different stages in foetal development. The linking of embryology and abortion provides scope for anti-choice activists, who were not slow to point out the incongruity of protecting the conceptus from medical research at 14 days, yet not protecting it from abortion until 24 weeks. As *The Times* put it:

> It seems illogical that such an illustrious committee [the Warnock Committee] should strongly condemn any experimentation on embryos after 14 days of growth, due to the possibility of pain, when, since 1967, over two million embryos, the majority with fully intact central nervous systems, have been fragmented by curettage/suction or forcibly expelled prematurely, a practice not only condoned but vociferously defended by society.[45]

Some years later, a letter to *The Times* made the same point. Responding to a letter calling for a review of NHS referral procedures, which had been signed *inter alia* by Mary Warnock, the writer argued that:

> Those who consider abortion as an option in the 'management of pregnancy', a social service rather than a killing must deny the right of the unborn. So perhaps those three members of the Warnock committee, including the chairman herself, who now so earnestly propose a 'fully comprehensive abortion service', might ponder upon why they sat for so long and moralised so earnestly upon the rights of a mere 14-day-old embryo.[46]

Similar arguments were heard both in Parliament – 'Is it not illogical of Parliament to provide protection for human embryos from two weeks on, yet not be concerned for the future of that pre-embryo at 18, 20, 24, 26 or 28 weeks?'[47] – and, to a lesser extent, in academic literature. Fortin, writing before the introduction of the Human Fertilisation and Embryology Act, argues that the legislative changes recommended by the Warnock Committee would, if implemented, result in a situation where 'the law might contain greater protection for the very early embryo *in vitro*, through controls on experimentation and restrictions on the period permissible for keeping the embryo alive, than the abortion law contains for the more developed foetus' (1988a, p. 55).

She suggests an alternative approach based on the work of philosopher, Michael Lockwood whereby a common limit of ten weeks (when the brain has reached a certain level of development) be adopted for both experimentation on embryos *in vitro* and abortion on demand (see Lockwood, 1985, p. 10). At that stage she suggests that the law would be improved by requiring those involved in any abortion decision relating to a foetus of more than ten weeks' development, to consider its particular stage of physical and mental development, with a view to assessing its claim to continued life, as opposed to the claims of the pregnant woman. Fortin envisages that compliance with such a requirement in cases of this kind could be ensured by the participation in the abortion decision of a fourth person, who would have to ensure that the claim of the foetus to continued life is balanced against the claim of the woman.

The issues involved in the control of embryo research are complex and difficult and I have not attempted to address the ethical merits of the legislation, nor indeed of the research it seeks to regulate. The concern which I have sought to highlight here regards whether recognition of the need to protect the embryo may foster a climate of foetal protectionism which will eventually lead to infringements of women's reproductive autonomy in other areas such as abortion.

CONCLUSIONS

Abortion is, in the first order, something done to fetuses/'unborn children', and only secondarily (at most), a procedure women undergo (Steinberg, 1991, p. 180).

The developments outlined above and the underlying assumptions which inform them, are both indicative and constitutive of a changing climate which could have negative implications for women's access to abortion services. Whereas the courts and legislator have as yet resisted the extension of foetal rights where they would infringe on the application of the Abortion Act, the potential for such extension remains and provides grounds for some concern. Whilst the pro-choice forces have been successful in defeating various attacks on the provision of abortion enshrined in the 1967 Act, considerable ground has been lost in popular assumptions about abortion. From this point the agenda becomes set within an essentially medical framework and the issue of what is at stake in the abortion debate centres essentially around the medical development of the foetus to the exclusion of broader, social issues. What seems to me to be still more worrying, however, is that the acceptance of a medical framework further entrenches medical control of abortion and stands against any initiative to claim decisional control for women. There is something particularly startling about the fact that MPs would vote to allow abortion of disabled foetuses until birth, yet refuse to allow abortion in the first twelve weeks on the authority of one doctor (as opposed to two). I have argued in the preceding chapters that it is medical control which now provides the most significant challenge to women's access to abortion, yet it is precisely this which remains unaddressed (see especially Chapters 4 and 5).

In Chapter 3, I argued that the construction of the woman seeking abortion was crucial to the form taken by the regulations introduced in the 1967 Abortion Act. The importance of the construction of woman in earlier debates was no doubt due, at least in part, to a greater focus on social factors. Now, with a near-exclusive focus on medical factors, the situation of the woman is pushed to one side and the foetus attains a greater centrality. Its construction as a small and vulnerable 'unborn child', divorced from the body of the woman, and pitted against her in an essentially adversarial relationship serves to legitimate the role of the doctor (backed by the State) to protect the foetus and to represent its interests against those of the woman.

7
The Regulation of Antiprogestin Terminations

These projections of absolute autonomy and independence of women is the reason why so many fight so hard against it . . . An antiprogestin drug could develop in the future in such a way that sudden decisions could be put into effect, so that spontaneous contacts from which no consequences are desired would become increasingly devoid of risk of pregnancy. This would likely change the behaviour of women entirely around reproduction and their sexual behaviour. They would be in a position to act and react like men, meaning they would, in every single case, be able not to let the consequences of sexual intercourse take place. I am convinced that in this framework the intensity of the reaction to this new drug becomes intelligible. More autonomy with regard to decisions in matters of reproduction and fertility always triggers fear (Retzlaff, 1993, p. 24).

Mifegyne has been developed within both the spirit and the letter of the law. In the UK, its usage as an abortifacient is strictly within the provisions of the Abortion Act 1967. This provides for the legal termination of pregnancy when clinically necessary and approved. The Mifegyne/prostaglandin in combination can therefore only be administered to women who fulfil the requirements of the 1967 Abortion Act. Usage is confined specifically to those hospitals and clinics approved and licensed under the Act for the termination of pregnancy. It is administered there only under medical supervision and only to women who agree to the treatment schedule. Mifegyne is therefore not available for general sale, nor through chemists nor on family doctors' prescription . . . The supply of Mifegyne is strictly controlled by Roussel. It is available only to those hospitals and clinics which have received instructions in its use and which conform to Roussel's specific conditions of supply (statement issued by Roussel UK, 1993).

INTRODUCTION

In the preceding chapters I have sought to demonstrate that the construction of abortion as primarily a medical matter has had a

124

substantial impact on the law which, in the last thirty years, has moved from a system of criminal prohibition to a decentralised network of medical control. This medicalisation has increasingly led to an apparent depoliticisation of abortion, defusing the conflict and controversy surrounding it. The extent of such medicalisation and depoliticisation in the 1990s was illustrated in the last chapter. Despite this appearance, I have asserted that abortion remains very much a political issue: the regulations governing its availability are underpinned by quite specific, discernible values which reflect certain attitudes to women and a clear value judgement as to who should control female fertility. Moreover, it was seen (particularly in Chapter 4) that the regulation of abortion continues to serve as a focal point for the deployment of power over women. Whilst the medicalisation of abortion law has had substantial benefits for ensuring women's access to abortion, it also poses substantial problems for that access. In this chapter, I would like to illustrate these arguments by way of an examination of the decision to license RU486 for use in Britain and the regulations introduced to govern its use.

Having first offered a brief introductory sketch of RU486, I shall go on to discuss reactions to the decision to license it for use in France, the US and Britain. In Britain, although the political significance of the debate as played out in Parliament (and to a lesser extent, outside it) was obscured by a focus on competing medical evidence as to the relative benefits of the drug, I argue that once again such depoliticisation is more apparent than real: fears regarding the control of abortion are the only convincing way of explaining the opposition to the drug amongst anti-choice activists. Abortion only remains depoliticised so long as its medicalisation is unchallenged. This foreshadows the conclusion reached in a fourth section, where I seek to address an apparent paradox: given the seeming simplicity of the antiprogestin procedure, why has this resulted in an accelerated regime of supervision and control? Finally, and on a more (cautiously) optimistic note, I shift from an examination of the present regulation of antiprogestins to an assessment of their potential to offer new ways of challenging the medical control of abortion.

BACKGROUND

The Development of RU486

RU486 is an anti-hormone drug or, more specifically, an antiprogestin. It binds to the progesterone receptors in the woman's uterus in order to block the production of progesterone and thus impair the womb's ability to hold on to a fertilised egg. The womb lining breaks down and the embryo is lost in the bleeding which follows. In order to improve its efficacy, RU486 has been combined with prostaglandins (PG), drugs which act to induce uterine contractions. The combination currently used in Britain, a first application of 600 mg of RU486, followed 36–48 hours later by a prostaglandin vaginal suppository, has a 94–7 per cent success rate.[1] RU486 is available for termination of pregnancies which have not exceeded nine weeks.[2] In the cases where abortion is not successfully induced, the woman will have a surgical abortion, normally by vacuum aspiration.

As yet, a comparatively low number of abortions have been performed in Britain using RU486/PG, and some GPs seem still to be unaware of its availability. The manufacturer, Roussel, estimated that for 1996, some 12,000 treatment packs would be distributed in the UK. Judging by figures for previous years, this represents under 20 per cent of those terminations which occur before nine weeks. In France, around 40,000 RU486 terminations take place each year which represents around half of all eligible cases taking up this form of treatment. The manufacturers anticipated that around 6,000 packs of RU486 would be distributed in Sweden during 1996.[3]

RU486/PG Compared to Conventional Abortion Techniques

In terms of effectiveness, complications, cost and the experience of the women who have used it, RU486 seems comparable to other early abortion techniques. It does, however, have its own peculiar advantages and disadvantages. One disadvantage is that an RU486/PG abortion takes more time than a surgical abortion, requiring two days or more and three trips to the clinic/hospital. This delay can be distressing for the woman who must carry with her the experience that she is in the process of ending a pregnancy. For this reason, a French gynaecologist involved with trials for RU486, Annie Bureau, has suggested that RU486/PG abortions are not suitable for all women (USPDA, 1990, p. 8). This delay has, on the other hand, also been cited as a positive part of the RU486/PG experience, giving women the possibility to

> transform the termination experienced as a failure into a positive reflection on one's fertility and sexuality. The time taken allows the event to sink in better, as part of the continuum of the life of the woman . . . RU gives women time to separate themselves from the pregnancy which they are giving up (UPSDA, 1990, p. 17).

Antiprogestins do have one major advantage over other methods of termination: they can be administered to the woman as soon as she knows that she is pregnant and has decided that she wants to have an abortion. For a surgical abortion a woman has to wait until at least six weeks from her last menstrual period. There seems to be some public consensus that early abortion is morally preferable to late abortion, as well as being safer, and often psychologically easier for the pregnant woman. One woman who had had an abortion using antiprogestins said that she chose it for this reason.

> I decided to choose the medical method because I could undergo the abortion much faster than if I had opted for a surgical abortion. I can't remember how many weeks it was, but, when I was told, it seemed quite horrific – the amount of time I would have had to have waited to have seen a gynaecologist (Furedi, 1994, p. 43).

From the evidence available it would seem, on balance, that antiprogestins have proved as safe as other methods of performing abortions, and may be a preferable alternative for some (but not all) women. However, a note of caution should be sounded by the cost of the drug which is substantially cheaper than a surgical termination. It is important to consider with caution the positive reaction of the NHS purchasers and providers, which should be read in this light.

Notwithstanding these concerns, most pro-choice commentators have come out cautiously in favour of the possibility of RU486/PG abortions and many women's groups are currently lobbying their governments and Roussel Uclaf for RU486 to be made available in their countries.

Licensing outside Britain

RU486/PG was first released on to the French market in September 1988. Distribution was suspended the following month by the manufacturers, Roussel Uclaf, amidst fears of an economic boycott by Catholic and anti-abortion groups and pressure from Hoechst, its principal shareholder. It was, however, swiftly reintroduced following the intervention of the French Minister of Health, Claude Evin, who maintained, in a phrase that has since become famous, that RU486 was the 'moral property of women' (Nau and Nouchi, 1988).

Roussel Uclaf, however, has shown a marked reluctance to distribute the product in other countries, and has declared itself unwilling to apply itself for a licence to market the drug, seemingly preferring to wait to be approached by the relevant government.[4] At the time of writing, the drug is only legally available in France, Britain and Sweden, although moves to license the drug in the US are also well under way.[5] According to the manufacturer, there are no plans to seek registration in any other country.[6]

In the United States, the debate surrounding antiprogestins has been explicitly party political and extremely acrimonious (Cole, 1989; Ricks, 1989; Lader, 1990; Chicoine, 1993). RU486 was opposed by both Presidents Reagan and Bush, who stopped all research on it at the National Institute of Health and forced the Food and Drug Administration (FDA) to put it on the proscribed list, blocking its entry into the country. Another Republican, Robert Dornan, unsuccessfully attempted to introduce legislation aiming to prohibit RU486, and to prevent its approval by the FDA (Lader, 1990, p. 21).[7] One of the first actions of Bill Clinton (three days after assuming responsibility as President) was to authorise testing of the drug within the US, with a view to granting it a product licence. At a hearing in July 1996, the FDA's Advisory Committee for Reproductive Health Drugs recommended the drug be approved for marketing in the US. While the FDA is not required to follow the panel's advice, it is highly uncommon for it to do otherwise. The drug would be marketed by Advances in Health Technology, Inc., an enterprise designated by the Population Council as the exclusive US distributor.[8] The drug's introduction on to the US market has been further delayed by reports that the businessman who acquired the rights to manufacture the drug has been convicted of fraud and forgery charges.[9]

BRITISH LICENSING OF RU486

Whereas in the US a storm of controversy has surrounded the drug, in Britain RU486 was introduced with a minimum of fuss. This has prompted one commentator to compare the British and US situations in the following terms: 'The NHS's distribution of RU 486 to any woman who qualifies for it is convincing evidence that in Great Britain equitable access to health care is more important than political pressures brought to bear by a vocal minority' (Chicoine, 1993, pp. 111–12). The characterisation of the availability of RU486 as 'NHS distribution to any woman who qualifies for it' is obviously mistaken, and this will be clearly seen below. However, this analysis is interesting in indicating once again the difference between the more explicit politicisation of abortion in the US, where the direct effect of political pressures brought to bear by identifiable individuals and groups is clearly visible.

In Britain, with some few exceptions, it seems that reactions to the drug have split down the traditional pro- and anti-choice lines. Two things are worth noting regarding reactions to the drug. First, the level of opposition to RU486 was relatively slight and the majority of arguments against the drug operated within a medical framework. Secondly, however, underlying reactions to the drug are hopes and fears regarding the control of abortion.

Medicalisation of the Political Debate

First then it is important to note that the introduction of antiprogestins did not provoke huge controversy in Britain. Conflict over the drug was not constructed as a matter for party politics as it was in the US. Opposition to RU486 has been far more muted in Britain, but has been present none the less. A largely unsuccessful and low-profile campaign was launched by the anti-choice groups, and the drug was debated in Parliament (albeit only after the decision to grant it a product licence for the British market had already been taken). Product licences are granted by the Minister of Health following advice from the Medicines Control Agency (MCA) and RU486 was licensed on 1 July 1991, ten months after an application had been submitted.[10] The fact that RU486 was licensed in Britain without any preceding discussion of the issue can itself be seen as a result of the fact that abortion is here again constructed as a medical rather than political issue – the decision was taken outside of the political arena on medical and economic criteria (safety and potential savings to the NHS).

After its licensing, however, some discussion of the issue was initiated in the House of Commons by Kenneth Hind (Con., W Lancs), then Secretary of the All Party Parliamentary Pro-Life Group. The pro- and anti-choice split is clearly seen in the parliamentary debates, where the lines of opponents and proponents of abortion are drawn clearly with Jo Richardson (Lab., Barking) joining the Under-Secretary of State for Health in speaking in defence of the granting of the product licence and Kenneth Hind, Bernard Braine (Con., Castle Point) and Ann Winterton (Con., Congleton) speaking against it.[11] However, the rhetoric adopted by the latter three is quite different in emphasis from that normally used, focusing on considerations of the health of the pregnant woman with only scant mention of the foetus. The arguments do not explicitly consider how the drug will effect women's control over their fertility. Rather MPs phrase their arguments within an essentially medical framework. Anti-choice MPs argue that 'women in their dilemma may be subjected to [RU486]'[12] with long-term dangers to their health, and long-term costs to the NHS.[13] This is countered by pro-choice MPs and government ministers who assert the safety of the antiprogestin termination ('nothing could be simpler and safer than that'),[14] the saving to the NHS[15] and the extra choice for women and doctors.[16]

This focus on arguments concerning women's physical health marks a shift in the anti-choice rhetoric. One could not be thought overly cynical for seeing this concern as a strategy for attempting to block the introduction of RU486, and for believing that the real motivation for so doing lies elsewhere. This move is also interesting in providing further illustration of the shift in anti-choice rhetoric to a concentration on the medical, already evident in the parliamentary debates at the time of the Alton Bill and the Human Fertilisation and Embryology Act (see Chapter 6). Again, both sides of the debate in Parliament increasingly make use of medical rhetoric and knowledges as the best way of putting across their arguments. This shift in focus away from the foetus also offers some support for an argument that I shall make below: antiprogestins make it more difficult for the anti-choice movement to rest their arguments on considerations of a foetus which is less easily represented as a recognisable 'baby' at this stage of gestational development (see p. 142). And again the anti-choice MPs run into problems in adopting medical rhetoric, as they fall open to challenge for lack of medical expertise.[17] Moreover, they face specific problems in that the weight of medical opinion stands against them. In an attempt to justify their opposition to the research claiming to have established the safety and efficacy of RU486, anti-choice MPs imply that the tests done have not been scientifically objective, as they have often been financed by Roussel or have involved at least one Roussel scientist.[18]

Understanding Opposition to RU486

It is abortion as an end rather than the means used to achieve it which has been the traditional focus of political dispute. The introduction of vacuum aspiration as an alternative to dilation and curettage (D&C) terminations provoked no debate. Antiprogestins only work early in the course of a pregnancy, and this should be a factor to recommend them to everyone. Why then did they encounter any opposition? In this section, I shall be looking in particular to the medicalisation of abortion and the related perceived need for medical control to explain opposition to the drug.

Anti-Choice Groups
The anti-choice campaigning groups have fought antiprogestins on all fronts, maintaining a more traditional line of argumentation, as well as seeking to deploy medical knowledges:

> We believe [RU486] will be physically and psychologically damaging to the women who take it (Nuala Scarisbrick, administrator of Life, in Prentice, 1990, p. 4).

> There will be more pressure on women to have abortions (Scarisbrick in Prentice, 1990).

> [RU486 is] chemical warfare on the unborn (SPUC leaflet, 'A Dose of Lies: False claims about RU486, the Abortion Drug').

Also present in some statements is an undercurrent of the need for abortion to be unpleasant as a deterrent to those women who take the decision to terminate a pregnancy too easily. This plays on the kind of construction of the woman who would seek to terminate a pregancy which was developed in Chapter 3. It also relates directly to fears regarding control of abortion. Phyllis Bowman (director of SPUC) said, 'We want to see the abortion law tightened up in this country and this drug is going to make people think it's easy to have one. We're against this philosophy of making abortions easier and easier' (Moorhead, undated, p. 1). SPUC's expert on RU486, Catherine Françoise, comments:

> You take a tablet to get rid of a headache. You take a tablet to stop getting pregnant. And now you take a tablet to get rid of a child . . . Terrifyingly, some people now talk of the death and destruction of the tiny unborn human life by a powerful chemical steroid as being more convenient (Sapsted, 1991, p. 41).

A still more extreme reaction comes from the US where a pro-life congressman stated:

> proponents of abortion want to replace the guilt suffered by women who undergo abortion with the moral uncertainty of self-deception . . . with the 'death pill', the taking of a pre-born life will be as easy and as trivial as taking an aspirin (in Ricks, 1989, p. 92).

Several commentators have raised the possibility that it is the belief that the abortion pill will make abortion less unpleasant which has created the hostility towards it. Implicit in this would seem to be the suggestion that women need to suffer in order to be deterred from reoffending (Dall'Ava Santucci, 1988; see also Ricks, 1989; Cook, 1990; Sapsted, 1991).

Also underpinning anti-choice opposition to the drug would seem to be certain worries about the issue of control. If the technical aspect of having an abortion becomes as easy as 'taking an aspirin' (and this construction implicitly carries with it images of self-treatment and even self-diagnosis), how is it to be controlled? Whereas some feminists have long advocated the practice of self-help terminations by menstrual extraction (see Chapter 4, pp. 55–6), antiprogestins seem to bring the possibility of self-induced abortion much closer to reality. Abortion by menstrual extraction relies on women who have experience with the method, working as part of a group, with access to certain equipment. More importantly, menstrual extraction presupposes the acceptance of a level of intimacy with one's own body and with the bodies of other women, that would be difficult for many who might find RU486 acceptable. As in the image conjured up above, it sounds as easy as taking an aspirin. So the introduction of RU486 seems to strike at the very basis of medicalised abortion – the level of technical control. Antiprogestins seem to embody the potential to render doctors redundant, and their monopoly untenable. One gynaecologist involved with the French trials for RU486 enthused that antiprogestins are revolutionary, as for the first time the doctor 'loses his primordial role.

He contents himself with saying if there is or is not a contraindication to taking RU and to overseeing the development of the abortion from a distance' (Aubeny, 1991, p. 33). She goes on to argue that RU486 will lead to the disappearance of hospitalisation and any invasive procedures, and present the possibility for the woman to take control as it is her own action which will bring about the abortion. If this is true then anti-choice fears seem well founded.

As will be seen below, the present regulation of RU486 in those countries where it has been introduced is strict, so the hopes expressed by Aubeny have little prospect of imminent realisation. However, her ideas do present exactly the kind of image that seems to underlie the fears of the anti-choice activists. Opposition to the pill does seem for the most part to reflect the idea that RU486 may 'privatise' abortion. A leader in the *Daily Telegraph* referred to RU486 as 'abortion on request'.[19] The American journal, the *New Republic*, carried an article which described RU486 as 'enabl[ing] women to perform abortions privately at home . . . a woman could take RU-486 safely and privately very soon after missing her period without ever knowing whether she was actually pregnant' (Kaye, 1986).

These kinds of fears have also been raised specifically in connection with s.3A of the Abortion Act (one of the amendments introduced by s.37 of the Human Fertilisation and Embryology Act) which gives the Secretary of State the power to authorise *classes* of places for the administration of such drugs (as opposed to having to issue individual licences, as is the case for other forms of termination, see pp. 160–1 below). Anne Widdecombe (Con., Maidstone) noted in the Houses of Commons:

> [this amendment] gives the Secretary of State powers to enlarge the classes of premises that will be licensed. I believe that that is merely a paving measure – even if it is not intended as such – for self-administered home abortion.[20]

It seems that opposition to antiprogestin terminations is underpinned by fears regarding the implications for control over abortion – that too much control may ultimately come to rest in the hands of the pregnant woman. After all, 'How could a state control swallowing?' (Goodman in Klein et al., 1991, p. 29).

Pro-Choice Reactions

> If this is a private and de-medicalized abortion experience, then the word 'private' has lost its definitional moorings (Klein et al., 1991, p. 112).

The majority of pro-choice supporters, who have expressed an opinion, seem to have come out cautiously in favour of the decision to license

RU486 for use in Britain, with both the National Abortion Campaign and the Birth Control Trust supporting it. Given the fears of the anti-abortionists that antiprogestins might result in freer access to abortion, this is not surprising. What is more intriguing is the idea of pro-choice opposition to antiprogestins.

Arguments which have been made against the drug are that it is less safe than conventional methods of early pregnancy termination such as vacuum aspiration, that it has as yet been inadequately tested, that women are being used as guinea pigs for industry and that the long-term effects of the drug will remain unclear for many years (Aktionsforum MoZ, undated; Klein et al., 1991; Raymond, 1991). These arguments are similar to those made by anti-choice MPs in Parliament, although in Parliament, specific opposition was expressed to the fact that it was *British* women who were being used as guinea pigs,[21] and the dangers of long-term effects were expressed not only in terms of dangers for women but also in terms of cost to the NHS.

As well as looking at the potential unknown side-effects and possible negative experiences of using the drug, the arguments put forward by those feminists who have proved hostile towards the licensing of the drug also focus in part on control. They argue that whereas RU486/PG terminations have been presented as involving a detechnicalisation and loosening of medical control, in fact quite the converse is true. Klein et al. put their claim strongly:

> In reality, the RU486/PG abortion method increases, rather than decreases the lack of privacy and the lack of women's control over the abortion experience. The only thing different about an RU486/PG abortion is the *rhetoric* of control which hardly matches the *reality* of strict and prolonged medical supervision. Measured by the number of doctor's visits, and the duration of time from visit one to visit three, or four (at which point the woman is back to square one of conventional abortion), we are talking about a non-private, extensively medicalized, and complicated abortion method (Klein et al., 1991, p. 29, emphasis in original).

Whilst this criticism originates from outside Britain, it seems to be no less applicable here and has been advanced in much the same form in an article in *Spare Rib* by one of the book's authors, Janice Raymond (1991). It is this seeming paradox – that worries regarding control are central to both pro- and anti-choice opposition to the drug – which I attempt to untangle in the following section regarding the regulation of antiprogestin terminations.

ANTIPROGESTINS AND PARADOXES OF MEDICAL CONTROL

I have argued above that the appearance of detechnicalisation offered by antiprogestin terminations has fuelled controversy at the introduction of RU486 and has drawn the lines between its opponents and proponents. Although arguments have been framed primarily in terms of medical safety, I have maintained that opposition has been motivated in large part by the fear that RU486 will give more control to women. Equally, where putting more control into the hands of women is seen as a positive thing, this has served as an argument in favour of antiprogestins.

In Britain, Roussel Uclaf, doctors involved in the trials of RU486 and politicians alike, have all been at great pains to dispel the idea that RU486 will contribute to increasing women's control over termination. In Parliament, every MP who spoke to support the introduction of RU486 emphasised that it would have to pass through the Abortion Act in the same way as other kinds of termination, and would be subject to exactly the same level of medical control:

> [RU486's] use will be confined to approved places and, as with other methods of abortion, will require the agreement of two doctors who will have to give their signature in good faith. It is not abortion on request (Jo Richardson, MP).[22]

> We are discussing a method of abortion. As it should be seen clearly as an abortion method, its use must be governed by the provisions of abortion legislation, and principally the Abortion Act. My right hon. Friend the Secretary of State has made it clear that he is licensing the drug only for use in conditions that are clearly set out in law – that is to say, that the prospect of an abortion must be agreed to by two doctors. It must be on defined grounds within the terms of the Act, it must be in licensed establishments – there is no question of it being available for use in unlicensed establishments by general practitioners (Stephen Dorrell, Under-Secretary of State for Health).[23]

> Usage is confined specifically to those hospitals and clinics approved and licensed under the Act for the termination of pregnancy. It is administered there only under medical supervision and only to women who agree to the treatment schedule. Mifegyne is therefore not available for general sale, nor through chemists nor on family doctors' prescription ... The supply of Mifegyne is strictly controlled by Roussel. It is available only to those hospitals and clinics which have received instructions in its use and which conform to Roussel's specific conditions of supply (Roussel statement, 1 June 1993).

All of this would seem to support Klein et al. and other feminists who have opposed the introduction of antiprogestins in their assertion that RU486 does not challenge the medical control of abortion. What particularly angers them is that RU486 has been represented as an essentially demedicalising procedure which will give more control to women whereas they contend that, on the contrary, it actually extends and entrenches medical control:

> All of the researchers and clinicians agree that RU486 will *never* be given without this medical management, yet they speak out of both sides of their mouths in simultaneously stating that RU486 gives women more control over abortion. The kind of medical supervision that RU486 requires is not physician oversight from afar, but a *highly medicalized treatment regimen* which is multi-stepped, time consuming, and for many women, pain-producing and long-suffering (Raymond, 1991, p. 35, emphasis in original).

In support of this argument, Klein et al. cite the pill's inventor Etienne-Emile Baulieu who, in the space of one article, writes 'RU486 could be a prototype of the second generation of ways of giving women more control of their fertility' and also that 'it should be given under strict medical supervision in specialized centers' (Klein et al., 1991, p. 25). Whilst for Klein et al. these two statements form a clear contradiction, I feel that it may be more usefully viewed as an apparent paradox which might be untangled with regard to the different forms of medical control which I outlined in Chapter 4. Antiprogestin abortions fall squarely within the terms of the Abortion Act, and are subject to all the same regulations as surgical abortions. As such, decisional control remains firmly in the hands of the medical profession: a woman seeking abortion will still need the certification of two doctors that her situation falls within one of the categories laid out in section 1 of the 1967 Act. What may be more interesting are the implications for technical, paternalistic and normalising control. These are considered below.

Technical Control
As was noted above, antiprogestins seemingly have the potential to detechnicalise the provision of abortion: their administration does not require the same level of training as a surgical abortion (although expertise will be necessary as back-up cover in case of complications). At present, however, it is true that in an important sense, as Klein et al. (1991) contend, antiprogestins serve to medicalise (rather than *de*medicalise) abortion. The increased medical control which forms the focus of their critique is represented by increases in a basic level of technical control: the woman requires more visits to hospital/clinic and,

like other terminations, the procedure must be performed at specifically authorised medical centres, under medical supervision which is, if anything, closer than that required for surgical terminations. One can add to this that the supply of the drug is very closely controlled and is subject to an extra level of administrative regulations introduced by the Secretary of State for Health. So, contrary to fears often expressed in the months preceding its introduction, RU486 will not be available over the chemist's counter without prescription, or with a prescription signed by a doctor. Neither will it be possible for the woman to take the drug to use 'in the privacy of her own home'. Even the enthusiasm of Elisabeth Aubeny (cited earlier as foreseeing the doctor as losing his primordial role) is dampened sufficiently for her to admit that 'the price paid for [RU486] is the increased medicalisation of medical terminations for women' (1991, p. 34).

Number of Hospital/Clinic Visits

Once a woman's request for termination has been granted, she will face three visits to the hospital/clinic where the termination takes place as opposed to one visit for a surgical termination. Two days after being given the RU486, she must return for the prostaglandins which will complete the termination. A third visit is deemed necessary for a medical examination to make sure that the abortion is complete and to monitor any side-effects.

Initially, there was some confusion as to what stages of the antiprogestin termination come within the term 'treatment for the termination of pregnancy' (per section 1(3) of the 1967 Act) and must therefore take place in a hospital or approved place. This point has since been clarified in a Department of Health circular:

> As with any other treatment for termination of pregnancy, both stages of this method (antiprogesterone tablets followed by prostaglandin pessary 36–48 hours later) must be administered in an NHS hospital/NHS Trust hospital or in one of the places approved by the Secretary of State under Section 1(3) of the 1967 Abortion Act, as amended, and specifically authorised to use this new method.[24]

Therefore both antiprogestin and prostaglandins must be given in accordance with the restrictions imposed by the 1967 Act. The interpretation adopted is not one which would be self-evident from a reading of the legislation as only in a very few cases will the prostaglandins themselves provoke the termination. Equally convincingly they could be seen as a pre-treatment, with the second stage (antiprogestins) being responsible for causing the termination. The official interpretation is the one which imposes the closest medical control. However, administration on an out-patient basis is in accordance with the Abortion Act, even in the small number of cases where the woman actually aborts outside the clinic.

The third foreseen visit to the hospital or clinic is not a requirement when the woman has a surgical abortion. For the latter, her check-up can be done by her GP or at a family planning clinic or advisory centre. David Baird, Professor of Reproductive Endocrinology at the University of Edinburgh who participated in many of the British trials involving RU486, contends that in medical terms this is not always necessary if you search for the products of conception by examining the woman vaginally before she leaves the hospital.[25] David Paintin (Emeritus Reader in Obstetrics and Gynaecology at St Mary's Hospital Medical School in London) comments:

> The development of medical services both within and outside the NHS is being restricted by prescribing rules, Department of Health regulations and the legal requirement to provide abortion within an NHS hospital. Clearly some regulation is necessary for patients' safety in relation to the use of drugs and the organisation of non-NHS facilities. But many of the regulations have been imposed for political reasons because ministers who are in charge of health and pharmaceutical manufacturers fear the small, but vehement, anti-abortion lobby (1994b, p. 48).

This points clearly to the depoliticising function of tighter medical control.

Medical Surveillance

Secondly, regulations ensure a closer level of medical surveillance over the woman while she is actually at the clinic/hospital. It is specified by Roussel that RU486 must be taken in the presence of the prescribing doctor. Further, the woman must be observed for at least two hours following administration of the drug and Roussel's conditions for issuing the drug prescribe that throughout the time a patient is on the premises a doctor must be present (not a requirement for surgical terminations). However, it seems that this level of control is unsupported by medical needs in the vast majority of cases, so long as medical back-up is available if something goes wrong.

The regulations imposed by the Department of Health and Roussel seem excessive not only in terms of medical need, but also in terms of the existing law. Following the case of *RCN* v. *DHSS*, it would seem that where the initial examination of the woman is done by doctors, pills could be handed over by a nurse or other medical personnel. As was seen in Chapter 5, those involved in performing terminations are protected by the terms of the Abortion Act where, per Diplock LJ, 'a registered medical practitioner . . . [accepts] responsibility for all stages of the treatment'.[26] Accordingly, so long as a doctor prescribed the treatment for the termination, remained in charge and accepted responsibility throughout, it seems that the pregnancy would be 'terminated by a registered medical practitioner' for the purposes of the 1967 Act, and any person taking part in the termination would be entitled to the protection afforded by section 1(1). This does not imply the need for a doctor to be present on the premises, to be the one who gives the woman the pills or to supervise her following administration, so long as there was cover provided in case of an emergency. Indeed, in the *RCN* case, Woolf J noted *obiter dicta* with explicit reference to the future possibility of chemical terminations that

> the registered medical practitioner must decide on the termination; the process must be initiated by him, and he must remain throughout responsible for its overall conduct and control *in the sense that any actions needed to bring it to a conclusion are done by appropriately skilled staff acting on his specific instructions, but not necessarily in his presence,* though he or another registered medical practitioner must be available to be called if required.[27]

This would suggest that a far less strictly controlled regime would still meet the existing statutory requirements. Again, restrictions imposed on access to antiprogestin terminations are not so much caused by statutory prohibition, as by the administrative and medical regulations governing their use.

Supply of RU486

There is a very tight control over the supply of the drug and to whom it may be given. Roussel are proud to claim that they can trace every individual pill from the factory through the hospital or clinic to the GP prescribing it. Each package of three RU486 tablets is labelled with three numbered stickers. One sticker goes on factory records, the second is retained in the hospital or clinic pharmacy, and the third goes on the woman's medical chart. It must be possible for the doctor or hospital pharmacist to account for all labels at any time. Roussel refuse to supply the drug unless doctors from a clinic attend a training seminar in its use. Further, they make detailed specifications as to how drugs must be stored, delivered and, if for any reason they are unused, returned.[28] One US doctor who requested a pack of RU486 as a last attempt to save a patient with advanced breast cancer (this being believed to be another potential use for the product), was requested to return the drug, when his patient eventually died before using it (Chalker and Downey, 1992, p. 220). These provisions speak clearly to fears that a black market may develop in the drug, and that it may thus become available outside of strict medical supervision.

Ministry of Health Regulations
The Minister of Health has issued some special regulations regarding the use of antiprogestins which would also seem to imply a tightening rather than loosening of medical control. First, outside of the NHS, antiprogestins are available only to women who live within one hour's travelling time of the clinic. This regulation is important as it serves to exclude non-resident women from using the drug. According to Chalker and Downey, provisions limiting the drug to British nationals were requested by Roussel (1992, p. 21), presumably to avoid further publicity of women travelling to Britain in order to receive early abortions. However, Marie Stopes clinics have now declared that they are able to offer early medical abortion to women from overseas, provided they are prepared to be treated on an in-patient basis and return to the clinic one week later for a check-up.[29] Secondly, it seems that antiprogestins may only be offered if the woman agrees for her own GP to be notified,[30] and he must be left sufficient time to respond with anxieties about the proposed treatment. Thirdly, a GP (not necessarily the woman's own) must agree to provide overnight cover. This is intended to ensure medical supervision following the termination.

With regard to the current regulations governing the use of antiprogestins then, it seems that basic technical control of the abortion procedure has been tightened, despite some evidence that such a degree of control is neither medically nor legally necessary. It seems likely that this very potential to demedicalise or detechnicalise abortion is responsible for the concrete *increase* in control, as it is this potential which has fostered the fears at its introduction. However, the foundations of such control seem less solid in this instance. Medical control of abortion is legitimated by the appearance of its necessity to ensure safety: the claim that only the medical professional can promise health. With antiprogestins it may become apparent that these two levels are out of step, and the medical monopoly seems untenable.

Paternalistic and Normalising Control
Whilst antiprogestins increase the level of basic technical control and medical surveillance over women having abortions, they may none the less be important at the level of making women feel more in control as the procedure depends more on their own active participation. A leading feminist gynaecologist, involved in the French trials leading to the introduction of the abortion pill there, noted 'with the abortion pill the woman isn't hospitalised or even undressed at the moment of

the abortion' (Bureau, in Simonnot, 1993b). Although women have to go through the same interviewing process to secure authorisation for their terminations, this may none the less have a significant effect on their experience of the abortion itself, and their relationship with the medical professionals involved in it. All ten of the women in Chantal Birman's 1989 study reported that their relationship with the medical profession was different and more positive than in the case of a surgical termination. Two women attributed this to the fact that they were part of a trial to test the drug and consequently things were better explained. Three others, however, asserted that the relationship was really different because they themselves were taking charge. One even talked of collusion with the doctor. Further, three of them noted that it was an advantage not to be so much at the mercy of the doctors who 'often want to make women suffer because they are usually against abortion and they inflict abortion as a punishment' (Birman, 1989, p. 8). Another woman cited by Chalker and Downey compared her RU486 termination with an earlier abortion, 'This time, I felt like I was in control, and taking the pills felt so much safer than having anesthesia and having some doctor poke at you with instruments' (1992, p. 211).

Abortion is also symbolically removed from medical control in that women are normally alone when they abort. Janet Callum relates her impression of a French clinic where women were having RU486/PG abortions:

> Some women felt that because there was no instrumentation, RU-486 was gentler and less intrusive, and they also appreciated not having to disrobe and lie down before a stranger. I observed women sitting quietly in a room together, reading magazines and talking. Occasionally one would excuse herself, walk into the bathroom and within about five minutes, emerge, her abortion completed. All expressed a profound appreciation at being 'in control', and several watched with rapt attention as the technician examined the products of conception (undated, p. 6).[31]

According to another study, the women who opted for medical termination were distinguished by their desire to be in control (Bachelot et al., 1991, p. 38; see also Sapstead, 1991, p. 41). Elisabeth Aubeny studied 75 women who had used this method of abortion. She notes:

> All emphasize the responsibility that they have to take . . . Instead of being passive as they are in vacuum aspiration, they manage their own abortions. By taking the tablet, the woman acts to trigger the process and supervises evacuation at home. In the vacuum technique, a doctor is in sole control. A woman can be virtually absent if she chooses general anesthesia. But RU 486 fits the needs of

responsible patients who can cope by themselves, as many women want to do (cited in Lader, 1990, p. 54).[32]

Whilst RU486 may lead to a present increase on the level of technical control, paradoxically it may simultaneously increase the woman's feeling of power and this may effect the nature of her relationship with the medical professionals she encounters – if not her GP, then the doctor who will be responsible for her termination. Further, RU486 may also have the potential to challenge the technical level of medical control of abortion in the future. As I have argued above, it is perceptions of this possibility which has provoked the fears motivating anti-choice opposition to it and led to the very tight regulation of the drug.

FEMINIST FUTURES?

Today, a strictly controlled pill, taken at hospital. But tomorrow, will it always be possible to exercise such a control? (Aubeny, 1991, p. 34).

In Chapter 6, I discussed the perceived need to protect the foetus from the pregnant woman, and the appointment of the doctor as the appropriate expert to represent the foetus's interests. This is closely related to the construction of abortion as an essentially medical event, requiring specialised knowledge and the idea of the woman as too irrational or irresponsible to be in control of her own termination. Whilst not wanting to overstate the importance of antiprogestins, I believe that they do have the potential to effect the abortion debate positively by challenging at least some of the assumptions about it which are rooted deep in sections of the public consciousness. Further, antiprogestin terminations may yet provide an extra impetus for streamlining medical procedures in a way that would further loosen medical control and improve women's access to early terminations.

'Foetal Protectionism' and Antiprogestins

Early abortions were traditionally seen by women as 'bringing on a late period'. Antiprogestins to a certain extent recreate this image of abortion. Berer writes that RU486 fulfils women's need when facing an unwanted pregnancy – to get a period (1993b, p. 18); Sapsted has described the final stage of the antiprogestin termination as 'a heavy period which expels the fertilised egg' (1991, p. 41). Coulet reports that some French women requesting antiprogestin terminations have described RU486 as 'the drug which brings periods back' (1993, p. 20), and Couzinet notes that 'Many women think of it as an induction of a menstrual period. Compared with classical abortion, the procedure is so much better tolerated emotionally by women' (in Cahill, 1987, p. 7).

The abortion debate in both Britain and the US has centred very much on the status of the foetus and its (non) personhood. An important anti-choice strategy has been to focus attention on fully-formed foetuses in later pregnancy, and much of their campaigning literature contains images of the developed older foetus. As has been seen, one anti-choice success of the 1988 Alton Bill campaigns was to shift attention on to late abortions (Steinberg, 1991). Antiprogestins, on the contrary, focus on early pregnancy. This has already been noted as a problem by US anti-choice groups. National Right to Life Committee president John Wilke comments, 'We're really very simplistic, visually-oriented people, and if what we destroy in there doesn't look human, then it will make our job more difficult' (in Kaye, 1986, p. 5).

With antiprogestins, abortion becomes more clearly part of a continuum which also includes contraception. The line between the two starts to blur, especially given that RU486 is in pill form and works in a way similar to the 'morning-after' pill (Outshoorn, 1990). In fact, in discussion of the abortion pill, very often the two treatments are confused.[33] This blurring of boundaries has been encouraged by RU486's developer, Etienne-Emile Baulieu, who describes his invention as a 'contragestive' ('to diffuse the strength of the word abortion'), arguing that it falls between abortion and contraception (1993, p. 4). In an article which examines the ethical implications of antiprogestins, Cahill argues that this is one of the more worrying implications of the drug: 'the line between abortifacient and contraceptive methods of birth control is obscured by rhetoric designed to make the drug more acceptable to those who already accept contraception prevention' (1987, p. 7).

However, what Cahill's argument in itself conceals is that a clear line drawn between abortion and contraception is not a natural or inevitable boundary but is itself historically specific and socially contingent. According to historian Barbara Brookes, the perception of a clear distinction between the two dates only from the 1920s (1988, p. 6). What changes with antiprogestin terminations is the following: with surgical abortion, the pregnant woman has to wait until at least six to eight weeks from her last menstrual period before the termination can take place. This gap has served to separate the two categories of abortion and contraception, keeping them distinct in both public consciousness and law. Indeed, British law has failed to provide any explicit distinction as to where contraception ends and abortion begins, a grey area long existing between the two (Tunkel, 1979; Douglas, 1991, pp. 95–6; Kennedy, 1988, Chapter 3).[34] Antiprogestins seem to have bridged this gap, to form a continuum between forms of contraception which prevent the egg from being fertilised (condom, spermicides, diaphragm, female condom), those which may prevent fertilisation or implantation (combined pill), those which may prevent implantation, or may dislodge the implanted embryo (IUD), and antiprogestins which cause the womb to shed its lining and hence the implanted embryo. The similarity between the functioning of antiprogestins and an IUD is marked: both interfere with the nurturing uterine environment sufficiently to prevent the continuation of pregnancy and to induce menstruation.

The Demystification of Abortion as a Specialised Medical Event

The role of the doctor in the medical termination changes from active to a more passive one. The doctor becomes a background figure, needed to supervise and to step in if anything goes wrong. It would seem that although the basic technical and bureaucratic control of abortion is currently greater in the case of antiprogestin terminations, that this control somehow becomes emptier and more artificial – it depends much more on stringent rules and bureaucracy than on accepted medical need. This is reflected in that, in practice, doctors do not always strictly abide by the rules:

> During the administration of the mifepristone, minimal supervision is required, and although the manufacturers tell us that the woman should be observed for two hours, in practice after the swallowing of the tablets the patient is allowed to leave after five to ten minutes. In the UK we have to administer these tablets in a licensed premises or in an NHS hospital. There is really no medical reason for this. This is purely a product of the legal requirement for termination of pregnancy (Baird, 1993, p. 5).

Logan describes how a significant part of the RU486/PG termination is carried out by nurses who administer the prostaglandin and do the vaginal examination with speculum (1994, p. 34). Likewise, as Jones notes, 'The use of mifepristone has enabled other doctors to distance themselves from the practice of abortion by leaving the work to nurses or junior medical staff' (1994, p. 22). It would seem to be just as safe for a nurse, midwife or trained lay person to administer both courses of treatment, given access to specialised medical help in case of need. This means that the traditional justification for the need for medical technical control – safety – would not ring true here. Antiprogestins seem to offer greater future potential for arguing for safe abortions, performed by trained lay personnel with medical personnel necessary only as backup.

Challenging Referral Procedures

A letter published in *The Times* shortly after the British licensing of RU486 called for a review of the existing referral procedures of the NHS.[35] As the letter points out, in the NHS in England and Wales, only 21 per cent of all abortions were performed within the first nine weeks of pregnancy, because of the lengthy procedures in some area health authorities. By 1995, this figure had reached 41 per cent of all terminations. The signatories argue that the introduction of early medical abortion, which can be used only until nine weeks from the woman's last menstrual period, provides the NHS with an exceptional opportunity to review its referral procedures so as to provide a fully comprehensive abortion service. Thus the importance of antiprogestins here is to provide an impetus for existing referral procedures to be expedited in order to make their use a possible option. This is an administrative matter and so has the advantage of not having to put abortion back on to the parliamentary agenda.[36] Some excellent examples in Britain already exist to show how successful a streamlining of referral procedures can be (see Glasier, 1993).

A more radical step would be to propose again the streamlining of referral procedures in Parliament. As was seen above (Chapter 6), in the 1990 parliamentary debates, the amendment tabled by Harriet Harman which sought to allow a woman to have an abortion following referral by just one doctor (as opposed to two) failed by a slim margin of only 28 votes. As antiprogestin terminations are dependent on an early referral, their existence within the NHS might provide one more argument for such an amendment in future debates and thus swing the balance. Claims that women should have the absolute right to elect to terminate early pregnancies might benefit in the same way. It is unlikely, however, that these issues will again receive parliamentary time in the near future.

Licensing of Other Premises

Under section 1(3)(A) of the Abortion Act,[37] the Secretary of State has power to authorise the use of specified abortifacient drugs in classes of places other than NHS hospitals. Although ministers have said that they have no immediate plans to make use of these powers,[38] as this amendment was introduced specifically by the Government, the possibility of future licensing of other premises is obviously already on the agenda.[39] This might mean that GPs' surgeries and eventually family planning clinics could be licensed to supply either the first or both courses of treatment. This would be beneficial for women, given that typically one will live nearer to a GP than to a hospital or specialised clinic. It also has a broader significance in driving a wedge into the power of the hospital doctors who, as was seen in Chapter 4, have a *de facto* monopoly on the provision of NHS terminations: it is the regulation that abortions must be performed on specially licensed premises which restricts the number of doctors who can perform them.

David Bromham (senior lecturer in obstetrics and gynaecology at St James' Hospital, Leeds) has suggested that family planning clinics might be particularly suitable for the provision of antiprogestin terminations (1994, p. 14; see also Baird, 1993, p. 6). The desirability of extending permission for treatment to be administered there or at GPs' surgeries will depend first and foremost on the perceived safety of such a move. If thought desirable, achieving this would depend on the political will of the Minister of Health. Given the current composition of the Government over recent years, the existence of such political will existing is probably limited. One Scottish organisation asked the Scottish Home and Health Department whether it could set up an abortion service in Edinburgh where women who presented for abortion to a large family planning clinic could be given the RU486 in that clinic and then admitted 48 hours later to the hospital for the administration of the prostaglandins. This would have meant that the family planning clinic would have had to have been recognised by the Secretary of State for Scotland as an approved place for termination of pregnancy. The Scottish Home and Health Department were reluctant to allow this to happen for reasons which, according to Glasier, are political: namely 'they do not want to rock the boat' (1993, p. 15).

CONCLUSIONS

Klein et al. argue that 'RU486/PG represents the epitome of a reproductive politics that makes no connection to the sexual politics of women's lives' (1991, p. 120). This is undoubtedly true in the sense that any kind of abortion does not on its own address the wider social (sexual) context within which women get pregnant. The availability of abortion is only ever part of the story and it can only be one part of a feminist politics of reproduction. It is also true that an antiprogestin termination will not be the right choice for some women. And as the RU486/PG termination is likely to be significantly cheaper than other forms of terminations, in the long term, there is need for vigilance in ensuring that women are left free to make our own decisions as to what kind of termination is to be chosen.

However, in another sense, Klein et al. must surely also be wrong. Antiprogestin terminations may connect with women's needs and perceptions in important ways. In particular, the availability of such an early method of abortion may have a positive effect on a woman's experience of her abortion. Further, whilst antiprogestins are indeed a method which currently entails a tighter level of technical control, this control seems in an important way to be more 'hollow' in that it is more dependent on rules and bureaucracy and less on a commonly perceived medical need. This increased technical control seems to be a result of fears generated by the seeming potential of antiprogestins to strike at the basis of this technical power.

Here it has been seen that the decision to license RU486 for use in Britain had little of the explicit political significance of the same measure in France or the US. What debate occurred here was instead cast within an essentially medical framework. Notwithstanding this, however, such dispute as did exist can only be adequately understood within a context of dispute as regards who should control female reproduction. Moreover, whereas RU486 was introduced with comparatively little controversy and contestation, it has been introduced only within a rigid framework of medical control and supervision: a far cry from 'NHS distribution of RU 486 to any woman who qualifies for it'.

POSTSCRIPT

While this book was in press, there was one further twist in RU486's tortuous history. On 8 April 1997, Roussel Uclaf announced that they had decided to suspend all production of the drug. All rights in it would be ceded to Edouard Sakiz, one of the doctors who had worked with Baulieu on the development of RU486, and former managing director of Roussel Uclaf. This decision can only be the result of the controversy which had dogged RU486 in France and, more recently, the USA and the threats of economic boycotts, feminist groups denounced the decision as a 'pro-life victory' (*Le Monde*, 10 April 1997). Maybe the final victory will not be that of the pro-life movement, however. Sakiz has announced his intention to set up a company called Excelgyn, to produce and to market the drug. He insists that this will be a non-profit making venture, stating that RU486 is different from other drugs: 'its a drug from which one should not make money' (*Le Monde*, 9 April 1997).

8
Conclusions

Yet law remains a site of struggle. While it is the case that law does not hold the key to unlock patriarchy, it provides the forum for articulating alternative visions and accounts. Each case of rape, sexual abuse, domestic violence, equal pay, and so on provides the opportunity for an alternative account to emerge. This account may not emerge in court (indeed it would be silenced there), nor in the media, nor in the formulation of reformed legislation, but it can and does emerge in women's writing and feminist groups . . . These resistant discourses are growing in power, and it is often law that provides a focal point for the voice to be heard (Smart, 1989, p. 88).

THE STORY SO FAR . . .

In the introduction to this book, I sketched out an argument which I have sought to sustain in the pages which followed. I have argued that the shift from a model of law based on criminal prohibition to a decentred network of medical control has (re)cast abortion as a narrow medical matter. Whilst it is true that threats to the 1967 Act remain in the form of periodic attacks in Parliament, it seems that a status quo has been broadly accepted and within this, abortion has become established as a matter for medicine rather than politics. It has been seen that this depoliticisation is real to the extent that important decisions regarding the provision of abortion have been shifted out of the public arena and left in the hands of medical professionals. However, I have argued that none the less abortion remains an important political issue and one deserving of a higher place on feminist agendas for reform. That abortion is a political issue is true both in terms of the values underpinning the existing rules governing the availability of abortion and also in the sense that the regulation of abortion provides particular sites and modes for the deployment of power over women. Finally, I have pointed to some of the major problems with continuing to accept the medical framework as the appropriate one for making decisions regarding the provision of abortion services. It seems to me that in Britain the most serious problem currently facing pro-choice politics is the relative powerlessness

147

of women in the face of medical authority and various consequences which stem from this.

In Chapter 2, I began my study of the law regulating abortion with some consideration of the statutory basis for legal terminations in Britain. I located the 1967 Abortion Act within the terms of the broad shift to 'governmentality' described by Foucault (1979a): as a tactic of management, surveillance and control of the population. In this instance, this is instituted through the medical profession who operate as 'parallel judges', able to offer a close evaluation of every individual case. I argued that, far from representing a straightforward loosening of power over women or being motivated by a desire to extend female autonomy and self-determination, the Abortion Act was actually in part motivated by a desire to regain control of a situation of mass, *de facto* resistance to the law and to assert a medical monopoly over the control of reproduction. The form of legislation adopted operates to fulfil these aims, strenuously avoiding the granting of substantive rights to women seeking abortion and passing almost total control to the medical profession. The Act represents a shift from a legal regulation based on criminal prohibition, to one based on a decentralised network of medical control over women. This is not to deny that the 1967 Act represented a gain for women, but rather to note that it simultaneously grounded a particular modality of power over them.

Foucault has contended that the new visibility of the population achieved through tactics of governmentality succeeded in constituting the individual for the first time as a 'case study', an object of inquiry and a new target of power. In Chapter 3, I examined the 'peripheral subject' constructed within the Abortion Act. The woman seeking abortion was constructed in terms of irrationality and instability: as either a selfish minor or a downtrodden and deranged victim of circumstance. Her very nature renders her unsuitable to make her own reproductive decisions; her inherent pathology grounds the need for the calm, rational and responsible figure of the doctor to take control of the situation. She is inherently in need of normalising medical supervision. The statute fails to challenge the notion of maternity as the female norm: abortion is only permitted when an exception can be made to this general rule. The constructions of unwanted pregnancy as an instance of individual pathology and of abortion as a wholly medical event have been integrally connected with the extension of a network of medical control over women.

In Chapter 4, I moved from a focus on the underlying motivations of the legislation to a consideration of how the medical control operated within its bounds actually functions in practice. In an attempt to provide a more differentiated model of power, I distinguished between:

- technical control (the medical monopoly over the performance of legal abortions),
- decisional control (the doctor decides who shall have access to abortion),
- paternalistic control (the sympathetic doctor imposes his own views) and
- normalising control (the doctor has access to details of the woman's 'private' world, and the power to locate her in a broader framework of understanding in order to produce an authorised account of her reality).

It was noted that some individual doctors have attempted to minimise the extent of this control over women, seeing the woman's desire for a termination as grounds enough for authorising it. In leaving control of abortion in the hands of the medical profession, however, women's access to abortion services becomes dependent on doctors' discretion. In practice this has had significant and enduring negative consequences for such access.

The medicalisation and medical control of abortion have been legitimated, entrenched and extended by law. Whilst not denying that abortion has medical aspects, I criticised the fact that the colonisation of law by medical knowledges has operated to the exclusion of other accounts and perspectives. The courts both accept and reinforce the medical control of abortion and hence medical power over women, as was seen in Chapter 5. The jurisprudence displays a clear judicial deference to medical authority and itself illustrates the influence of medicalisation, making use of medical constructions. As the law becomes dependent on medical concepts and definitions (for example, viability), or creates its own constructions based on its perceptions of medical reality (for example, good medical practice), then expert medical witnesses are necessarily drawn into the courts to guide judicial interpretations. However, judicial respect for medical authority has not been entirely negative for women. It was significant here that medical control of abortion has in many ways served to protect, rather than to impinge upon, female autonomy. The law operates to protect the medical relationship from outside challenge. Where it is less useful is in protecting women within this relationship as was seen in cases such as *Re S* and *Re W*. In terms of the regulation of abortion, the case of Barbara Whiten has staged a confrontation between medical discretion and female autonomy to provide a challenge which finds the legal protection offered to women to be greatly lacking.

In Chapter 6, I examined section 37 of the Human Fertilisation and Embryology Act 1990 in the light of the broader assumptions which underlie it. I argued that the reforms introduced by this section display the same tension with regard to medicalisation as the case law: although they have been widely greeted as a pro-choice victory, on another level they also constitute a defeat. In this sense I argued that the framework for debate has shifted away from a broader social framework which includes discussion of women's circumstances and needs to a predominantly medical framework, focusing on the (medically defined) status of the foetus. I highlighted two specific problems. First, I argued that the parliamentary debates display a worrying assumption of foetal separation which has remained largely unchallenged. Secondly, whilst the acceptance of abortion as an area of medical knowledge has helped to defend the ambit of the 1967 Act, and to secure a comparatively high upper time limit for terminations of 24 weeks, it cannot but have contributed to the climate which saw the failure of those proposed amendments seeking to loosen medical control over access to abortion and to allow women greater autonomy in early pregnancy.

In Chapter 7, I looked at the use of antiprogestins in procuring terminations and the legal and medical framework which has been established to regulate them. I argued that what discussion there was regarding the decision to license RU486 for use in Britain was conducted primarily in medical terms and this obscured the drug's potential political significance and contributed to the relative lack of controversy which greeted its licensing for the British market. However, it became clear that such depoliticisation remains an appearance and not a reality: whilst coded in medical terms, the reactions of pro- and anti-choice groups can only be understood within a context of an ongoing struggle over control of women's fertility. Further, I noted that although RU486/PG terminations were initially seen as a way of demedicalising abortion, their introduction has resulted in an increased degree of medical control and supervision. I argued that the regulations governing the use of antiprogestins were a reaction to fears regarding the potential of the drug to decrease medical control. Over and above these regulations, however, I argued that RU486 may yet have significant potential for challenging certain aspects of medical control and medicalisation.

In the light of this analysis, it seems clear that the medicalisation of abortion has served largely to remove it from the public sphere, whilst also greatly influencing what discussion of it remains within that arena. However, as I have emphasised throughout, it is still relevant to view the regulation of abortion in Britain as a political issue. This is true in two senses. First, the existing legal rules governing the availability of abortion were predicated on the desire to establish a network of control capable of regulating both abortion and the women who seek it, whilst safeguarding the medical monopoly over it. This is seen in terms of the statute, the judicial protection of a medical monopoly, and in other rules and regulations such as those introduced to govern the supply of antiprogestin terminations. Secondly, the form taken by the regulations ensures that women are constantly vulnerable to medical power: the element of control inherent in the doctor–patient relationship is entrenched and extended.

However, a rather different model of power than one which focuses on violence or coercion is essential for such an analysis. The model of power which has emerged in this work is one not of state prohibition, but a more regulatory model: a shifting and decentralised network of medical power, the operation of which is justified by specific, gendered constructions of the nature of the woman seeking to terminate a pregnancy and the expert knowledge of medical professionals. Legal regulation stands not in opposition to this medical regulation but functions in a symbiotic relationship with it, adopting medical knowledges and norms, legitimating and entrenching a sphere of medical discretion. The operation of power has been largely concealed in that the encoding of abortion law in medical terms contributes to a growing appearance of depoliticisation: abortion becomes a site for scientific knowledge and expert control. This serves to protect the status quo, with the legal framework for such medical control, and the exceptional judicial intervention serving to legitimise the normal run of medical practice and control. As Dreyfus and Rabinow comment:

> Political technologies advance by taking what is essentially a political problem, removing it from the realm of political discourse, and recasting it in the neutral language of science. Once this is accomplished the problems become technical ones for specialists to debate (1982, p. 196).

Although law formally retains ultimate authority for itself, its power is deployed only in exceptional cases.

Abortion activists on both sides of the political fence have embraced medicalisation, working within the medical framework and adopting medical knowledges and rhetoric where this has seemed the most effective way of influencing the political debate and legislation. Anti-choice activists have used medical knowledges very effectively, using medical accounts of the physiological development of the foetus and photographs which purport to show it at an advanced stage of pregnancy. The *pièce de résistance* of this genre is the (largely discredited) pseudo-scientific film *The Silent Scream*, which purports to show an ultrasound imaging of a twelve-week foetus being aborted. Narration is provided by Dr Bernard Nathanson, 'sober, bespectacled, leaning professorially against the desk', providing medical authority for the images (Petchesky, 1987, p. 59; see also Hartouni, 1991, pp. 36–7).[1] In a similar vein is the SPUC campaign which produced leaflets and colour postcards with a developed foetus sucking its thumb, 'showing the baby's humanity in words and pictures' (see p. 115). I argued that although this is not a new tactic, its power has been increased due to the invention of techniques which allow the photographing of the foetus *in utero*. Advanced medical technology is used to produce an image which emphasises all that is baby-like about the foetus – like a baby, it is shown as existing whole and separate from the body of the pregnant woman. This mirrors the shift in the political debate which has come to revolve around the (medically defined) status of the foetus, with the body of the pregnant woman completely occluded.

The anti-choice movement has also produced expert witnesses to testify to a medically proven form of illness following termination: post-abortion trauma or syndrome. This has been the object of a private Commission organised by anti-choice MPs under Lord Rawlinson[2] and a repeated subject of parliamentary questions by anti-choice MPs.[3] Anti-choice MPs have also tabled many parliamentary questions dealing with various other medical aspects of abortion. In just one month of 1993, David Alton MP requested information on the links between abortion and chlamydia,[4] infertility,[5] spontaneous miscarriages in subsequent pregnancies,[6] maternal deaths,[7] how often it was necessary to give blood transfusions following abortion,[8] the incidence of perforations and ruptures of the uterus[9] and the procedures for reporting of physical complications following abortion.[10]

Nevertheless, it seems that the weight of medical opinion in Britain is in favour of allowing abortion (within certain medically controlled circumstances and limits) and that, on balance, medicalisation has led to a facilitation of women's access to abortion. Britain was among the first western countries to legalise abortion and the medical framework adopted by the law helped to minimise potential opposition and political controversy. Since 1967, doctors have grown increasingly liberal in the provision of abortion and the courts have refused to check this development. Specialist non-NHS clinics have been established in areas where senior NHS doctors are less liberal and block the performance of abortions in 'their' hospitals. As was seen in Chapter 4, the removal of purchasing powers to District Health Authorities and GPs has resulted in a steady increase in the percentage of terminations which are state funded. Administrative attempts to restrict the number of abortions (for example where the Department of Health altered notification forms to omit reference to the woman's environment) seem likewise to have been unsuccessful (see p. 86). Britain has a relatively high upper time limit for abortion, which was enshrined in statute in 1990 because it coincided with viability (primarily a medical event). Finally, that antiprogestins arrived on the British market with only minor protests preceding their introduction testifies to the extent to which abortion has come to be seen as an essentially medical, rather than political, matter.

WHAT'S WRONG WITH MEDICALISATION?

Given that medicalisation has brought such obvious gains for women, why would one seek to challenge it? Notwithstanding the above, medicalisation also presents two integrally connected problems. First, there is the problem of the medical framework itself. In the same way that the adoption of a rights framework for debate has been criticised for the marginalisation of consideration of broader social issues, so too has the pre-eminence of medical knowledges and the acceptance of a medical framework for debate marginalised discussion of other factors. As the law has been colonised by medical knowledges, other understandings of abortion have been excluded from it. Secondly, this acceptance of a medical framework seems to make any possibility of loosening the medical grip on the control of abortion appear ever more remote and thus contributes to the maintenance of the concrete problems which stem from such medical control outlined in Chapter 4.

Marginalisation of Non-Medical Factors

Whilst feminist commentators have recognised that the language of rights has been useful and politically empowering for the women's movement (as for many minority groups), recent years have seen an increasing degree of unease with regard to its invocation.[11] The use of rights in the formulation of claims has been criticised for a number of reasons including their focus on individuals as opposed to social structures (Himmelweit, 1988, p. 42; Kingdom, 1991, p. 62) and on narrow legal solutions rather than wide-ranging social reform. Thus, if and when such rights are attained, this can present a problem as solved, although history clearly shows that an improvement in women's formal legal position does not automatically lead to an improvement in women's social and economic position (Kingdom, 1991, p. 47). I would argue that medicalisation poses similar problems and that the problems posed by the adoption of a medical rhetoric are now more pressing in the case of abortion. At the parliamentary level and, to a large extent, also within the rhetoric of the campaigning groups, the rights discourse is being superseded by the use of medical discourse and a deployment of medical knowledges.

As Carol Smart has contended, law has a particular claim to truth which is indivisible from its expression of power, operating not simply in its material effects (judgements), but also in its ability to disqualify other knowledges and experiences (1990a, p. 5). This further enhances the significance of the colonisation of law by medical knowledges. The 1967 Act marked a landmark victory for the medical discourse or paradigm, constructing abortion as falling primarily within the sphere of medical, rather than moral or religious authority (as in Ireland), or as a matter of a constitutional conflict between a woman's right to privacy and the State's interest in protecting foetal life (as in the United States). This victory has been consolidated in more recent years: the medicalisation of abortion has become so grounded in our common-sense perception of it, that it becomes difficult even to begin to imagine an alternative legal context to that of medical control. In this sense a clear evolution between the parliamentary debates of 1966–7 and those of 1990 has been seen. Whilst the former contain much discussion of women and broader social factors, the latter are characterised by their strong medical focus. The acceptance of abortion as something which falls within the realm of the medical has become so firmly entrenched that anyone wishing to be heard in the debates is under pressure to adopt medical discourse. Other voices are silenced. Neatly illustrating this is a comment made to one of the writers in a volume on cultural studies: 'how can you do any research on abortion, you've never studied medicine' (Fyfe, 1991, p. 169).

One example of the ability of medical knowledges to disqualify other accounts was seen in Chapter 6 with the adoption of 24 weeks as the upper time limit for abortion in 1990. As was seen, this rested on the significance attributed to the medical construction of 'viability' and the assertion that any other cut-off point would simply be 'arbitrary'. As I asserted above, to accept this one factor of viability as the decisive cut-off point ignores women's complex decision making and awareness of broader social considerations. As Maureen McNeil argues, the adoption of viability as a dividing line

> shifts the focus of decision-making away from women who, in opting for or against abortion, make complex evaluations of their particular circumstances and of the social sustainability of new life. Such decisions have little to do with what medical science can sustain technologically. Saying that it is theoretically possible to plug a 24-week-old fetus into life support apparatuses is very different from saying that you personally will take primary responsibility for supporting – in every sense – a child through to adulthood (1991, p. 156).

Other examples were found in the jurisprudence. In Chapter 5, I discussed the case of *C* v. *S*, which concerned Robert Carver's attempts to prevent his pregnant ex-girlfriend from terminating her pregnancy. The major issue to be debated in court was neither S's situation, nor her claim to self-determination and how that can be weighed against Carver's interests. Rather the legal issue was constructed as a narrow medical one, revolving around the point of viability and the boundaries of medical discretion. Again, this led to a favourable verdict for S, but the tremendous political importance of the decision was defused. The legal problem to be decided is defined in medical terms.

The process of focusing a debate is also (inevitably) one of narrowing it: any way of formulating a question equally occludes other possible formulations. This is an essential process for law, which is not able to deal with infinite complexity. It must simplify and reduce an issue to manageable proportions before it can begin to deal with it. However, whilst it is not 'wrong' to view abortion as a medical phenomenon, other important ways of conceptualising it are obscured by the dominance of the medical framework. I would contend that the current statute does more than simply omit consideration of social factors. Rather, as was seen in Chapter 3, by its very structure, the law focuses attention on to what is *different* and *medically* (broadly construed) significant about the particular woman's situation. Abortion is illegal: the question is what is peculiar about this woman or this pregnancy that should justify its performance? This obscures consideration of much of what has been central to feminist accounts of abortion: what may be *similar* in the situation of women which contributes to the existence of unwanted pregnancy.[12] Even in so far as the Abortion Act does take account of social factors (in that the doctor can take account of the 'woman's actual or reasonably foreseeable circumstances'), these are individualised, reconstructed as exceptions which are particular to the situation of the individual woman and only by virtue of this fact gain their medical (and hence legal) relevance. As was seen in Chapter 5, this is true even where doctors make their recommendation for termination on the grounds of the so-called 'statistical argument':[13] doctors are legally required to take an individualised decision (see pp. 85–6). It remains implicit in the law that women should only be allowed to have abortions if they fit into one of the 'abnormal' categories: if they are somehow distinguished from the 'normal', family-oriented, maternal woman with a normal pregnancy.

In dealing with social problems which particularly affect certain individuals, the makers of public policy have always to make a choice, or to strike a balance, between dealing with the problem on a social level (through welfare measures, preventative campaigns) and on an individual level (through treating the individual, criminal sanctions, individual benefits). For example, unemployment can be seen as a social, structural problem: for whatever reason, there will inevitably be a certain number of people in our society who are without work. Alternatively, it can be seen as an individual problem: the individual is unemployed because she is underskilled or insufficiently motivated. The way in which unemployment is conceptualised has vital implications for how we seek to deal with it. If it is due to structural factors, it is only by addressing these that unemployment will be eradicated or mitigated. If it is because of an individual laziness or inadequacy, then effort must be directed at reforming the individual. In fact, our system of welfare benefits rests on a dual conception which incorporates aspects of both of these viewpoints: accepting the inevitability of unemployment and hence the need to pay benefits, but at the same time introducing carrot-and-stick measures to encourage the individual into the labour market and training schemes to enhance her chances within it.

Central to feminist writing on abortion has been an emphasis on the broad, structural factors which contribute to the incidence of unwanted pregnancy and which make abortion more than an individual matter – a refusal to abstract the issue of abortion from the context of women's concrete situations and lived experiences. Such writings have raised not merely individual, medical considerations (are the requirements for abortion justified by this case history?) but also reflect the more general, social issues involved in discussion about unwanted pregnancy. The problem of understanding abortion has thus been one of simultaneously grasping both individual and social factors, of understanding that abortion is at once a decision arising from intimate and personal circumstances, yet at the same time is influenced by important structural givens which relate to the particular situations of women in a given society at a given time. The nature of reproduction is thus simultaneously recognised as both social *and* individual, operating both at the core of social life, as well as within and upon women's individual bodies (Petchesky, 1984a, p. 2).

Socialist feminist writers like Ros Petchesky in the US and Elizabeth Kingdom in Britain have suggested that pro-choice campaigns might be usefully reformulated with a focus on women's needs (Petchesky, 1984a) or circumstances (Kingdom, 1992). Within these general categories they would include the need to consider such matters as the availability of safe and efficient contraception, sex education, the difficulty for women to take control of their own sexuality and refuse intercourse where it is not desired, social pressures such as stigma attached to mothering outside of marriage, financial and economic considerations, and the massive loss of freedom experienced by individual women on having a child. Within the present, medicalised legal construction, the essential problem is perceived as one of how far doctors' freedom to terminate pregnancies should be legally controlled. Once some provision has been made in this direction and an acceptable 'compromise' reached, the problem seems solved, the state's responsibilities fulfilled. When the problem is relocated within the context of women's lives, the issue becomes one of unwanted pregnancy and attention is uncomfortably refocused on to problems which are less easily (and cheaply) addressed: poverty, poor child benefits, lack of childcare facilities, inadequate social provision for the physically and mentally disabled, failure to provide adequate sex education and contraception, women's lack of control in sexual relations and, above all, our hugely disproportionate share in the costs and responsibilities of childcare.[14] Medicalisation (and the casting of law in medical terms) has aided the apparent depoliticisation of abortion. This may have improved access to abortion services, but it has directed debate firmly away from discussion of how such social factors might be addressed.

Entrenchment of Medical Control

The acceptance of a medical framework for debate works against any loosening of medical control: the more abortion becomes seen as a medical decision, the more difficult it becomes to see this decision as one which fundamentally belongs to women rather than to doctors. In 1990 MPs voted to maintain a relatively high upper limit in the law and in certain instances (including in cases of foetal disability) they voted that abortion should be allowed until the moment of birth, in this respect making the Abortion Act amongst the *most* liberal of western abortion statutes. At the same time, MPs refused to allow abortions prior to 12 weeks either on request or where authorised by only one doctor, retaining the strictest medical control and situating the Abortion Act amongst the *least* liberal of western abortion statutes. This voting pattern is consistent only if one locates it within a context of medicalisation and medical control. Law leaves a broad scope for medical discretion, but this implicit acceptance of abortion as a site of privatised, expert, medical knowledge can only have contributed to the failure of the proposals to loosen such control in early pregnancy. Likewise, antiprogestins were licensed for use in Britain on the basis of repeated assurances that they would be issued only through the most strictly controlled medical channels. As a result, women in Britain may have the possibility to use this method, but only within the very tight limits of a cumbersome, highly medicalised system of supervision and control. The licensing of RU486 thus widens the medical choices open to women acting in conjunction with their doctors, but allows the exercise of this choice only under an even tighter medical control.

It has been evident that medical control of abortion brings its own attendant problems, and these were outlined in Chapter 4. It remains true that one's chance of obtaining NHS funding for a termination is dependent on where one lives, and the bias of either the senior doctors in local NHS hospitals or, increasingly, the priorities of GP fundholding practices or senior administrators who purchase block contracts for services. Further, it seems that there is little control over how a woman will be treated by the GP and hospital workers encountered in her attempt to obtain an NHS termination. Finally, whereas the woman acting in conjunction with her doctor is comparatively well protected legally in the courts against outside interference (by state or third party), she has less protection against her own doctor (see Chapter 5). In practice, this has resulted in a situation where women who are sufficiently knowledgeable to approach a clinic, and who have the necessary money to fund their own terminations, will have access to safe, legal abortion, in a relatively sympathetic environment. The same is not necessarily true for younger women, women of minority ethnic groups or others who are lacking the same resources in terms of money and knowledge of how the system operates. The entrenchment of medical control leaves women's access to termination as discretionary, and the treatment received as dependent on medical goodwill. Inevitably, the worst consequences of this will fall upon the most vulnerable – and least vocal – groups of women. With the possibility of obtaining NHS funding for a termination dependent on geography, and the likelihood of a sympathetic reception from one's GP largely a matter of luck, it seems that the most pressing problem now facing a feminist politics of abortion is that of medical control.

CHALLENGING MEDICALISATION AND MEDICAL CONTROL: THE ROLE OF LEGAL REFORM

The above analysis raises a clear problem for a pro-choice politics. It seems that the most effective way of protecting and entrenching women's access to abortion services has been to embrace an essentially medical framework, deploying medical knowledges and constructions. This is a language and argumentation which seems to have been most effectively 'heard' within the existing legal structures and which is least susceptible to challenge or dispute. To phrase claims in the language of medical need also serves to depoliticise them, giving them all the weight of an apparent objectivity. However, it is difficult to see how medical knowledges can be deployed without reinforcing the construction of abortion as essentially a medical phenomenon, thus marginalising other accounts and entrenching the idea that control should rest in medical hands. Moreover, addressing medical power is especially difficult given the form that it takes and the fact that its operations are often barely apparent: only in the most extreme cases can such power be understood in the terms proposed by some feminist writers such as MacKinnon (1983a) as coercion or violence against women. Its operation is rather grounded in medical knowledge, and the medical claim to define the patient's best interests. For abortion, moreover, such power is grounded not only by the notion of the doctor as the expert most able to help the pregnant woman, but equally by the idea that he is most in touch with the interests of the foetus, and by his construction in other areas of obstetrics and gynaecology as the 'foetal protector' (see pp. 52–3).

The problem of the power imbalance inherent in the medical relationship should not be confined to discussion of abortion, but in this instance it is particularly acute. Confronted with an unwanted pregnancy, the doctor may be hostile to the woman's request and decide not to authorise her termination. And only for abortion (and some infertility treatments) does the doctor have a statutorily entrenched right to refuse to treat on the grounds of conscientious objection. On a general level, patients' representation groups have fought for certain legal structures and procedures which aim to restrict medical discretion and to protect the patient. Academic commentators have likewise called for a statute to lay down the rights of patients (Montgomery, 1992a, p. 94) or for the transformation of John Major's Patient's Charter into more specific, enforceable rights (Longley, 1993, Chapter 5). What is perhaps not evident, however, is how far law is capable of addressing such operations of medical power and how far the acquisition of legal rights would go towards adequately protecting women's access to abortion services. In the remaining pages, I would like to make some tentative suggestions regarding how useful recourse to law can be in this instance. I will very briefly outline some of the potential legal reforms which might serve to improve the position of the 'patient' within the specific case of the regulation of abortion. I will then go on to question whether law is the most effective way of addressing the problems which have been highlighted above. Should legal reform provide the basis for feminist campaigns in this area? Or would a focus on medical practice be more beneficial? In a final section, I will return to consideration of legal reform as a focal point for feminist campaigns, this time from a slightly different perspective.

Legal Strategies: Possibilities and Problems
Various possible legal reforms have been suggested as ways of improving the power imbalance within the medical relationship or giving women some legal protection within it. These have typically focused on the level of decisional control, although some have also looked to doctors' technical monopoly over the performance of terminations. The issue of conscientious objection has also received some attention.

Challenging Decisional Control
The central demand of the women's movement (and, in particular, the National Abortion Campaign) has been that women should be credited with the responsibility and maturity to make their own reproductive decisions, and thus should be entitled to authorise their own terminations. In 1995, NAC launched a campaign for abortion on request. This would obviously have a significant effect on the power relationship between the woman seeking abortion and her doctor, not only in terms of removing his decisional control, but also lessening the potential for exercise of paternalistic and normalising control. Women are currently vulnerable to the exercise of such power as a result of being dependent on the doctor for a referral. Recognising this decision as one

which belongs fundamentally to all women would also focus attention on abortion as a collective issue, involving all women rather than just a marginal and deviant minority.

Such a reform has at least two shortcomings. First, without anything more it leaves doctors' technical control (and the problems which stem from it) intact. Secondly, and more importantly, it has little possibility of success in the current political climate. Amendments suggested in 1990 attempted far more limited measures and even these were unsuccessful (p. 114). The limiting of these demands to the first twelve weeks of pregnancy was no doubt designed to maximise support – opinion polls have consistently shown that a greater number support a 'woman's right to choose' when this is confined to the first trimester (Francome, 1991). Moreover, elective termination in early pregnancy is now the norm in western Europe. Another possible measure, and one which came close to succeeding in 1990, was to remove the requirement of a second signature, and thus to allow women to decide in conjunction with just one doctor. This was narrowly defeated (by 228 votes to 200). I noted that the introduction of antiprogestins provides one more argument in favour of such reform (p. 144).

Challenging Technical Control
Abortion is one of the only medical procedures where it is explictly provided that treatment must be performed by a registered medical practitioner. This technical control has been important in grounding the other types of medical power seen in Chapter 4. Doctors' decisional control over access to abortion services and the authority which enhances their paternalistic and normalising control is closely tied to their technical expertise and monopoly over the performance of abortions. The question which now arises is whether this technical monopoly should be removed, and (early) abortion governed in the same way as any other medical procedure: that is, that it would not be deemed illegal, unless the practitioner holds herself out as having skills or qualifications which she does not.[15] A first problem and area for closer investigation would be the possibility of ensuring the safety of women seeking termination. Again, however, such a reform would have no chance of success at the present time.

There may, however, be a possibility for challenging doctors' monopoly of technical control over terminations, by allowing them to be performed within established medical structures by a wider group of trained professionals. It has been seen that prostaglandin terminations are already largely performed by nurses, with the doctor in a largely background, supervisory role. I have also argued that antiprogestins may in the future provide a basis for a larger number of people to be able to perform terminations: the most obvious first step would be to allow the administration of the first stage of treatment by

GPs in their surgeries and trained personnel in family planning clinics. This kind of potential extension was clearly in the minds of ministers in 1990, when the Government proposed an amendment which now allows the Secretary of State to authorise *classes* of places to carry out terminations (see p. 132). Increasing the number of potential providers loosens the medical monopoly. Quite possibly, it would have a significant effect on the power context were the abortionist to be a nurse or midwife rather than a doctor. The executive board of the American College of Obstetricians and Gynaecologists has recommended that non-physicians be trained to do abortions in 'collaborative settings alongside physicians' – at present nearly all states have laws which, like the Abortion Act, limit the performance of abortions to trained medical practitioners.[16]

Conscientious Objection
The Abortion Clinics (Access) Bill was introduced into Commons in May 1993 by Harry Cohen MP (Lab., Leyton).[17] The Bill was introduced at a time of concern at the arrival in Britain of 'Operation Rescue' and more militaristic, US-style tactics on the part of anti-choice activists. Its main thrust was the prohibition of interference with and intimidation or harassment of clients or employees entering abortion clinics. However, the Bill also contained a clause which put the onus on general practitioners to inform women what sort of counselling is available and might be helpful to them. Such a requirement might provide a small step towards attempting to address the power imbalance within the medical relationship, by refusing to allow the doctor complete agenda-setting power, and giving the woman greater information. Statute could provide that a doctor, acting as a conscientious objector under the Act would not be able simply to refuse a woman's request for abortion but at that point would have to inform her of the reason for such refusal and refer to her a colleague who is not a conscientious objector. This would protect doctors who wished to exercise their right to conscientious objection, whilst mitigating the impact of this on the women who approach them for terminations.

An alternative to this was a suggested amendment to s.37 of the Human Fertilisation and Embryology Act 1990 which foresaw that doctors wishing to exercise their right to conscientious objection under s.4 of the Abortion Act would have to register on a list which would be available to women before approaching a GP. This was rejected on the grounds that it might lead to discrimination against doctors who hold such views. The utility of any such changes would, in any case, be limited unless introduced in conjunction with a loosening of doctors' decisional control. Under the current legislation the doctor can, without claiming to be a conscientious objector, still block the woman's request: the power to certify whether the conditions laid down in s.1 of the Abortion Act are fulfilled remains his.

There is also an argument for raising the issue of conscientious objection in the law courts rather than Parliament. The only people who can make use of the right of conscientious objection as defined in s.4(1) of the Abortion Act are those who 'participate in treatment' authorised by the Act. This obviously covers the medical staff who actually perform abortions. However, according to Lord Keith, in the House of Lords' decision in the case of *Janaway* (see p. 182), the Abortion Regulations (1968, SI 1968/390, now SI 1991/490) do not seem to view the signing of the green form as part of the treatment for the termination of pregnancy, since regulation 3(2) states, 'Any certificate of an opinion referred to in s.1(1) of the Act shall be given *before the commencement of the treatment* for the termination of the pregnancy to which it relates' (my emphasis). As the Regulations demand that the green form must be signed *before* the commencement of the treatment for the termination of pregnancy, then it seems to be impossible to see the signing of the green form as *part* of that treatment. And if signing the form is not part of that treatment, then the s.4(1) defence cannot apply to it.

If it is right that s.4(1) does not apply in this context, then it remains to be established whether the GP owes a *duty* to the woman to sign the green form and refer her to a consultant. Schedule 2 of the NHS (General Medical Services) Regulations 1992 (SI 1992 No 635), para 12 provides that

> 12(1) Subject to paragraphs 3, 13 and 44 a doctor shall render to his patients all necessary and appropriate personal medical services of the type usually provided by general medical practitioners.
> (2) The services which a doctor is required by sub-paragraph (1) to render shall include the following . . .
> . . . (d) arranging for the referral of patients, as appropriate, for the provision of any other services under the Act.

The provision of services involving the termination of pregnancy is one of the 'other services' under the 1977 NHS Act (ss.1 and 3). So it would seem that legally GPs have not merely a duty to refer to a colleague, but rather they have a duty to sign the green form and refer to a consultant, when in their medical opinion, the woman fits within the terms of s.1(1) of the Abortion Act.

This interpretation is not that adopted by the Department of Health in their guidelines regarding the purchase of abortion services (see pp. 56–8):

All GPs who have an objection, for reasons of conscience, to recommending termination should quickly refer a woman who seeks their advice about a termination to a different GP. Prompt action should be taken in order to reduce the likelihood of a late termination. If doctors fail to do so, they could be alleged to be in breach of their terms of service.[18]

It is difficult to see on what basis the Department feels that referral to a colleague is demanded by the terms of service, but referral for abortion services is not.

Whether a court would find in favour of a plaintiff in such a case remains unclear. If there is one lesson to be taken from the decisions in *Bourne* and the *RCN* case it is the degree of creativity of which judges are capable where this is necessary to protect a defendant doctor. The potential plaintiff should recognise that the courts are very reluctant to convict doctors unless bad faith can be proved. Moreover, the above provision makes it possible for a GP's employer to take action against him, not for the patient who feels that she has been wrongly treated. The plaintiff also would face a problem in that whether or not a woman should be granted a termination remains a matter for the doctor to decide. The GP who refuses to refer her may claim that, in any case, in his clinical opinion, the woman did not have grounds under the 1967 Act.[19]

Non-Legal Reform

However, whilst the above proposals accept a focus on legal reform as the most effective means of achieving change, it is by no means clear that this is true. Neither is it clear that the acquisition of legal rights would be sufficient to secure women's access to abortion. It seems that those reforms which have even the slightest chance of success in the current political climate would be seriously limited in their impact. Further, it remains a dilemma for feminist campaigns that, once enacted, legislation is in the hands of individuals and agencies far removed from the values and politics of the women's movement. It is thus never possible to know with any certainty what effect a certain reform will have in practice. This has led Carol Smart to warn feminists to beware the 'siren call of law'. Even where feminists are critical of law, she argues, we are all too often seduced by it, attempting to use it pragmatically in the hope that new law or more law might be better than the old law (1989, p. 160). Whilst this does not lead Smart to the conclusion that law must remain unchallenged (and I shall return to this below), she does suggest that it is important not to resort unproblematically to law. It is possible that other (non-legal) strategies might be more useful.

Something which has emerged clearly during the course of this book is the importance of medical practice in determining access to abortion services. Medical practice is itself by no means coherent, unitary and unchanging. Rather it consists of varying practices which are constantly evolving and developing. It has been seen that legal developments have often followed changes at this level rather than vice versa: not only in the sense that medical groups have had an important influence on the development of legislation, but also that the judiciary has adopted medically determined standards of 'good practice' in judging medical conduct, and the law has become ever more dependent on medical concepts and knowledges. As such, it may be that the authority of medicine is more significant than the precise content of legal rights. It is medical practice which will have the greatest influence on the availability of abortion, in terms of doctors' willingness to perform and authorise terminations, and their treatment of the women who approach them.

That the acquisition of legal rights may be insufficient to address such problems can be seen in the French situation. French law grants women the right to define themselves as in a 'situation of distress' and thus to authorise their own abortions within the first twelve weeks of pregnancy. All French women have the right to have such terminations funded by the state. However, women are still dependent on doctors for the performance of such abortions, and this, combined with the low time limit foreseen by the law and public spending cuts, means that 65 per cent of abortions in the Paris region are privately funded and 5,000 French women travel abroad each year (to Spain, Britain or the Netherlands) to terminate their pregnancies (Simonnot, 1993a, 1993b; see also Allison, 1994). The situation of practical access to abortion would thus appear to be worse in France than it is in Britain, despite the more liberal statutory provisions regarding early termination. Joni Lovenduski and Joyce Outshoorn argue that the effects of abortion legislation are far less important than a network of good medical facilities. They point to the examples of Sweden and the United States, both countries with liberal legislation. In Sweden, the scrupulous provision of adequate facilities makes access to abortion a reality for women. In the United States, on the other hand, access to abortion is often severely restricted (1986, p. 4; see also Ketting and van Praag, 1986). It is thus particularly important to think about how improvements can be made at the level of medical practice.

De-privatisation of Knowledge

An important aspect of the medicalisation of reproduction is the privatisation of knowledge regarding it which has become concentrated in medical hands. One priority is a de-privatisation or proliferation of knowledge: an attempt to readdress the power imbalance inherent in the medical relationship, by strengthening the position of the patient within it. Greater awareness of the practical realities of access to abortion, of reproductive biology and of different abortion techniques are essential here. This has long been part of feminist strategies: it is the aim of books such as the Boston Health Collective's *Our Bodies, Ourselves*, and more recently *A Book of Women's Choices* (see pp. 55–6). The idea is that knowledge will strengthen women and lessen the power imbalance within the medical relationship. This is most important where women currently have least knowledge and are most vulnerable: for example, young women and ethnic minority women, especially those who do not speak English. The most effective way to reach such women may be (as a first step) through public information campaigns, better and earlier sex education in schools and well-women clinics.

Exploiting Elements of Resistance within the Medical Profession
Medical practice is by no means unitary: the medical profession consists of different groups and individuals, and instances of resistance to the hegemonic medical control over abortion have also come from *within* it. A few noteworthy doctors have been amongst the leading campaigners who have fought for women to be allowed more control. Many more, at the grass-roots level, have allowed women to make their own reproductive decisions, and have viewed their role as one of facilitating such choices. Especially important is the fact that non-NHS charitable clinics developed precisely to oppose the monopolistic power of senior gynaecologist/obstretricians who were in a position to deny the possibility of NHS terminations in the hospitals which they control. These clinics have provided inexpensive terminations and have guaranteed a more sympathetic reception and a more woman-centred service. Thus, the situation of practical access to abortion has improved over the last thirty years in no small part because of the actions of some doctors and sections of the medical profession who have done much to try to further women's reproductive autonomy, taking as their starting point the need to listen to women (and often being very much marginalised within the profession for so doing).[20] As such, both the greater education of doctors and the support of such clinics remain important.

A Return to Law: Challenging Medicalisation and the Construction of Alternative Visions
However, an appreciation of the limits of law reform and a recognition of the importance of influencing medical practice is not in itself an argument that one should abandon the law as a site of struggle. As has been clear throughout the present work, the law regulating abortion

cannot be understood merely in terms of its concrete, material effects but must be seen also in terms of its importance as an institutionalised and formalised site of power struggles, with a power to prefer certain accounts, to define and to disqualify (Smart, 1989, 1990a). Law does not merely reflect reality, it also contributes to constructing our perception of it, lying at the root of some of the most commonplace assumptions which people make in ordering their daily lives. Equally, it will have influence on doctors: it is surely true that the more liberal provisions of the Abortion Act contributed to doctors' changing attitudes towards abortion. Smart has thus argued that feminists *do* need to engage with the law, maintaining that it is precisely law's power to define which must become the focus of feminist strategies: it is in its ability to offer a redefinition or alternative truth that feminism offers political gains (1989, pp. 164–5). Law operates as an important 'authorised discourse' which silences women by privileging other accounts of reality (Eisenstein, 1988 p. 4; Smart, 1989, 1990a). Engagement with the law is thus important as a process of the public formulation of claims and alternative visions.

In this book, I have attempted to outline a specific understanding of abortion, to show how this has been fostered by the law and to point to some of the problems of this current understanding. The possible legal reforms outlined above are not in themselves sufficient for countering the problems of medical power and ensuring women's access to abortion. However, the challenge they pose to the current status quo in terms of their reconceptualisation of women, women's role in society, abortion and the medical relationship is important. Indeed, in this sense, the challenge they pose is nothing if not radical.

In the 1960s, abortion law reformers spoke in powerful and angry terms of the hypocrisy of a law that effectively allowed abortions for the rich but not to the poor, leaving the latter to choose between unwanted maternity or the danger of the backstreets. Today, with improved access to abortion services and an apparent depoliticisation of abortion, such tones are muted and alternative accounts of abortion are often lacking. Abortion law remains a particular site of conflict for definitional struggle. However, what seems to have become central to such dispute is the definition of the conceptus – as foetus or baby, embryo or 'unborn child' – and the fixing of one point where it can be said to acquire personhood. Increasingly, medical science has been accepted as the final arbiter of this point. The attribution of one status to the foetus, of one point whereby its rights or interests can be allowed to override those of the woman is, however, only one possible construction of the crucial issue of what is at stake in the abortion debate. It is important to dislodge the foetus from its central place in the debates and to reintroduce consideration of women and our lived experiences. The introduction of broader, social circumstances will implicitly involve a challenge to the medicalisation of the debates, and a (re)emphasis of knowledges other than the strictly medical. It will also require a challenge to the way in which the female subject upon which the law is currently predicated is to be constructed.

Arguably the most powerful speech in the 1990 debates came from the New Right Conservative MP and vocal advocate of abortion rights, Theresa Gorman. Gorman refused the medical framework and rather attacked those who oppose abortion:

> What motivates those who persist in trying to amend a woman's right in these affairs is theology . . . These motives form one of the deepest, most misogynous strands in human society. For centuries theologians have equated sex with sin and celibacy with grace. They have regarded women as little more than flower pots in which future children, preferably boy children, are reared. Time and again we hear people pay lip-service to a woman's rights in this, yet when it comes down to it they legislate to give priority to the rights of the foetus that she carries . . . The concept of a woman having a right to control her sexuality, let alone enjoy it, is anathema to them . . . If the Pied Piper of Mossley Hill [David Alton] had his way, he would lead the House and the country back to the time when women were the victims of their sexuality – perpetually pregnant, physically worn down, old before their time, unable to find time to develop the other talents with which they were born and always subservient to a man and to the demands of the family . . . This is supposedly a liberal society and we should accord to the women of that society the maturity and ability to make decisions about such matters for themselves.[21]

Whilst anti-choice MPs increasingly deploy medical argumentation, Gorman here asserts that their underlying motivation is actually religious or moral – hence she implicitly challenges its relevance. She insists on a repoliticisation of abortion, relocating it within a context of (male) power over women's lives. However, this speech, where a pro-choice position is overtly informed by feminist arguments, remains the exception rather than the rule in parliamentary debates.[22] Outside Parliament, the pro-choice movement has a low profile. Compared with the anti-choice groups, its membership is small, and it operates on a tight budget. Its strategy has been essentially one of reactive campaigns, with a capacity to mobilise large numbers of women only when the status quo established in the 1967 Act is challenged. The pro-choice movement is, in one sense, a victim of its own success: the establishment of relatively good access to safe, legal abortion. However, in the absence of a more pro-active stance on the part of the pro-choice movement, it is difficult to see how medical power can be effectively challenged.

CONCLUSIONS

In this book, I have described the *pre-eminence* of medical knowledges, the consequent *marginalisation* of other accounts and the *shift* to a medical model of control. The choice of terminology has been deliberate – it is not a question of the complete replacement of religious, moral and social discourses by the medical, but rather a matter of the gradual readjustment of the balance between them and recodification of the law in these terms. I have here expressed concern that such medicalisation has been inadequately challenged, and that its pre-eminence has been established on the basis of the occlusion of other accounts. At the same time, I have recognised the problems and dangers inherent in challenging it.

In 1993, Diane Munday, an early and active member of the Abortion Law Reform Association, was interviewed in an article commemorating 25 years since the entry into force of the Abortion Act. She expressed her sadness that

> Britain, which pioneered abortion legislation, now lags behind the rest of Europe where abortion on request in the first three months of pregnancy is available in 13 countries. Here, 'rigid' legal requirements remain in place, which led to many abortions being carried out much later in pregnancy than necessary (Hunt, 1993).

Various factors are implicated here including the one which Munday goes on to highlight: the existence of a well-organised and active anti-choice campaign. Whereas pro-choice activists and academics have been most alert to the risks posed by the anti-choice groups, the Church or the State, however, less attention has been paid to the problems posed by the highly medicalised model of British abortion law. In accordance with the hopes expressed by David Steel in 1967, women have been delivered 'into the hands of the medical profession'.[23] Whilst medicalisation has helped to extend access to abortion, such access remains tightly grasped in the deadlock of medical control.

Medicalisation has been the greatest strength of the British abortion law and its greatest weakness. It has simultaneously depoliticised the extension of women's access to abortion services, defused political conflict and left women dependent on the vagaries of medical discretion and good will. Smart has written that law is often an important focal point against which resistant voices can be raised (1989, p. 88). The current regulation of abortion and the situation of practical access to it gives a much clearer focal point for opposition to the anti-choice groups. In this sense it is important for feminists to make explicit the gender politics which underlie the current regulation of abortion: to argue that who controls abortion *remains* a deeply and inherently political matter. It is political because it concerns how as women we are able to live our lives and control our own fertility. This is a matter of fundamental importance for men and women alike in deciding how we wish to order our society. If the law regarding abortion is to be improved, it is essential for the feminist movement to take a more pro-active stance towards it. An essential part of this is to challenge the basic assumptions underlying the current regulation of abortion: the medicalisation and the construction of women seeking abortion which underpins it. Uncomfortable, risky and difficult as it may be, this inevitably involves an attack on the status quo.

Appendix 1
The Abortion Act 1967

1967 Chapter 87. An Act to amend and clarify the law relating to termination of pregnancy by registered medical practitioners. [27 October 1967]

BE IT ENACTED by the Queen's most Excellent Majesty, by and with the advice and consent of the Lords Spiritual and Temporal, and Commons, in this present Parliament assembled, and by the authority of the same, as follows: –

Medical Termination of Pregnancy
1. (1) Subject to the provisions of this section, a person shall not be guilty of an offence under the law relating to abortion when a pregnancy is terminated by a registered medical practitioner if two registered medical practitioners are of the opinion, formed in good faith –
(a) that the continuance of the pregnancy would involve risk to the life of the pregnant woman, or of injury to the physical or mental health of the pregnant woman or any existing children of her family, greater than if the pregnancy were terminated; or
(b) that there is a substantial risk that if the child were born it would suffer from such physical or mental abnormalities as to be seriously handicapped.
(2) In determining whether the continuance of a pregnancy would involve such risk of injury to health as is mentioned in paragraph (a) of subsection (1) of this section, account may be taken of the pregnant woman's actual or reasonably forseeable environment.
(3) Except as provided by subsection (4) of this section, any treatment for the termination of pregnancy must be carried out in a hospital vested in the Minister of Health or the Secretary of State under the National Health Service Acts, or in a place for the time being approved for the purposes of this section by the said Minister or Secretary of State.
(4) Subsection (3) of this section, and so much of subsection (1) as relates to the opinion of two registered medical practitioners, shall not apply to the termination of a pregnancy by a registered medical practitioner in a case where he is of the opinion, formed in good faith, that the termination is immediately necessary to save the life or to prevent grave permanent injury to the physical or mental health of the pregnant woman.

Notification

2.–(1) The Minister of Health in respect of England and Wales, and the Secretary of State in respect of Scotland, shall by statutory instrument make regulations to provide –

(a) for requiring any such opinion as is referred to in section 1 of this Act to be certified by the practitioners or practitioner concerned in such form and at such time as may be prescribed by the regulations, and for requiring the preservation and disposal of certificates made for the purposes of the regulations;

(b) for requiring any registered medical practitioner who terminates a pregnancy to give notice of the termination and such other information relating to the termination as may be so prescribed;

(c) for prohibiting the disclosure, except to such persons or for such purposes as may be so prescribed, of notices given or information furnished pursuant to the regulations.

(2) The information furnished in pursuance of regulations made by virtue of paragraph (b) of subsection (1) of this section shall be notified solely to the Chief Medical Officers of the Ministry of Health and the Scottish Home and Health Department respectively.

(3) Any person who wilfully contravenes or wilfully fails to comply with the requirements of regulations under subsection (1) of this section shall be liable on summary conviction to a fine not exceeding one hundred pounds.

(4) Any statutory instrument made by virtue of this section shall be subject to annulment in pursuance of either House of Parliament.

Application of Act to visiting forces etc.
3. omitted

Conscientious objection to participation in treatment

4.–(1) Subject to subsection (2) of this section, no person shall be under any duty, whether by contract or by any statutory or other legal requirement, to participate in any treatment authorised by this Act to which he has a conscientious objection:

Provided that in any legal proceedings the burden of proof of conscientious objection shall rest on the person claiming to rely on it.

(2) Nothing in subsection (1) of this section shall affect any duty to participate in treatment which is necessary to save the life or to prevent grave permanent injury to the physical or mental health of a pregnant woman.

(3) In any proceedings before a court in Scotland, a statement on oath by any person to the effect that he has a conscientious objection to participating in any treatment authorised by this Act shall be sufficient evidence for the purpose of discharging the burden of proof imposed upon him by subsection (1) of this section.

Supplementary provisions

5.–(1) Nothing in this Act shall affect the provisions of the Infant Life (Preservation) Act 1929 (protecting the life of the viable foetus).

(2) For the purposes of the law relating to abortion, anything done with intent to procure the miscarriage of a woman is unlawfully done unless authorised by section 1 of this Act.

Interpretation

6. In this Act, the following expressions have meanings hereby assigned to them:–

> "the law relating to abortion" means sections 58 and 59 of the Offences Against the Person Act 1861, and any rule of law relating to the procurement of abortion;
>
> "the National Health Service Acts" means the National Health Service Acts 1946 to 1966 or the National Health Service (Scotland) Acts 1947 to 1966.

Short title, commencement and extent

7.–(1) This Act may be cited as the Abortion Act 1967.

(2) This Act shall come into force on the expiration of the period of six months beginning with the date on which it is passed.

(3) This Act does not extend to Northern Ireland.

Appendix 2
The Abortion Act 1967, as amended in 1990[1]

Medical Termination of Pregnancy

1. (1) Subject to the provisions of this section, a person shall not be guilty of an offence under the law relating to abortion when a pregnancy is terminated by a registered medical practitioner if two registered medical practitioners are of the opinion, formed in good faith –

(a) **that the pregnancy has not exceeded its twenty-fourth week and that the continuance of the pregnancy would involve risk, greater than if the pregnancy were terminated, or of injury to the physical or mental health of the pregnant woman or any existing children of her family; or**

(b) **that the termination is necessary to prevent grave permanent injury to the physical or mental health of the pregnant woman; or**

(c) **that the continuance of the pregnancy would involve risk to the life of the pregnant woman, greater than if the pregnancy were terminated; or**

(d) that there is a substantial risk that if the child were born it would suffer from such physical or mental abnormalities as to be seriously handicapped.

(2) In determining whether the continuance of a pregnancy would involve such risk of injury to health as is mentioned in paragraph (a) **or (b)** of subsection (1) of this section, account may be taken of the pregnant woman's actual or reasonably forseeable environment.

(3) Except as provided by subsection (4) of this section, any treatment for the termination of pregnancy must be carried out in a hospital vested in the Minister of Health or the Secretary of State under the National Health Service Acts, or in a place for the time being approved for the purposes of this section by the said Minister or Secretary of State.

(3A) **The power under subsection (3) of this section to approve a place includes power, in relation to treatment consisting primarily in the use of such medicines as may be specified in the approval and carried out in such manner as may be so specified, to approve a class of places.**

(4) Subsection (3) of this section, and so much of subsection (1) as relates to the opinion of two registered medical practitioners, shall not apply to the termination of a pregnancy by a registered medical practitioner in a case where he is of the opinion, formed in good faith, that the termination is immediately necessary to save the life or to prevent grave permanent injury to the physical or mental health of the pregnant woman.

Notification
2. omitted (provisions unaltered)

Application of Act to visiting forces etc.
3. omitted (provisions unaltered)

Conscientious objection to participation in treatment
4. omitted (provisions unaltered)

5. (1) No offence under the Infant Life (Preservation) Act 1929 shall be committed by a registered medical practitioner who terminates a pregnancy in accordance with the provisions of this Act.

(2) For the purposes of the law relating to abortion, anything done with intent to procure a woman's miscarriage (or in the case of a woman carrying more than one foetus, her miscarriage of any foetus) is unlawfully done unless authorised by section 1 of this Act and, in the case of a woman carrying more than one foetus, anything done with intent to procure her miscarriage of any one foetus is authorised by that section if –

(a) the ground for termination of the pregnancy specified in subsection (1)(d) of that section applies in relation to any foetus and the thing is done for the purpose of procuring the miscarriage of the foetus, or

(b) any of the other grounds for termination of the pregnancy specified in that section applies.

Interpretation
6. omitted (provisions unaltered)

Short title, commencement and extent
7. omitted (provisions unaltered)

Notes

CHAPTER 1

1. See in particular Andrea Dworkin (1983) and Catharine MacKinnon (1983a, 1983b, 1991). For a critical response to MacKinnon's early writings on abortion, see especially Joffe (1984) and Petchesky (1984).
2. Here there is also an overlap with abortion in terms of heated discussion as to the rights and wrongs of foetal sex selection or the abortion of disabled foetuses: the 'responsible mother' is one who wishes to give birth to a healthy child, who accepts certain constraints on her conduct in order to do so, and will abort a foetus should it prove to be 'defective' (see McNally, undated).
3. I am grateful to Liz Kingdom who has reminded me of this point on several occasions.

CHAPTER 2

1. This was provided in the form of drafting assistance, the granting of extra parliamentary time and arrangements to move the Bill to another Standing Committee when it looked like its progress would be held up by long discussions on the Employment Agencies Bill. The reform of abortion would seem to be one of a variety of reforms introduced at this time where although the Government was favourable to an issue being brought before Parliament it did not wish to take the initiative itself. Between 1952 and 1967 there had been several previous attempts to reform the law (see footnote 6 below), all of which had been talked out and failed for lack of time.
2. The first Abortion Law Reform Association conference, 15 May 1936, in Brookes (1988, p. 95).
3. H.C. Deb. Vol. 750 Col. 1372, 1967 (13 July). Here again the Abortion Act seems to fit in with other contemporary measures. The Matrimonial Property Act laid down that women's work whether inside or outside of the home should be considered as a contribution towards buying the family assets, when they came to be divided on divorce. The Equal Pay Act 1970, introduced by Barbara Castle during her time as Secretary of State for Employment and Production, laid down the principle of same wages for same work. The Divorce Act 1969 established the right of a couple to have a divorce after two years apart where both partners wanted it, or five years' separation where one partner did not agree. The

Family Planning Act 1967 provided for the provision of family planning facilities on the NHS.

4. Price, H.C. Deb. Vol. 750 Col. 1372, 1967 (13 July).
5. The Committee was required: 'To enquire into the prevalence of abortion, and the law relating thereto, and to consider what steps can be taken by more effective enforcement of the law or otherwise, to secure the reduction of maternal mortality and morbitity arising from this cause.' The Committee's report was published in March 1939. No further action followed.
6. The attempts at reform were introduced by Joseph Reeves MP (House of Commons, 1952); Lord Amulree (House of Lords, 1954); Kenneth Robinson (House of Commons, 1961); Reneé Short (House of Commons, June 1965); Lord Silkin (House of Lords, November 1965), Wingfield Digby (House of Commons, February 1966). For more discussion of these initiatives, see Dickens (1966, pp. 123–31) and Richards (1970, Chapter 5).
7. Previously English law had distinguished between abortion before and after quickening. This had been the position in common law, and was enshrined in the first statute regulating abortion, Lord Ellenborough's Act 1803, which made abortion a felony in the case of abortion after quickening, but only a misdemeanour where it occurred before that point. The distinction was removed by the Offences Against the Person Act 1837, which largely established the form followed by the modern law. Quickening was the point at which the foetus was thought to become ensouled (when the soul entered the body). It also marked the point when the woman might feel the first stirring inside her. Quickening was believed to occur at around twelve weeks, although this was believed to be earlier for a male foetus than a female one.
8. This exception reflects the second purpose of the Act: to legalise the operation of craniotomy – crushing the impacted foetal skull, inevitably causing foetal death – which was widely practised to save the life of the pregnant woman before caesarian sections became commonplace.
9. The Abortion Act and Infant Life (Preservation) Act were explicitly 'uncoupled' by s.37(4) of the Human Fertilisation and Embryology Act (1990). See Chapter 6 for more discussion of this reform.
10. [1938] 3 All ER 615.
11. [1938] 3 All ER 615 at 619.
12. [1948] 1 BMJ 1008
13. [1958] Crim LR 469; [1958] 1 BMJ 1242.
14. The *Lancet*, 29 March 1884.
15. *R* v. *Newton and Stungo* [1958] Crim LR 469; [1958] 1 BMJ 1242.
16. Robinson, H.C. Deb. Vol. 634 Col. 858, 1961 (10 February).
17. For an account of the formation of the ALRA, see Jenkins (1960), Hindell and Simms (1971), Greenwood and Young (1976) and Brookes (1988).
18. Ferris reports the official annual death rate but argues that many death certificates were disguised to conceal abortions in order to protect the good name of the family (1966, pp. 73–5). The Birkett Committee quoted figures of 411–605 deaths per year associated with abortion (this also includes non-criminal terminations). Dickens puts the number of

deaths from criminal abortions in excess of 200 per year (Dickens, 1966, p. 113) and Glanville Williams hints at a still higher figure (1958, p. 194).

19. Jeger, H.C. Deb. Vol. 749 Cols 977–8, 1967 (29 June).
20. In the House of Lords Debates, Lord Strange argues that 'nearly every woman in this condition [of unwanted pregnancy] would be in a state bordering on suicide', H.L. Deb. Vol. 277 Col. 1235, 1966 (23 October).
21. H.C. Deb. Vol. 732 Cols 1098–9, 1966 (22 July).
22. H.C. Deb. Vol. 732 Col. 1115, 1966 (22 July). David Owen is now a member of the Social Democratic Party.
23. McNamara, H.C. Deb. Vol. 732 Col. 1124, 1966 (22 July).
24. H.C. Deb. Vol. 732 Cols 1141–2, 1966 (22 July).
25. The Birkett Committee estimated 54,000 p.a. (Jenkins, 1960, p. 33). Hordern (1971, p. 2) says 120,000–175,000.
26. Steel, H.C. Deb. Vol. 732 Col. 1075, 1966 (22 July).
27. See the case of *R* v. *Mills* [1963] 1 QBD 522; [1963] 1 All ER 202, following *R* v. *Scully* (1903) 23 NZLR 380. See also the case of *Peake* (1932) 97 JPN 353.
28. See Wells, H.C. Deb. Vol. 732 Col. 1080, 1966 (22 July); Deedes, H.C. Deb. Vol. 732 Col. 1091, 1966 (22 July); Hobson, H.C. Deb. Vol. 732 Col. 1132, 1966 (22 July); Braine, H.C. Deb. Vol. 747 Col. 455, 1967 (2 June).
29. Steel, H.C. Deb. Vol. 732 Col. 1075, 1966 (22 July).
30. This function of the doctor as a source of moral authority is detailed by Foucault in two books: *Madness and Civilisation* and *Birth of the Clinic*. In the former he notes that the introduction of the doctor into the asylum was based more on his moral authority than on his medical knowledge, 'his absolute authority in the world of the asylum . . . insofar as, from the beginning, he was Father and Judge, Family and Law – his medical practice being for a long time no more than a complement to the old rites of Order, Authority and Punishment' (1989a, p. 272, see also 1980d).
31. Mahon, H.C. Deb. Vol. 747 Col. 502, 1967 (2 June).
32. For example, Steel, H.C. Deb. Vol. 732 Col. 1076, 1966 (22 July); H.C. Deb. Vol. 750 Col. 1348, 1967 (13 July); Owen, H.C. Deb. Vol. 732 Col. 1116, 1966 (22 July); Dunwoody, H.C. Deb. Vol. 732 Col. 1096, 1966 (22 July).
33. H.C. Deb. Vol. 750 Col. 1349, 1967 (13 July).
34. Steel, H.C. Deb. Vol. 171 Col. 210, 1990 (24 April).
35. H.C. Deb. Vol. 732 Col. 1116, 1966 (22 July). See also Steel, H.C. Deb. Vol. 732 Col. 1076, 1966 (22 July). Bernard Dickens makes the same point as an argument for reform (1966, p. 133).
36. See Keown (1988, pp. 90–5) for the same objections from the British Medical Association, the Royal College of Obstetricians and Gynaecologists and the Medical Women's Federation. That a doctor should not be forced to carry out a termination when he does not wish to do so is also enshrined in section 4 of the Abortion Act which provides for the possibility of conscientious objection to providing treatment under the Abortion Act except when the operation is necessary to save the

woman's life or to prevent grave, permanent injury to her health, see below (pp. 161–3).

37. The idea that the women might fabricate charges is put forward several times in the parliamentary debates (see Chapter 3, p. 45) and also in the Birkett Report which suggested that in a great number of cases, 'girls and women made the allegation of rape falsely' (Brookes, 1988, p. 117).

38. Compare this to the formula put forward by the Royal College of Obstetricians and Gynaecologists (RCOG) who suggested that the law might also provide that the practitioner could take into account such circumstances, whether past, present or prospective as were in the doctor's opinion relevant to the physical or mental health of the woman or of the child if born (Keown, 1988, p. 92) and the joint report of the RCOG and British Medical Association which argued for a subclause which contained almost exactly the wording as that eventually adopted (Keown, 1988, p. 97).

39. H.L. Deb. Vol. 285 Col. 1419, 1967 (23 October).

40. Section 1(4) provides that this restriction shall not apply when a registered medical practitioner is of the opinion, formed in good faith, that termination is immediately necessary to save the life, or to prevent grave, permanent injury to the physical or mental health of the pregnant woman. Section 1(3) was amended in 1990 to allow the relevant authorities to approve simultaneously a 'class of places' for the performance of terminations where performed primarily by the use of medicines.

41. S.I. 1968 no. 390, issued the same day as the Abortion Act came into force, currently S.I. 1991 no. 499.

42. Although, as has been seen above, attempts to prevent or control abortions by way of the criminal law had proved a visible failure.

43. See the following chapter for some examples of the way in which the figure of the woman seeking abortion is 'pathologised' and constructed as in need of medical control.

44. In terms of the success of the legislation, it will be seen in subsequent chapters that this attempted colonisation of medical lines of control was, in many ways, unsuccessful. It seems likely that the notification procedure is not always taken seriously by doctors with significant under-reporting of abortions performed, see Walsworth-Bell (1992) and Abortion Review, Winter 1992, no. 46. In particular, the judiciary are largely unwilling to police medical action under the 1967 Act (see Chapter 5).

CHAPTER 3

1. An interesting example of this which will be discussed later is David Alton's choice of rhetoric in Parliament in the 1988 and 1990 debates (see p. 110). Although in his (1988) book, Alton gives priority to religious and moral arguments (starting the chapter on abortion by quoting Mother Theresa), in Parliament he relies far more on medical knowledges to found his arguments.

2. Similarly, Paul Ferris notes the very real need for caution on the part of the reformers:

> A constant danger for abortion-law reformers, as it used to be for advocates of birth control, is that they should appear to be condoning immorality. This is why their propaganda plays up the unwanted pregnancies among married women, and says as little as it can about the thousands of single girls who have abortions. It is easier to make a respectable case in public for the weary mother of half a dozen children than for a girl of eighteen who slept with two men last week. The reformers' dilemma lies in the risk that any system which makes it easier for the mother of six to have an abortion is liable to be applied to a promiscuous teenager (1966, pp. 154–5).

3. Lyons, H.C. Deb. Vol. 732 Col. 1089, 1966 (22 July).
4. Mahon, H.C. Deb. Vol. 750 Col. 1356, 1967 (13 July).
5. See, for example, the comments of Knight, H.C. Deb. Vol. 749 Col. 932, 1967 (29 June); Glover, H.C. Deb. Vol. 749 Col. 971, 1967 (29 June).
6. Since its introduction, Knight has been one of the loudest critics of the 1967 Act. More recently, she gained attention for her success in securing an amendment to the 1994 Criminal Justice Act forbidding the use of foetal ovarian tissue in infertility treatments.
7. Knight, H.C. Deb. Vol. 732 Col. 1100, 1966 (22 July).
8. Knight, H.C. Deb. Vol. 749 Col. 926, 1967 (29 June).
9. Knight, H.C. Deb. Vol. 732 Cols 1101, 1102–3, 1966 (22 July).
10. Maude, H.C. Deb. Vol. 732 Col. 1121, 1966 (22 July).
11. Mahon, H.C. Deb. Vol. 749 Col. 1046, 1967 (29 June).
12. Deedes, H.C. Deb. Vol. 732 Col. 1092, 1966 (22 July).
13. The clause sought to allow abortion to 'a pregnant woman being a defective or becoming pregnant while under the age of 16 or becoming pregnant as a result of rape'.
14. H.C. Deb. Vol. 730 Col. 1075, 1966 (22 June).
15. H.C. Deb. Vol. 750 Col. 1350, 1967 (13 July). This is presumably based on the official statistics of 35–40 deaths per year, which I cited in Chapter 2. As I explained there, there is every indication that the real figure was far higher, see Chapter 2, endnote 18.
16. See, for example, Strange, H.L. Deb. Vol. 274 Col. 1235, 1966 (23 May).
17. By mutual agreement with the ALRA, Silkin dropped his Bill so that the reformers could concentrate on getting the Steel Bill through the House of Commons (see Hindell and Simms, 1971, p. 154).
18. Dunwoody, H.C. Deb. Vol. 732 Col. 1096, 1966 (22 July).
19. Lyons, H.C. Deb. Vol. 732 Col. 1089, 1966 (22 July).
20. H.C. Deb. Vol. 747 Col. 496, 1967 (2 June).
21. H.C. Deb. Vol. 732 Col. 1115, 1966 (22 July).
22. H.C. Deb. Vol. 749 Cols 977–8, 1967 (29 June).
23. H.L. Deb. Vol. 277 Col. 1235, 1966 (23 October).
24. H.C. Deb. Vol. 732 Col. 1113, 1966 (22 July).

25. See Thomson (1995) for an exposition of medical discourse concerning women in the nineteenth century, and the way that these perceptions connect with the regulation of abortion.
26. Doctors are referred to as 'medical men', 'professional medical gentlemen' and 'professional men'. They are always referred to as 'he' within the 1966–7 debates.
27. Steel, H.C. Deb. Vol. 747 Col. 463, 1967 (2 June).
28. Mahon, H.C. Deb. Vol. 750 Col. 1352, 1967 (13 July).
29. Raglan, H.L. Deb. Vol. 274 Col. 591, 1966 (10 May).
30. Lyons, H.C. Deb. Vol. 732 Col. 1090, 1966 (22 July).
31. Steel, H.C. Deb. Vol. 747 Col. 464, 1967 (2 June).
32. Hobson, H.C. Deb. Vol. 747 Col. 531, 1967 (2 June).
33. See especially the speech of Theresa Gorman, cited at p. 167.
34. H.C. Deb. Vol. 732 Col. 1129, 1966 (22 July).
35. H.C. Deb. Vol. 732 Col. 1104, 1966 (22 July).
36. H.L. Deb. Vol. 276 Col. 1108, 1966 (22 July).
37. H.C. Deb. Vol. 732 Col. 1144, 1966 (22 July).
38. H.C. Deb. Vol. 732 Col. 1098, 1966 (22 July).
39. H.C. Deb. Vol. 749 Col. 1059, 1967 (29 July).
40. H.C. Deb. Vol. 750 Col. 1346, 1967 (13 July).
41. There is much debate in Parliament on this issue, which revolves around the number of 'healthy' foetuses which must be sacrificed in order to pick out 'damaged' ones. This appears to give official sanction to the notion that the lives of the disabled are of less value than the able-bodied. For example, Peter Mahon, Labour MP for Preston S:

    > It is argued that if a mother has a particular disease in pregnancy . . . there is a chance that her child will be deformed in some way. But *the real tragedy would be that a large number of perfectly normal unmaimed human lives are to be sacrificed for the sake of one who would be born with some physical deformity.* What kind of morality is that? H.C. Deb. Vol. 750 Col. 1358, 1967 (13 July), my emphasis.

    Likewise: 'Surely it would be more reasonable to have the odd malformed child than to take the risk of killing a normal foetus' Galperin, H.C. Deb. Vol. 749, Col. 1065, 1967 (29 June). For a strong criticism by a disabled feminist of the provision of abortion for reason of foetal disability, see Morris (1991).
42. Winstanley, H.C. Deb. Vol. 749 Col. 1059, 1967 (29 June).
43. H.C. Deb. Vol. 749 Col. 1055, 1967 (29 June).
44. H.C. Deb. Vol. 749 Col. 1057, 1967 (29 June).
45. I.e. under section 1(1)(a) Abortion Act 1967, continuance of the pregnancy would involve risk of injury to her mental health. There is also some contention as to whether abortion in case of rape might still be permissible on the basis of the pre-existing common law, and notably *R* v. *Bourne* (see pp. 79–81). On the issue of whether *Bourne* was completely superseded by the Abortion Act see Smith and Hogan (1988, p. 372).
46. Wells, H.C. Deb. Vol. 732 Col. 1086, 1966 (22 July).

47. Hobson, H.C. Deb. Vol. 732 Col. 1138, 1966 (22 July).
48. The judge also has to point out that it is open to the jury to convict in the absence of corroboration if satisfied that the testimony is true.
49. H.C. Deb. Vol. 750 Col. 1349, 1967 (13 July).

CHAPTER 4

1. H.C. Deb. Vol. 171 Col. 205, 1990 (24 April).
2. This was practised well into this century under the Mental Defectives Act 1913 for unmarried mothers on the grounds of moral imbecility or feeble-mindedness.
3. However, Hudson (1987) relates the case of a woman who developed obsessive behaviour as a result of living with a sadistic husband. The recommended medical 'cure' was to operate on her. Roberts (1985, p. 33) gives the example of another woman who, following an illness which consisted of a refusal to do any housework, was given a course of six ECT treatments and subsequently discharged as 'well' again.
4. Indeed, medical science is fundamental in *constituting* the individual human organism. As Foucault has argued, medicine was the first to study the individual as such. Furthermore, as Foucault (1979b) and more recently Laqueur (1990) have argued, medical science is central to our understanding of the individual as essentially coded male/female.
5. Marjorie Tew has suggested that infant mortality was already in decline when obstetricians took over birth and that the increasing hospitalisation of birth, the focus upon abnormality and the employment of medical technology has actually slowed down the decrease in the infant mortality rate (in Bridgeman, 1993c, p. 33; see also Gardner, 1981, p. 130; Foster, 1995).
6. Wendy Savage was suspended from her post as Honorary Consultant in Obstetrics and Gynaecology to Tower Hamlets Health Authority in 1985 for alleged incompetence. In her 1986 book she forcefully argues that she was a victim of an ongoing power struggle about who controls childbirth and her real crime had been to give women too much autonomy in the process. See also Young (1981), for an account of the difficulty of finding room to express female or feminist values within medicine.
7. See Petchesky (1987); Wells (1993). See Fortin (1988a) and pp. 75–7 below for the spilling over of such ideas into the legal arena.
8. Since April 1996, GP fundholders have also been responsible for the purchase of abortion services (see pp. 57–8 for more discussion of this).
9. Although, as will be seen below, GPs may now choose to purchase abortion services for their patients from the non–NHS sector.
10. Hordern indicates one possible reason for this when he cites a family doctor who said that a consultant gynaecologist was 'much less likely to see at first hand, as do general practitioners, the day to day struggles of the ill-housed, impoverished mother of a young family, whose husband may be sick or unemployed or ne'r do well' (1971, p. 30).
11. Under the Venereal Diseases Act 1917.

12. *Royal College of Nursing* v. *Department of Health and Social Security* [1981] 1 All ER 545 (HL), discussed in Chapter 5 below (pp. 96–8).
13. 5–10 per cent of first trimester terminations may be followed by minor complications of which the most common are infection, pain and bleeding due to incomplete evacuation. Many of these complications are self-limiting but up to 3 per cent may result in hospital admission (Diggory, 1991).
14. See Chapter 7. RU486 (mifepristone) is an abortion drug, developed by a French company, Roussel-Uclaf. It is available in Britain up to the ninth week of pregnancy, and would seem to require far less expert medical control than any other method of abortion. A woman using this method of termination would not need anaesthetic, and can receive treatment as an out-patient.
15. Even though at that time there were only 460 of these in the country (MacIntyre, 1973, p. 127).
16. Except in an emergency, under s.1(3) of the Abortion Act:

> any treatment for the termination of pregnancy must be carried out in a hospital vested in the Minister of Health or the Secretary of State under the National Health Service Acts, or in a place for the time being approved by the said Minister or the Secretary of State.

17. On or around the day that a woman expects to begin menstruating, the contents of the uterus are suctioned out by way of a cannula. This will lighten and shorten menstruation and if an egg has been fertilised during the preceding weeks it will be removed at the same time. Menstrual extraction is also known as menstrual regulation or menstrual evacuation.
18. This fear abated somewhat following the election of President Clinton and the Supreme Court's decision in *Planned Parenthood* v. *Casey*, 112 Sup. Ct. 2791 (1992), which was less restrictive than had been anticipated.
19. The DPP also argued that it was impossible for a doctor to believe in good faith that a given pregnancy was potentially injurious to a woman's health if she was not even known to be pregnant.
20. Quoted by the DPP in a letter of 13 March 1979, see Tunkel (1979, p. 253). This is also the conclusion reached by the Lane Committee which was commissioned by the Government to investigate the operation of the Abortion Act (Department of Health and Social Security, 1974, p. 36).
21. This right extends to doctors and nurses, not to administrative staff such as secretaries, see *Janaway* v. *Salford AHA* [1988] 3 All ER 1051. Where the GP is part of a fund-holding practice, this extends to a right not to purchase abortion services (see below, pp. 57–8).
22. Around 12 per cent of these terminations were performed in non-NHS agencies on NHS patients. The statistics are taken from the annual reports issued by the Office of Population Censuses and Surveys.
23. In 1993, 10,878 terminations of a total of 11,001 performed were funded by the NHS, H.C. Deb. Vol. 247 Col. 55–6w, 1994 (18 July).
24. Taken from OPCS Abortion Statistics, HMSO AB Series no. 20 and Office for National Statistics Monitors AB 96/5 and AB 96/6. 'NHS agency'

terminations are those carried out on an NHS patient in the private sector (i.e. funded by the NHS but not carried out on NHS premises).

25. Under regulation 20(3) and (4) of the NHS (Fundholding Practices) Regulations 1996.
26. Health Service Guidelines: Guidance on fundholder purchase of terminations of pregnancy, HSG (95) 37.
27. Six of the regional offices of the Department of Health responded to my letter asking for more information on this point. In all of these, some GP fundholding practices had informed the relevant regional office of the Department of Health that they would not be purchasing abortion services: twelve fundholding practices each in Trent Region and Northern and Yorkshire Region, sixteen in North Thames Region, five in South and West Region, over nine in South Thames Region and over one hundred practices in the West Midlands Region.
28. Letters received from Trent, South and West, and West Midlands regions, October 1996; Northern and Yorkshire regions, November 1996; South Thames Region, January 1977; telephone conversation with Philip Melville of the North Thames Regional Office of the Department of Health, 30 November 1996.
29. There is, however, a statutory duty under section 4(2) of the Abortion Act to participate in any treatment necessary to save the life or prevent grave permanent damage to the physical or mental health of the pregnant woman. See Smith and Hogan (1988, pp. 373–4) for the same duty at common law, following *R* v. *Bourne*. See Brazier for the contention that there may also be a duty to discuss the possibility of amniocentesis with a view to abortion for women of over 35 (1992, p. 308).
30. *The Times*, 7 June 1990.
31. The report identified four factors which contributed to delay: non-recognition of pregnancy, the decision to seek an abortion, locating and obtaining medical agreement and a clinic or hospital to carry out the operation and waiting for admission after agreement has been confirmed.
32. H.C. Deb. Vol. 171 Col. 247, 1990 (24 April).
33. *R* v. *Smith* [1974] 1 All ER 376, discussed in Chapter 5 below (pp. 83–5).
34. One member of the MWF dissented, believing that the decision should belong to the pregnant woman.
35. *The Times*, 15 April 1991.
36. See Arney (1982, p. 183) for the same assertion with regard to the US.
37. *The Times*, 21 June 1989.
38. This idea that a desire to terminate a pregnancy is an illness reflects a common assumption that deviant behaviour in females often arises from psychological problems (see Smart, 1976, Chapter 6). One might also think back to Oakley's assertion that pregnancy in itself has increasingly become seen as a state of pathology (1984, Chapter 1).
39. The *Guardian*, 9 May 1994.

CHAPTER 5

1. The *Observer*, 15 September 1996.

2. Fortin continues:

> The expansion of biological and medical knowledge about the needs of the unborn child show that it is at its most vulnerable at the earliest stages of its gestational development and that foetal abuse or neglect at this time, may do serious and permanent structural damage. It is now well known, for example, that the excessive consumption of drugs or alcohol and the excessive smoking of cigarettes by the pregnant mother is hazardous to the health of her unborn child. There are many other sources of potential harm; safeguards are now commonly taken against unsuitable or inadequate maternal diet and workplace hazards such as exposure to radiation or harmful chemicals of various kinds (1988a, p. 75).

3. *Re F* [1988] 2 WLR 1288, [1988] 2 All ER 193. The courts refused a local authority's application for an order to restrain a pregnant woman who was mentally disturbed, had a history of drug use and led a 'nomadic existence'.

4. *D (a minor) v. Berkshire County Council and others* [1987] 1 All ER 20. A woman who was a registered drug addict and had taken drugs throughout her pregnancy, gave birth to a baby born with drug withdrawal symptoms. The local authority obtained care and control of the child by order of the juvenile court on the grounds that, *inter alia*, the mother's abuse of her own bodily health during pregnancy had avoidably impaired or neglected the child's proper development, see Bainham (1987) and Fortin (1988b).

5. [1992] 4 All ER 671. See Thomson (1994a) for a discussion of this case and Widdett and Thomson (1997) for more recent developments.

6. *Re T (refusal of medical treatment)*, NLJ, 7 August 1992 at 1126. No legal basis is offered for this possible qualification.

7. The judge refers to the case of *Re A.C.* (1990) A 2d 1235, where an order to perform a caesarian section was granted by a trial judge against the woman's wishes. However, he seemed to be unaware that the Court of Appeals had later overturned and roundly condemned the decision.

8. See Morgan (1992), Young (1993), Bridgeman (1993b, 1993c), Wells (1993) and Draper (1993).

9. The *Guardian*, 13 April 1994.

10. For discussion of two of these cases, *Norfolk and Norwich Health Care (NHS) Trust* v. *W, Rochdale Health Care (NHS) Trust* v. *C* (Fam.), unreported (3 July 1996), see Widdett and Thomson (1997).

11. The *Guardian*, 14 October 1992.

12. *The Times*, 14 October 1992.

13. The High Court judgment was reported as *Re J*, the Court of Appeal judgment as *Re W* [1992] 4 All ER 627.

14. Under *Gillick* v. *West Norfolk and Wisbech Area Health Authority* [1985] 3 All ER 403, a child of under 16 with the necessary intelligence and understanding can consent to medical treatment; however, she does not have the ability to refuse treatment. In the latter case, other parties

(and notably parents) can give consent on her behalf, even when the child has explicitly refused consent to a procedure.

15. 3 All ER [1938] 615.
16. An amendment aiming to extend the Abortion Act to Northern Ireland was firmly rejected in 1990, by 267 to 131 votes. All MPs representing Northern Irish constituencies (all of whom are male) voted against the reform. As several of them commented, it was the first issue to unite them for some time. In 1995, 1,548 Northern Irish women travelled to Britain to terminate their pregnancies (ONS Monitor, AB 96/5).
17. Cited approvingly in *Newton* v. *Stungo*, Crim. L.R. [1958] 469, and *Bergmann and Ferguson, BMJ* 22 May 1948, 1008.
18. Pp. 41–2, 1846 [709] xxiv.
19. At 619. See the same distinction made at 617 and 621.
20. *BMJ* 22 May 1948, 1008–9. This case would appear to extend the test as laid down in *Bourne*, demanding not that a belief be reasonable, but merely that it be honest.
21. Crim. L.R. [1958] 469. See Harvard (1958) for more detail of the facts of this case.
22. See also the case of *R* v. *Sumner* (1958) Glamorgan Assizes, discussed in Harvard (1958, p. 600).
23. *Royal College of Nursing* v. *Department of Health and Social Security* [1981] 1 All ER 545, at 554.
24. [1978] 2 All ER 987 at 992. Cited approvingly by Donaldson MR in *C* v. *S* [1987] 1 All ER 1230, at 1243.
25. [1974] 1 All ER 376, 1 WLR 1510, 58 Cr App Rep 106.
26. Abortion (Amendment) Regulations 1976 (SI 1976/15).
27. S.1(2) of the Abortion Act which states, 'In determining whether the continuance of a pregnancy would involve such risk of injury to health as is mentioned in paragraph (a) of subsection (1) of this section, account may be taken of the pregnant woman's actual or reasonably foreseeable environment.'
28. The original notification form had left a space for non-medical grounds. See Hordern (1971, p. 275) for a copy of this form.
29. Compare this with the standard of medical negligence as established by *Bolam* v. *Friern Hospital Management Committee* [1957] 2 All ER 118 at 121: 'A doctor is not guilty of negligence if he has acted in accordance with a practice accepted as proper by a responsible body of medical men skilled in that particular art'. Again the court must judge the actions of doctors against the standards of their peers.
30. (1989) 59 DLR (4th) 609, per Bernier JA, at 613. He continues:

> A person who freely does an act must assume its consequences. Pregnancy is not in itself an infringement of the physical integrity of a woman, an interference with her body, but a function which is a fundamental part of her nature. The rule of nature is that a pregnancy must be carried to term. The right to voluntarily terminate it constitutes an exception to this general rule. To arbitrarily have recourse to this without reasonable grounds constitutes at any stage of a pregnancy

> an abuse of right. On the other hand, a woman is entitled to an abortion if there are reasonable grounds for doing this in the light of the stage of pregnancy. The further advanced the pregnancy, the more serious and peremptory must be the grounds . . . But when the interests of the mother are contrary to those of her unborn child, when she wishes to terminate her pregnancy in a situation where the public interest is not involved, it is unquestionably the right of the father, on serious and reasonable grounds, to oppose the abortion. This legal interest is based on the very fact of conception of which both the father and mother were the cause. It is his child as much as it is the mother's, neither more, neither less.

See Graycar and Morgan (1990, pp. 218–19) on this case.

31. [1978] 2 All ER 987.
32. Per Baker P at 989. Cited approvingly in *C* v. *S* [1987] 1 All ER 1230, at 1238.
33. The decision goes against the prediction of an earlier article in the *Modern Law Review* which foresaw the necessity of consent, at least where the couple were cohabiting. O'Neill and Watson argued that

> It seems quite feasible that the court might hold, not only that it has a duty to protect the unborn child, but also that the child's father has a right to request that it do so. If sympathy ever guides a court in coming to its decision on law, such sympathy might well, in the case of an abortion apparently 'on demand', guide the court towards a decision in favour of the father (1975, p. 184).

34. *Paton* v. *UK* [1980] ECHR 408. The Commission (the preliminary screening body for the Court) held that the right to respect for family life cannot be interpreted so widely as to confer on the father a right to be consulted or to make applications about an abortion his wife intends to have performed. Grubb (1990, p. 157) has argued, however, that this case may not be the last word at this level, as the decision was narrowly expressed: Mrs Paton was only eight weeks pregnant and the Commission made it clear that it was not concerned with balancing the rights of a mature foetus with those of the woman, for this was a case where the pregnancy was in its initial stages. Further, the Commission restricted its decision to cases where there is a 'medical indication' for abortion in the interests of the woman's life or health. For example, it specifically excluded from its consideration abortions performed on eugenic grounds.
35. [1987] 2 WLR 1108, [1987] 1 All ER 1230.
36. Indeed Mr Paton would have been in a stronger position to make such a claim as he was married to the pregnant woman, and thus would have been the child's legal guardian. Further, Baker clearly dismisses the possibility that the putative or illegitimate father could have any rights at all in such a case: *Paton* v. *BPAS* [1978] 2 All ER 987, at 990.
37. *C* v. *S* could no longer occur in the same form as s.37 of the Human Fertilisation and Embryology Act has specifically uncoupled the

application of the Abortion Act from that of the Infant Life (Preservation) Act and introduced a fixed upper time limit of 24 weeks into the Abortion Act (except in the presence of some specified contraindications). It is worth noting that although Carver lost this case in the courts, he won it out of them: S felt unable to go through with the termination following all the publicity surrounding the case.

38. The following cases were referred to (at 1239): *R* v. *Handley* (1874) 13 Cox CC 79, a child was considered to have been 'born alive' when it existed as a live child, breathing and living by reason of its breathing, through its own lungs alone, without deriving any of its living or power of living by or through any connection with its mother. *R* v. *Poulton* (1832) 5 C&P 329, 172 ER 997, even the fact of a child having breathed was said not to be conclusive proof of it having been in 'a living state'. In *R* v. *Enoch* (1833) 5 C&P 539, 172 ER 1089 and *R* v. *Wright* (1841) 9 C&P 754, 173 ER 1039, the judge directed the jury that to be alive there must be, in addition to breathing, a circulation independent of the mother.

39. The *Sunday Express*, 4 August 1996.

40. The *Guardian*, 6 August 1996.

41. Ms Allwood eventually lost all eight of the babies.

42. Section 37(5) of the Human Fertilisation and Embryology Act, amending the wording of section 5(2) of the Abortion Act.

43. For a clear and detailed exposition of the problems raised by the current wording of the Act, see Morgan and Lee (1991, pp. 55–60).

44. See Conservative MP Anne Widdecombe, in the *Guardian* (7 August 1996) and letters to the *Guardian* (7 and 8 August 1996).

45. *News of the World*, 11 August 1996.

46. Crown Office Reference No: CO 2619.96.

47. The Health Authority's statement that it would not transmit SPUC's offer of financial help to A was made on 5 August, SPUC's application to the court was made at just after 4 p.m. on 6 August.

48. *Associated Provincial Picture Houses Ltd* v. *Wednesbury Corporation* [1948] 1 KB 233.

49. [1990] 1 AC 109.

50. [1990] 1 QB 770 (CA).

51. A116 paragraph 74.

52. Telephone conversation with Brendan Garrard, SPUC, 5 September 1996.

53. *Sidaway* v. *Board of Governors of the Royal Bethlehem Hospital* [1985] AC 871.

54. *R* v. *Smith* [1974] 1 All ER 376. See pp. 83–5 above.

55. [1981] 1 All ER 545 (QBD, CA and HL).

56. The procedure for abortion by medical induction is as follows: a doctor inserts a catheter into the woman's uterus and subsequent steps are carried out either in whole or in part by nursing staff, who may be responsible for connecting a pump to the catheter which would feed the prostaglandins into the woman, and monitoring the process which could take anything up to 30 hours. The prostaglandins serve to induce

uterine contractions which will expel the foetus and terminate the pregnancy.
57. See also Woolf J at 553:

> the registered medical practitioner must decide on the termination; the process must be initiated by him, and he must remain throughout responsible for its overall conduct and control in the sense that any actions needed to bring it to a conclusion are done by appropriately skilled staff acting on his specific instructions, but not necessarily in his presence, though he or another registered medical practitioner must be available to be called if required.

58. See Hoggett:

> The obvious intention of the Act is to protect not only the doctor but any person who takes part in an abortion, such as nursing and theatre staff, and any person who procures or supplies instruments or other abortifacients knowing that they are to be used 'with intent to procure the miscarriage of any woman' (1968, p. 254).

59. The one area where it *may* advance them is the liberalisation of the administration of drugs in antiprogestin terminations (see Chapter 7 below).
60. In the Court of Appeal decision, Lord Denning criticised this, commenting: 'If the Department of Health want the nurses to terminate a pregnancy, the Minister should go to Parliament to get the statute altered . . . that is the way to amend the law and not by means of a departmental circular' (557).
61. [1985] 3 All ER 403. In this case, the House of Lords upheld the right of doctors to give contraceptives and contraceptive advice to minors, even in the absence of parental consent. This case also established the principle that the ability of a child under the age of 16 to give her consent to medical treatment and advice depends on her level of understanding and intelligence.
62. The *Independent*, 22 May 1991.
63. Alexander McCall Smith in *The Times*, 28 May 1991.
64. *T* v. *T and another* [1988] 1 All ER 613 at 621, *Re G, The Times*, 31 January 1991.
65. The *Observer*, 27 March 1994.
66. See reports in the *Guardian*, the *Independent* and *The Times*, 22 December 1995.
67. A copy of the standard consent form is included in Brazier (1992, p. 76).
68. These two defences seem very similar, but in practice there is one important difference: in the first the burden of proof is on the patient to establish that the surgeon's assumption of consent was not reasonable, in the second, the burden of proof is on the surgeon to establish that the intervention was reasonable and necessary to save the life of the patient

or to prevent grave and permanent injury to her health (see Brazier, 1992, p. 91).

69. *Bolam* v. *Friern Hospital Management Committee* [1957] 2 All ER 118 at 122.

70. *The Times,* 12 September 1993; Thomson (1994b, p. 13).

71. Notwithstanding this, Mrs Whiten might take some encouragement from the fact that another woman has been awarded damages of around £10,000 from the same Health Authority (North Nottinghamshire) after she was given an abortion without her consent: *Abortion Review*, Summer 1996, no. 60.

CHAPTER 6

1. H.C. Deb. Vol. 171 Col. 214, 1990 (24 April).

2. These were introduced by Norman St John-Stevas (1969), Godman Irvine (1970), Michael Grylls (1973 and 1974), James White (1975), William Benyon (1977), Bernard Braine (1978), John Corrie (1979), Enoch Powell (1984), Ken Hargreaves (1985 and 1986), Alistair Burt (1987), David Alton (1988) and Douglas Houghton (House of Lords, 1989). For more on attempts to reform the Abortion Act, see Keown (1988 and Mills and Sheldon (forthcoming).

3. Eighteen weeks was chosen as the lowest limit which might be realistically attainable – this reflects a strategy of cutting away 'salami' fashion at the law, gradually paring down the time limit on abortions.

4. See also McNeil (1991, p. 151) on press panics during the period of debate over the Alton Bill which reinforced the enhanced status of the foetus.

5. One persistent point of imprecision in the law is that it does not specify when the 24 weeks will be deemed to begin. As Murphy (1991) argues, there are four distinct stages which may be argued to mark the critical date: date of the last period prior to conception (LMP), date of fertilisation, date of implantation, or when the embryo reaches two weeks old.

6. H.C. Deb. Vol. 171 Col. 199, 1990 (24 April). An article in *The Times* (24 April 1990) cited Widdecombe as promising a lapse in the parliamentary Pro-Life campaign 'at least until after the general election' (which eventually took place in April 1992).

7. OPCS, HMSO Abortion Statistics 1988, series AB no. 15.

8. H.C. Deb. Vol. 171 Col. 172, 1990 (24 April); see also at Col. 175.

9. See Braine, H.C. Deb. Vol. 171 Col. 217, 1990 (24 April); Alton, H.C. Deb. Vol. 174 Col. 1206, 1990 (21 June); Alton, H.C. Deb. Vol. 171 Col. 228, 1990 (24 April).

10. Amess, H.C. Deb. Vol. 171 Col. 255, 1990 (24 April).

11. Kellett-Bowman, H.C. Deb. Vol. 171 Col. 175, 1990 (24 April).

12. H.C. Deb. Vol. 171 Col. 223, 1990 (24 April).

13. H.C. Deb. Vol. 171 Cols 241–2 1990 (24 April). The speech made by the Rev. Ian Paisley stands in clear contrast to this trend, drawing heavily on religious arguments, H.C. Deb. Vol. 174 Cols 235–9, 1990 (21 June).

14. The most clear use of feminist discourse is made by Theresa Gorman, H.C. Deb. Vol. 171 Col. 231, 1990 (24 April), quoted at length below, at p. 167.

15. H.C. Deb. Vol. 171 Col. 221, 1990 (24 April). See also; Alton (1988), where he quotes at length from Paula Conor of Feminists Against Eugenics; and Duffy, H.C. Deb. Vol. 171 Col. 252, 1990 (24 April): 'Free and easy abortion is in the interests of men because it removes the problem of pregnancy, and women are well aware of that.'
16. H.C. Deb. Vol. 171 Col. 201, 1990 (24 April).
17. H.C. Deb. Vol. 171 Col. 248, 1990 (24 April).
18. H.C. Deb. Vol. 171 Col. 204, 1990 (24 April); see also Steel, H.C. Deb. Vol. 171 Cols 206–7, 1990 (24 April); Harman, H.C. Deb. Vol. 171 Col. 262, 1990 (24 April).
19. The *Guardian*, 23 April 1990.
20. For example, Bottomley, H.C. Deb. Vol. 171 Col. 173, 1990 (24 April); Clarke, H.C. Deb. Vol. 171 Col. 267, 1990 (24 April). See also the references in note 18 above.
21. Harman, H.C. Deb. Vol. 171 Col. 262, 1990 (24 April).
22. *The Times* (2 June 1990):

> do our legislators truly intend the unborn to be destroyed well beyond viability, for any other cause than to save the life of the mother? The answer may, of course, be 'yes'; and – if so – we will have moved from discussion of abortion to that of euthanasia.

23. Kellett-Bowman, H.C. Deb. Vol. 171 Col. 241, 1990 (24 April).
24. Braine, H.C. Deb. Vol. 171 Col. 216, 1990 (24 April).
25. Braine, H.C. Deb. Vol. 171 Col. 215, 1990 (24 April). See also Smyth, H.C. Deb. Vol. 171 Col. 241, 1990 (24 April); Clarke, H.C. Deb. Vol. 171 Cols 264, 267, 1990 (24 April); Amess, H.C. Deb. Vol. 171 Col. 255, 1990 (24 April); Alton, H.C. Deb. Vol. 171 Col. 223, 1990 (24 April).
26. Gorman, H.C. Deb. Vol. 171 Col. 232, 1990 (24 April): 'I would far rather trust the woman and her medical adviser [to decide]'; Primarolo, H.C. Deb. Vol. 171 Col. 248, 1990 (24 April): 'Abortion is a medical decision and a woman's choice'; Nicholson, H.C. Deb. Vol. 171 Col. 250, 1990 (24 April): 'up to 12 weeks the mother's wish, in conjunction with her general practitioner's decision, should be sufficient to allow her an abortion'.
27. Emma Nicholson has since moved to the Liberal Democratic party.
28. See, for example, Richardson, H.C. Deb. Vol. 171 Col. 187, 1990 (24 April); Nicholson, H.C. Deb. Vol. 171 Col. 250, 1990 (24 April).
29. See also the contributions to Franklin et al. (1991). Franklin (1991) has written that the concept of 'foetal personhood' is both ontological and teleological in that it focuses on not only the foetus's present status, but also its human potentiality. These two elements are frequently confused and conflated in the debates.
30. Joyce Outshoorn cites the Book of Jeremiah: 'Before I formed you in the womb/I knew you/and before you were born/I consecrated you' (1992, p. 1).
31. Information from SPUC leaflet 'White Flower Sunday'.
32. Alison, H.C. Deb. Vol. 174 Col. 1180, 1990 (21 June).

33. Braine, H.C. Deb. Vol. 171 Col. 217, 1990 (24 April).
34. Doran, H.C. Deb. Vol. 171 Col. 213, 1990 (24 April).
35. MacKay, H.C. Deb. Vol. 171 Col. 243, 1990 (24 April).
36. Cormack, H.C. Deb. Vol. 171 Col. 208, 1990 (24 April), my emphasis.
37. Widdecome, H.C. Deb. Vol. 171 Col. 192, 1990 (24 April), my emphasis.
38. H.C. Deb. Vol. 171 Col. 249, 1990 (24 April).
39. For an excellent, detailed commentary on the Act, see Morgan and Lee (1991).
40. The *Guardian*, 24 April 1990.
41. See Brazier (1988, p. 9) for discussion of the invocation of abortion in the arguments used by opponents and proponents of research.
42. The *Guardian*, 23 April 1990.
43. It is interesting to note that s.37 (dealing with abortion) chose to adopt a fixed period of 24 weeks, thus translating a medical event into a fixed period to meet the (legal) requirement for precision and certainty. However, s.3 (dealing with embryo research), wrote the biological event itself (the appearance of the primitive streak) into the statute. This is presumably due to the greater ease with which the latter can be identified with any accuracy.
44. H.C. Deb. Vol. 171 Col. 265, 1990 (24 April).
45. *The Times*, 24 July 1984.
46. *The Times*, 17 July 1991.
47. Duffy, H.C. Deb. Vol. 171 Col. 252, 1990 (24 April). See also Alton, H.C. Deb. Vol. 171 Col. 223, 1990 (24 April).

CHAPTER 7

1. Rodger and Baird (1987); UK Multicentre trial (1990); Baulieu (1993); Baird (1993, p. 5); Aubeny (1993).
2. RU486 can also be used to improve the efficiency of prostaglandin terminations (13–20 weeks) and to soften and dilate the cervix prior to mechanical cervical dilation for vacuum aspiration. These uses will not be considered here.
3. Information provided in two letters from Angela Davey, Head of Medical Information Services, Hoechst Marion Roussel, dated 25 July and 2 August 1996.
4. Roussel Uclaf list the following factors as prerequisites for a decision to apply for a product licence: abortion must be legal, the right to abortion must be accepted by public, political and medical opinion; the request must be made by official and medical bodies; the distribution circuit must be very strictly controlled; approved clinics must exist; a suitable prostaglandin must be available on the market; a strict medical follow-up of the patient must be part of the clinical protocol (Roussel press release, 29 July 1992). See Thoss (1993) and Retzlaff (1993) for the problems this has caused regarding the possible introduction of RU486 in Germany.
5. See *Abortion Review*, Winter 1997, no. 62, p. 17.
6. Letter from Angela Davey.

7. It also seems likely that the FDA's initial import ban on the drug was a direct result of pressure brought to bear by four US Congressmen, see Chicoine (1993, pp. 94–5).

8. *Reproductive Freedom News*, Volume V, no. 13, 26 July 1996.

9. See *Abortion Review*, Winter 1997, no. 62, p. 17.

10. The fact that this period is substantially shorter than the norm of 17 months provoked allegations that the drug had been 'fast-tracked': Winterton, H.C. Deb. Vol. 195 Col. 894, 1990 (22 July); Braine, H.C. Deb. Vol. 195 Col. 888, 1990 (22 July); Hind H.C. Deb. Vol. 195 Col. 885, 1990 (22 July).

11. The exception to this was Dale Campbell-Savours MP who, although a member of the Life lobby, spoke in favour of the pill as a means of preventing later abortions.

12. Braine, H.C. Deb. Vol. 195 Col. 890, 1991 (22 July). Note the construction of the traumatised and misguided woman, who needs to be protected from abortion.

13. See Hind, H.C. Deb. Vol. 195, Cols 884–7, 1991 (22 July); Braine, H.C. Deb. Vol. 195, Cols 888–92, 1991 (22 July); Winterton, H.C. Deb. Vol. 195 Cols 895–6, 1991 (22 July).

14. Richardson, H.C. Deb. Vol. 195, Col. 892, 1991 (22 July).

15. Richardson, H.C. Deb. Vol. 195, Col. 893, 1991 (22 July).

16. Richardson, H.C. Deb. Vol. 195, Cols 892, 894, 1991 (22 July); Thurnham, H.C. Deb. Vol. 195, Col. 897, 1991 (22 July); Dorrell, H.C. Deb. Vol. 195, Col. 899, 1991 (22 July).

17. 'I am surprised that lay persons should so question the work of the Medicines Control Agency, which is held in the highest regard and undertook proper testing', Thurnham, H.C. Deb. Vol. 195 Col. 897, 1991 (22 July).

18. See Hind, H.C. Deb. Vol. 195 Col. 884, 1991 (22 July). MPs make similar accusations of partiality on the part of the French government's decision to license the pill, given that they own a 36 per cent share in Roussel: Braine, H.C. Deb. Vol. 195 Col. 888, 1991 (22 July); Winterton, H.C. Deb. Vol. 195 Col. 895, 1991 (22 July). See also SPUC's leaflet, *RU486: Update and Implications*.

19. 21 July 1991. Cited by Richardson, H.C. Deb. 1991 Vol. 195, Col. 892, 1991 (22 July).

20. H.C. Deb. Vol. 174 Col. 1193, 1990 (21 June).

21. Hind, H.C. Deb. Vol. 195 Col. 888, 1991 (22 July); Braine, H.C. Deb. Vol. 195 Col. 889, 1991 (22 July); Winterton, H.C. Deb. Vol. 195 Col. 895, 1991 (22 July); Amess, H.C. Deb. Vol. 195 Col. 898, 1991 (22 July).

22. H.C. Deb. Vol. 195 Col. 892, 1991 (22 July). See also Thurnham, H.C. Deb. Vol. 195, Col. 897, 1991 (22 July); Clarke, H.C. Deb. Vol. 174 Col. 1199, 1990 (21 June).

23. H.C. Deb. Vol. 195, Col. 899, 1991 (22 July).

24. Department of Health, PL/CMO (91) 9, PL/CNO (91) 4, issued by the Chief Medical Officer.

25. Although he does feel that a follow-up visit is necessary for post-abortion counselling and contraceptive advice (1993, p. 6).

26. *Royal College of Nursing of the United Kingdom* v. *Department of Health and Social Security* [1981] 1 All ER 545 at 571.
27. Ibid. at 553, my emphasis.
28. See Roussel release, *Conditions of Supply for Mifegyne (Mifepristone).*
29. *Abortion Review*, Spring (1994), no. 51.
30. There seems to be some confusion on this point. The Department of Health states that there is no requirement that the woman be referred by her GP, rather the relevant procedure is that the woman must demonstrate that she has medical cover for follow-up (letter to Leonora Lloyd, 26 April 1993). However, it seems that (at least some) clinics are applying this to mean that they must inform her GP (for example, Paintin, 1994a, p. 10).
31. The privacy might also be experienced as a more negative aspect. Birman notes that 'by increasing the sense of individualism, RU 486 may well make the women's isolation and solitude worse, at a time when they are battling with a painful and harrowing situation' (Birman, 1989, p. 8).
32. Not all women will experience such control as a positive thing. One woman told Dr Aubeny, 'You see everything that takes place and that's difficult, I would have preferred the doctor to have taken complete charge of everything' (in Lader, 1990, p. 55).
33. See, for example, Campbell-Savours, H.C. Deb. Vol. 195 Col. 898, 1991 (22 July).
34. Ricks (1989, p. 72) makes the same point with regard to US law.
35. 9 July 1991. The letter was signed *inter alia* by MPs, members of the Birth Control Trust, Mary Warnock and Janet Radcliffe Richards.
36. As such the response from Bernard Braine MP accusing the signatories of the letter as 'by implication . . . calling for a change in the law to allow abortion on demand' was incorrect (*The Times*, 17 July 1991).
37. Introduced by section 37(3) of the Human Fertilisation and Embryology Act 1990.
38. Dorrell, H.C. Deb. Vol. 195 Col. 899, 1991 (22 July) and letter of 9 March 1993 from Department of Health to Leonora Lloyd (National Abortion Campaign).
39. 'A question was asked earlier about what type of premises would be used for administering such a drug. It is possible that the pill could be administered in a GP's surgery under the supervision of a registered medical practitioner. The patient would still have to return two days later to be given the pessary', Clarke, H.C. Deb. Vol. 174 Col. 1199, 1990 (21 June).

CHAPTER 8

1. A panel of New York medical experts have contested the scientific validity of the film, on the grounds, *inter alia,* that the frantic movements of the foetus are caused by speeding up the film and that the size of the foetus as it appears in the film is nearly twice the size of a normal twelve-week foetus (Petchesky, 1987, pp. 60–1).

2. Members of the Commission included anti-choice campaigners David Alton, Margaret White and Catherine Françoise. See National Abortion Campaign (1993b) and *Abortion Review*, Spring 1993, no. 47.
3. Alton, H.C. Deb. Vol. 209 Col. 603w, 1992 (17 June); Spink, H.C. Deb. Vol. 212 Col. 69w, 1992 (19 October).
4. H.C. Deb. Vol. 217 Col. 477w, 1993 (22 January).
5. H.C. Deb. Vol. 217 Col. 813w, 1993 (28 January).
6. H.C. Deb. Vol. 217 Col. 813w, 1993 (28 January).
7. H.C. Deb. Vol. 217 Col. 722w, 1993 (27 January).
8. H.C. Deb. Vol. 217 Col. 477w, 1993 (22 January).
9. H.C. Deb. Vol. 217 Col. 698w, 1993 (26 January).
10. H.C. Deb. Vol. 217 Col. 536w, 1993 (25 January).
11. See especially Liz Kingdom (1985, 1991, 1992); Carol Smart (1989); Sue Himmelweit (1988) and Ros Petchesky (1984a). For a defence of the use of rights, see especially Adelaide Villmoare (1991); Martha Minow (1989) and Patricia Williams (1988). Joyce Outshoorn (1992) has argued that this preoccupation with rights may be a peculiarly Anglo-American one. She cites the very different formulation of claims by the German and Dutch women's movements, which focus more on control over one's body (1988, p. 207).
12. Compare this with the French law, as drafted by Simone Veil, which foresees that legal abortion should be accompanied by a coherent policy on contraception, abortion and improved education, see Allison (1994, p. 230).
13. Statistically speaking, to continue a pregnancy poses greater risk to the woman's health than an early termination and therefore termination is authorised by s.1(1)(a) of the Abortion Act.
14. One might also think here of the costs that childcare imposes on individual families (even in the exceptional cases of two or more adults genuinely sharing equally in childcare responsibilities) as opposed to costs borne by the wider society.
15. There is some room for doubting whether an abortion would be lawful at common law in any case: this would depend on whether it were seen to amount to a 'maim'.
16. *Abortion Review*, Spring 1994, no. 51. Unlike Britain, US law contains no specifications regarding *where* terminations may be performed. This means that the potential of RU486 to privatise abortion becomes much more real. Doctors will be able to perform terminations in their surgeries. This has obvious advantages in a country where abortion clinics have become such focal points for dissent. However, as Therese Murphy has pointed out to me, it may also serve to mark doctors who provide terminations in their surgeries as particularly easy targets for attack by militaristic anti-choice groups.
17. See H.C. Deb. Vol. 225, Cols 241–4, 1993 for the Bill's first reading.
18. No. 7, Guidance on fundholder purchase of termination of pregnancy, HSG (95) 37.

19. Following *R* v. *Smith* (1974), the doctor would have had to examine the woman to be able to convince the court that he had formed an opinion in good faith (see pp. 83–5).
20. As the Wendy Savage case clearly demonstrated, see Savage (1986), and note 6, Chapter 4, above.
21. Gorman, H.C. Deb. Vol. 171 Cols 229–33, 1990 (24 April).
22. Indeed, as I noted in Chapter 6, it is perhaps anti-choice MPs who have made the greater use of explicitly feminist rhetoric in Parliament (see p. 111).
23. H.C. Deb. Vol. 750 Col. 1349, 1967 (13 July).

APPENDICES

1. The amendments introduced by s.37 of the Human Fertilisation and Embryology Act are recorded in **bold**.

Bibliography

Abortion Law Reform Association (1997) *A Report on NHS Abortion Services* (London: Abortion Law Reform Association).

Aitken Swan, I. (1977) *Fertility Control and the Medical Profession* (London: Croom Helm).

Aktionsforum MoZ (1992) *RU 486 – un choix qui n'en est pas un* (leaflet).

Alberman, E. and Dennis, K. (eds) (1984) *Late Abortions in England and Wales* (London: Royal College of Obstetricians and Gynaecologists).

Allison, M. (1994) 'The Right to Choose: Abortion in France', 47 *Parliamentary Affairs*, no. 2 (April) 222–37.

Alton, D. (1988) *What Kind of Country?* (Basingstoke: Marshall Pickering).

Arney, W. (1982) *Power and the Profession of Obstetrics* (Chicago: University of Chicago Press).

Aubeny, E. (1991) 'Introduction à la table ronde sur l'avortement précoce par Ru 486 + prostaglandines' in *Neuvièmes journées nationales d'études sur l'avortement et la contraception* (Creil: Association Nationale des Centres d'Interruption de Grossesse et de Contraception).

Aubeny, E. (1993) 'Clinical Experience in France – New Developments in Medical Abortion', in Furedi A. (ed.) *Medical Abortion Services: European Perspectives on Anti-progestins* (London: International Planned Parenthood Federation).

Bachelot, A., Cludy, L. and Spira, A. (1991) 'IVG par RU 486 et IVG par aspiration' in *Neuvièmes journées nationales d'études sur l'avortement et la contraception* (Creil: Association Nationale des Centres d'Interruption de Grossesse et de Contraception).

Bainham, A. (1987) 'Protecting the Unborn – New Rights in Gestation', 50 *Modern Law Review* 361–8.

Baird, D. (1993) 'Clinical Trials – the UK Experience', in Furedi, A. (ed.) *Medical Abortion Services: European Perspectives on Anti-progestins* (London: International Planned Parenthood Federation).

Barrett, M. and Roberts, H. (1978) 'Doctors and their Patients: the Social Control of Women in General Practice', in Smart, C. and Smart, B. (eds) *Women, Sexuality and Social Control* (London, Henley and Boston: Routledge and Kegan Paul).

Baulieu, E.-E. with Rosenblum, M. (1991) *The Abortion Pill* (London, Sydney, Auckland and Johannesberg: Century).

Baulieu, E.-E. (1993) 'Putting Anti-progestins in Context: How RU 486 Works', in Furedi, A. (ed.) *Medical Abortion Services: European Perspectives on Anti-progestins* (London: International Planned Parenthood Federation).

Berer, M. (1993a) 'Abortion in Europe from a Woman's Perspective', *Progress Postponed: Abortion in Europe in the 1990s* (London: International Planned Parenthood Federation).

Berer, M. (1993b) 'Women's Views on Anti-progestin Abortion', in Furedi, A. (ed.) *Medical Abortion Services: European Perspectives on Anti-progestins* (London: International Planned Parenthood Federation).

Birman, C. (1989) The Experiences of Women having an Abortion with RU 486, *Women's Global Network for Reproductive Rights* (October–December) 7–9.

Birth Control Trust (1987) *Reducing Late Abortions: Access to NHS Services in Early Pregnancy* (London: Birth Control Trust).

Birth Control Trust (1990) *The Abortion Pill (Mifepristone/RU 486): Widening the Choice for Women* (London: Birth Control Trust).

Boston Women's Health Book Collective (1971) *Our Bodies, Ourselves* (New York: Simon and Schuster).

Bourne, A. (1962) *A Doctor's Creed: The Memoirs of a Gynaecologist* (London: Gollancz).

Brazier, M. (1988) 'Embryo's "Rights": Abortion and Research', in Freeman, M.D.A. (ed.) *Medicine, Ethics and the Law* (London: Stevens & Sons).

Brazier, M. (1992) *Medicine, Patients and the Law* (Harmondsworth: Penguin).

Bridgeman, J. (1993a) 'Old enough to Know Best?', 13 *Legal Studies* 69–80.

Bridgeman, J. (1993b) 'Medical Treatment: the Mother's Rights', *Family Law* 534–5.

Bridgeman, J. (1993c) 'Demanding Reproductive Control?', in Feminist Legal Research Unit (ed.) *Body Politics: Control v Freedom: the Role of Feminism in Women's Personal Autonomy* (Liverpool: University of Liverpool).

Bromham, D. (1994) 'Setting up Services', in Furedi, A. (ed.) *Running an Early Medical Abortion Service* (London: Birth Control Trust).

Brookes, B. (1988) *Abortion in England, 1900–1967* (London, New York and Sydney: Croom Helm).

Cahill, L.S. (1987) '"Abortion Pill" RU486: Ethics, Rhetoric and Social Practice', *Hastings Center Report* (October–November) 5–8.

Callum, J. (unpublished) *RU-486 and Early Termination Abortion* (Atlanta: Federation of Feminist Women's Health Centers).

Cameron, I.T. and Baird, D.T. (1988) 'Early Pregnancy Termination: a Comparison Between Vacuum Aspiration and Medical Abortion Using Prostaglandin or the Antiprogestogen RU 486', 95 *British Journal of Obstetrics and Gynaecology* (March) 271–6.

Campbell, J. (1992) Letter, 305 *British Medical Journal* 589.

Chalker, R. and Downey, C. (1992) *A Woman's Book of Choices: Abortion, Menstrual Extraction, RU 486* (New York and London: Four Walls, Eight Windows).

Chicoine, D. (1993) 'RU486 in the United States and Great Britain: a Case Study in Gender Bias', XVI *Boston College International and Comparative Law Review*, No. 1, 81–113.

Cole, L.A. (1989) 'The End of the Abortion Debate', 138 *University of Pennsylvania Law Review*, 217–23.

Cook, R. (1990) 'The Moral Property of Women?', 17 *People*, No. 3, 12.

Cossey, D. (1982) *Abortion and Conscientious Objection* (London: Birth Control Trust).

Coulet, M.-F. (1993) 'Anti-Progestins in France: Questions Women Ask', in Furedi, A. (ed.) *Medical Abortion Services: European Perspectives on Anti-progestins* (London; International Planned Parenthood Federation).

Dall'Ava Santucci, J. (1988) 'Punition', *Le Monde*, 29 October.

Daud, S. (1993) 'Abortion, Contraception and Ethnic Minorities', *Progress Postponed: Abortion in Europe in the 1990s* (London: International Planned Parenthood Federation).

Davies, C. (1975) *Permissive Britain: Social Change in the Sixties and Seventies* (London: Pitman).

Davies, V. (1991) *Abortion and Afterwards* (Bath: Ashgrove Press).

Davis, K. (1988a) *Power Under the Microscope: Towards a Grounded Theory of Gender Relations in Medical Encounters* (Amsterdam: Foris Publications).

Davis, K. (1988b) 'Paternalism Under the Microscope', in Todd, A.D. and Fisher, S. (eds) *Gender and Discourse: The Power of Talk* (Norwood and New Jersey: Ablex Publishing Company).

Department of Health and Social Security (1974) *Report of the Committee on the Working of the Abortion Act*, chaired by The Hon. Mrs Justice Lane, cmnd 5579 (London: HMSO).

Dickens, B.M. (1966) *Abortion and the Law* (Bristol: MacGibbon and Kee Ltd).

Diggory, P. (1991) *Abortion – an Introduction: Guidance on Technique, Complications and the Provision of Services* (London: Birth Control Trust).

Donzelot, J. (1979) *The Policing of Families: Welfare versus the State* (London: Hutchinson and Co. Ltd).

Douglas, G. (1991) *Law, Fertility and Reproduction* (London: Sweet and Maxwell).

Douzinas, C. and McVeigh, S. (1992) 'The Tragic Body: the Inscription of Autonomy in Medical Ethics and Law', in Wheeler, S. and McVeigh, S. (eds) *Law, Health and Medical Regulation* (Aldershot and Brookfield, Vermont: Dartmouth Publishing Co.).

Draper, H. (1993) 'Women, Forced Caesarians and Antenatal Responsibilities', in Feminist Legal Research Unit (ed.) *Body Politics: Control v Freedom: the Role of Feminism in Women's Personal Autonomy* (Liverpool: University of Liverpool).

Dreyfus, H. and Rabinow, P. (1982) *Michel Foucault: Beyond Structuralism and Hermeneutics* (Brighton: Harvester).

Duncan, S. (1994) 'Disrupting the Surface of Order and Innocence: Towards a Theory of Sexuality and the Law', 2 *Feminist Legal Studies* 3–28.

Dworkin, A. (1983) *Right Wing Women: The Politics of Domesticated Females* (London: The Women's Press).

Easlea, B. (1981) *Science and Sexual Oppression* (London: Weidenfeld and Nicolson).

Ehrenreich, B. and English, D. (1978) *For Her Own Good: 150 Years of the Experts' Advice to Women* (London: Pluto).

Eisenstein, Z. (1988) *The Female Body and the Law* (Berkley, Los Angeles and London: University of California Press).

Farrant, W. (1985) 'Who's for Amniocentesis? The Politics of Prenatal Screening', in Homans, H. (ed.) *The Sexual Politics of Reproduction* (Hampshire: Gower).

Ferris, P. (1966) *The Nameless: Abortion in Britain Today* (London: Hutchinson).

Fitzpatrick, P. (1987) 'Racism and the Innocence of Law', in Fitzpatrick, P. and Hunt, A. (eds) *Critical Legal Studies* (Oxford: Basil Blackwell).

Fitzpatrick, P. (1997) 'Relational Power and the Limits of Law', in K. Tuori, Z. Bankowski and J. Uusitalo (eds) *Law and Power: Critical and Socio-Legal Essays* (Liverpool: Deborah Charles).

Fortin, J. (1988a) 'Legal Protection for the Unborn Child', 51 *Modern Law Review* 54–83.

Fortin, J. (1988b) 'Can you Ward a Foetus?', 51 *Modern Law Review* 768–75.

Foster, P. (1995) *An Unhealthy Relationship: Women and the Healthcare Industry* (Milton Keynes: Open University Press).

Foucault, M. (1979a) 'Governmentality', *m/f*, No. 3, July, 5–21.

Foucault, M. (1979b) *The History of Sexuality: Volume 1: An Introduction* (Harmondsworth: Penguin).

Foucault, M. (1980a) 'Body/Power', in Gordon, C. (ed.) *Michel Foucault: Power/Knowledge. Selected Interviews and Other Writings, 1972–1977* (Hemel Hempstead: Harvester Press).

Foucault, M. (1980b) 'Two lectures', in Gordon, C. (ed.) *Michel Foucault: Power/Knowledge. Selected Interviews and Other Writings, 1972–1977* (Hemel Hempstead: Harvester Press).

Foucault, M. (1980c) 'Truth and Power', in Gordon, C. (ed.) *Michel Foucault: Power/Knowledge. Selected Interviews and Other Writings, 1972–1977* (Hemel Hempstead: Harvester Press).

Foucault, M. (1980d) 'The Politics of Health in the Eighteenth Century', in Gordon, C. (ed.) *Michel Foucault: Power/Knowledge. Selected Interviews and Other Writings, 1972–1977* (Hemel Hempstead: Harvester Press).

Foucault, M. (1989a) *Madness and Civilization: A History of Insanity in the Age of Reason* (London and New York: Tavistock and Routledge).

Foucault, M. (1989b) *The Birth of the Clinic* (London and New York: Routledge).

Foucault, M. (1991) *Discipline and Punish: The Birth of the Prison* (London: Penguin).

Francke, L. (1980) *The Ambivalence of Abortion* (Harmondsworth: Penguin).

Francome, C. (1984) *Abortion Freedom: A Worldwide Movement* (London: Allen and Unwin).

Francome, C. (1986) *Abortion Practice in Britain and the United States* (London: Allen and Unwin).

Francome, C. (1991) *Abortion and Public Opinion* (London: Abortion Law Reform Association and National Abortion Campaign).

Franklin, S. (1991) 'Fetal Fascinations: New Dimensions to the Medical-Scientific Constructions of Fetal Personhood', in Franklin, S., Lury, C. and Stacey, J. (eds) *Off-Centre: Feminism and Cultural Studies* (London: Harper Collins Academic).

Franklin, S., Lury, C. and Stacey, J. (eds) (1991) *Off-Centre: Feminism and Cultural Studies* (London: Harper Collins Academic).

Friedson, E. (1970) *Profession of Medicine: A Study of the Sociology of Applied Knowledge* (Chicago, London: University of Chicago Press).

Furedi, A. (ed.) (1994) *Running an Early Medical Abortion Service* (London: Birth Control Trust).

Furedi, A. (ed.) (1995) *The Abortion Law in Northern Ireland: Human Rights and Reproductive Choice* (Belfast: Family Planning Association Northern Ireland).

Fyfe, W. (1991) 'Abortion Acts: 1803–1967', in Franklin, S., Lury, C. and Stacey, J. (eds) *Off-Centre: Feminism and Cultural Studies* (London: Harper Collins Academic).

Gallagher, J. (1987) 'Prenatal Invasions and Interventions: What's Wrong with Fetal Rights', 10 *Harvard Women's Law Journal* 9–58.

Gardner, K. (1981) 'Well Women Clinics: a Positive Approach to Women's Health', in Roberts, H. (ed.) *Women, Health and Reproduction* (London: Routledge and Kegan Paul).

Glasier, A. (1993) 'Provision of Medical Abortion in the UK – Organisation and Uptake', in Furedi, A. (ed.) *Medical Abortion Services: European Perspectives on Anti-progestins* (London: International Planned Parenthood Federation).

Gordon, C. (ed.) *Michel Foucault: Power/Knowledge. Selected Interviews and Other Writings, 1972–1977* (Hemel Hemstead: Harvester Press).

Graycar, R. and Morgan, J. (1990) *The Hidden Gender of Law* (Annandale: Federation Press).

Greenhalgh, P. (1992) 'The Doctor's Right to Choose', 305 *British Medical Journal* 589.

Greenwood, V. and Young, J. (1976) *Abortion in Demand* (London: Pluto).

Grubb, A. (1990) 'Abortion Law in England: the Medicalization of a Crime', 18 *Law, Medicine and Health Care*, Nos. 1–2, Spring–Summer, 146–61.

Hall, M.H. (1990) 'Changes in the Law on Abortion', 301 *British Medical Journal* 1109–10.

Hartnell, V.H. (1993) 'Medical Termination of Pregnancy and the Future Provision of Termination Services', 19 *British Journal of Family Planning* 143–4.

Hartouni, V. (1991) 'Containing Women: Reproductive Discourse in the 1980s', in Penley, C. and Ross, A. (eds) *Technoculture* (Minneapolis and Oxford: University of Minnesota Press).

Harvard, J.D.J. (1958) 'Therapeutic Abortion', *Criminal Law Review* 600–13.

Himmelweit, S. (1988) 'More than "a Woman's Right to Choose"?', *Feminist Review*, No. 29, Spring, 38–55.

Hindell, K. and Simms, M. (1971) *Abortion Law Reformed* (London: Peter Owen).

Hoggett, A.J.C. (1968) 'The Abortion Act 1967', *Criminal Law Review* 247–58.

Homans, H. (1985) 'Discomforts in pregnancy: traditional remedies and medical prescriptions', in H. Homans (ed.) *The Sexual Politics of Reproduction* (Hants: Gower).

Hordern, A. (1971) *Illegal Abortion: the English Experience* (Oxford, New York: Pergamon Press).

Hudson, D. (1987) 'You Can't Commit Violence Against an Object: Women, Psychiatry and Psychosurgery', in Hanmer, J. and Maynard, M. (eds) *Women, Violence and Social Control* (Hampshire: Macmillan).

Hunt, L. (1993) 'Stigma and Secrecy that Marked a Different World', The *Independent*, 27 April.

Illich, I. (1977) *Disabling Professions* (London: Marion Boyars Publishers Ltd).

Jenkins, A. (1960) *Law for the Rich* (London: Victor Gollancz).

Joffe, C. (1984) 'Comments on Mackinnon', *Radical America*, March–June, 68–9.

Jones, I. (1994) 'Setting up the Services', in Furedi, A. (ed.) *Running an Early Medical Abortion Service* (London: Birth Control Trust).

Kane, A. (1990) 'Anti-Abortionists Defeated', 7 *Socialist Action*, May–July, 18–20.

Kaye, T. (1986) 'Are you for RU486?', *The New Republic*, 27 January.

Kennedy, I. (1988) *Treat Me Right: Essays in Medical Law and Ethics* (Oxford: Clarendon Press).

Keown, J. (1987) 'Selective Reduction of Multiple Pregnancy', *New Law Journal* 1165.

Keown, J. (1988) *Abortion, Doctors and the Law: Some Aspects of the Legal Regulation of Abortion in England from 1803 to 1982* (Cambridge: Cambridge University Press).

Ketting, E. and van Praag, P. (1986) 'The Marginal Relevance of Legislation Relating to Induced Abortion', in Lovenduski, J. and Outshoorn, J. (eds) *The New Politics of Abortion* (London: Sage Publications).

Kingdom, E. (1985) 'Legal Recognition of a Woman's Right to Choose', in Brophy, J. and Smart, C. (eds) *Women-in-Law: Explorations in Law, Family and Sexuality* (London: Routledge and Kegan Paul).

Kingdom, E. (1991) *What's Wrong with Rights? Problems for Feminist Politics of Law* (Edinburgh: Edinburgh University Press).

Kingdom, E. (1992) 'Problems with Rights', paper presented at conference, *The Rights of Women* (European University Institute, Florence, 17 October 1992).

Kitzinger, S. (1978) *Women as Mothers* (Oxford: Martin Robertson).

Klein, R., Raymond, J.G. and Dumble, L.J. (1991) *RU 486: Misconceptions, Myths and Morals* (Melbourne: Spinifex).

Lacey, N., Wells, C. and Meure, D. (1990) *Reconstructing Criminal Law: Critical Perspectives on Crime and the Criminal Process* (London: Weidenfeld and Nicolson).

Lader, L. (1990) *RU 486: The Pill That Could End the Abortion Wars and Why American Women Don't Have It* (Reading, Massachussetts: Addison-Wesley Publishing Co. Ltd).

Lapping, B. (1970) *The Labour Government 1964–70* (Harmondsworth: Penguin).

Laqueur, T. (1990) *Making Sex: Body and Gender From the Greeks to Freud* (Cambridge, Massachusetts and London: Harvard University Press).

Lewis, J. (1984) *Women in England, 1840–1950* (London: Wheatsheaf Books).

Lockwood, M. (1985) 'Where Does Life Begin?', in Lockwood (ed.) *Moral Dilemmas in Modern Medicine* (Oxford: Oxford University Press).

Logan, A. (1994) 'Provision and Practice', in Furedi, A. (ed.) *Running an Early Medical Abortion Service* (London: Birth Control Trust).

Longley, D. (1993) *Public Law and Health Service Accountability* (Buckingham and Philadelphia: Open University Press).

Lovenduski, J. and Outshoorn, J. (1986) *The New Politics of Abortion* (London: Sage Publications).

McDonnell, K. (1984) *Not an Easy Choice: A Feminist Re-examines Abortion* (Toronto: The Woman's Press).

MacIntyre, S.J. (1973) 'The Medical Profession and the 1967 Abortion Act in Britain', 7 *Social Science and Medicine* 121–34.

MacIntyre, S.J. (1977) *Single and Pregnant* (London: Croom Helm).

MacKinnon, C. (1983a) 'The Male Ideology of Privacy: A Feminist Perspective on the Right to Abortion', 17 *Radical America*, July–August, 23–35.

MacKinnon, C. (1983b) 'Feminism, Marxism, Method and the State: Towards Feminist Jurisprudence', 8 *Signs: Journal of Women in Culture and Society* 635–58.

MacKinnon, C. (1991) 'Reflections on Sex Equality Under Law', 100 *Yale Law Journal*, No. 5, March, 1281–328.

McKnorrie, K. (1985) 'Abortion in Great Britain: One Act, Two Laws', *Criminal Law Review* 475–88.

McNally, R. (undated) *A Foucauldian Analysis of Abortion for Foetal Handicap*, unpublished MA thesis (Brunel University).

McNeil, M. (1991) 'Putting the Alton Bill in Context', in Franklin, S., Lury, C. and Stacey, J. (eds) *Off-Centre: Feminism and Cultural Studies* (London: Harper Collins Academic).

Martin, E. (1987) *The Woman in the Body: a Cultural Analysis of Reproduction* (Milton Keynes: Open University Press).

Mason, K. (1990) *Medico-Legal Aspects of Reproduction and Parenthood* (Aldershot: Dartmouth Publishing Company).

Merchant, C. (1980) *The Death of Nature: Women, Ecology and the Scientific Revolution* (San Francisco: Harper and Row).

Millns, S. and Sheldon, S. (forthcoming) 'Abortion', in Cowley, P.J. (ed.) *The Conscience of Parliament: Moral Issues in British Politics* (London: Frank Cass).

Minow, M. (1989) 'Beyond Universality', *University of Chicago Legal Forum*, 115–38.

Montgomery, J. (1989) 'Medicine, Accountability and Professionalism', 16 *Journal of Law and Society* 319–39.

Montgomery, J. (1992a) 'Rights to Health and Health Care', in Coote, A. (ed.) *The Welfare of Citizens* (London: Rivers Oram Press).

Montgomery, J. (1992b) 'Doctors' Handmaidens: the Legal Contribution', in Wheeler, S. and McVeigh, S. (eds) *Law, Health and Medical Regulation*, (Aldershot: Dartmouth Publishing Company).

Moorehead, J. (undated) 'Boycott Call for Abortion Pill Firm's Products', in National Abortion Campaign (ed.) *RU486: a Collection of Articles and Press Cuttings on the 'Abortion Pill'* (London: National Abortion Campaign).

Morgan, D. (1990) 'Abortion: the Unexamined Ground', *Criminal Law Review* 687–694.

Morgan, D. (1992) 'Re S', 142 *New Law Journal* 1448.

Morgan, D. and Lee, R. (1991) *Guide to the Human Fertilisation and Embryology Act* (London: Blackstone).

Morris, J. (1991) 'Abortion: Whose Right to Choose?', *Spare Rib*, October, 16–18.

Murphy, J. (1991) 'Cosmetics, Eugenics and Ambivalence: the Revision of the Abortion Act 1967', *Journal of Social Welfare and Family Law*, No. 5, 375–93.

National Abortion Campaign (1993a) 'New Anti-Abortion Bill', *For Urgent Action*, 12 February.

National Abortion Campaign (1993b) 'Anti-Abortionists' Fake Commission', *For Urgent Action*, 12 February.

National Abortion Campaign (undated) *RU486: a Collection of Articles and Press Cuttings on the 'Abortion Pill'* (London: National Abortion Campaign).

Nau, J.-Y. and Nouchi, F. (1988) 'Une loi providentielle . . .', *Le Monde*, 31 October.

Neustatter, A. and Newson, G. (1986) *Mixed Feelings: The Experience of Abortion* (London, Sydney and New Hampshire: Pluto).

Newdick, C. (1995) *Who Should We Treat? Law, Patients and Resources in the N.H.S.* (Oxford: Oxford University Press).

Oakley, A. (1981) 'Normal Motherhood: an Exercise in Self-Control?', in Hutter, B. and Williams, G. (eds) *Controlling Women: the Normal and the Deviant* (London: Croom Helm).

Oakley, A. (1984) *The Captured Womb: A History of the Medical Care of Pregnant Women* (Oxford: Blackwell).

O'Neill, P.T. and Watson, O. (1975) 'The Father and the Unborn Child', 38 *Modern Law Review* 174–85.

Outshoorn, J. (1988) 'Abortion Law Reform: a Woman's Right to Choose?', in Buckley, M. and Anderson, M. (eds) *Women, Equality and Europe* (Hampshire: Macmillan).

Outshoorn, J. (1990) 'Changing Meanings of Abortion and Gender in the Light of Recent Developments in Reproductive Technology in the Netherlands', paper presented at the *Social and Political Science Conference* (London).

Outshoorn, J. (1992) 'The Body and Reproductive Rights', paper presented at the conference *The Rights of Women* (European University Institute, Florence, 17 October 1992).

Paintin, D. (1993) 'Legal Abortions in 1992 in England and Wales', *Abortion Review*, Winter, 1.

Paintin, D. (1994a) 'Introduction', in Furedi, A. (ed.) *Running an Early Medical Abortion Service* (London: Birth Control Trust).

Paintin, D. (1994b) 'Conclusions', in Furedi, A. (ed.) *Running an Early Medical Abortion Service* (London: Birth Control Trust).

Petchesky, R.P. (1984a) *Abortion and Woman's Choice: The State, Sexuality, and Reproductive Freedom* (New York and London: Longman).

Petchesky, R.P. (1984b) 'Abortion as Violence Against Women: a Feminist Critique', *Radical America*, March–June, 64–8.

Petchesky, R.P. (1987) 'Foetal Images: the Power of Visual Culture in the Politics of Reproduction', in Stanworth, M. (ed.) *Reproductive Technologies: Gender, Motherhood and Medicine* (London: Polity).

Pfeffer, P. (1985) 'The Hidden Pathology of the Male Reproductive System', in Homans, H. (ed.) *The Sexual Politics of Reproduction* (Hants: Gower).

Prentice, T. (1990) 'French Hope to Market Abortion Pill in Britain', *The Times*, 23 July.

Price, D. (1988) 'Selective Reduction and Foeticide: the Parameters of Abortion', *Criminal Law Review* 199–210.

Randles, T. (1991) 'The Alton Bill and the Media's Consensual Position', in Franklin, S., Lury, C. and Stacey, J. (eds) *Off-Centre: Feminism and Cultural Studies* (London: Harper Collins Academic).

Raulet, G. (1983) 'Structuralism and Post-Structuralism: an Interview with Michel Foucault', 55 *Telos* 195–211.

Raymond, J. (1991) 'RU 486: a Medical Miracle?', *Spare Rib*, February, 34–7.

Retzlaff, I. (1993) 'Anti-Progestins – a Feminist Medical View', in Furedi, A. (ed.) *Medical Abortion Services: European Perspectives on Anti-progestins* (London: International Planned Parenthood Federation).

Richards, P. (1970) *Parliament and Conscience* (London: Allen & Unwin).

Ricks, S. (1989) 'The New French Abortion Pill: the Moral Property of Women', 1 *Yale Journal of Law and Feminism*, No. 1, Spring, 75–99.

Roberts, H. (1985) *The Patient Patients: Women and Their Doctors* (London, Boston, Melbourne and Henley: Pandora Press).

Rodger, M. and Baird, D.T. (1987) 'Induction of Therapeutic Abortion in Early Pregnancy with Mifepristone in Combination with Prostaglandin Pessary', The *Lancet*, 19 December, 1415–18.

Rothman, B.K. (1986) *The Tentative Pregnancy: Prenatal Diagnosis and the Future of Motherhood* (New York: Viking).

Sapsted, A.-M. (1991) 'Abortion: the New Pill', The *Sunday Times Magazine*, January 6.

Savage, W. (1982) 'Taking Liberties with Women: Abortion, Sterilization, and Contraception', 12 *International Journal of Health Services*, No. 2, 293–307.

Savage, W. (1986) *A Savage Enquiry: Who Controls Childbirth?* (London: Virago).

Science and Technology Sub Group (University of Birmingham) (1991) 'Feminism and Abortion: Pasts, Presents and Futures', in Franklin, S., Lury, C. and Stacey, J. (eds) *Off-Centre: Feminism and Cultural Studies* (London: Harper Collins Academic).

Scully, D. (1980) *Men Who Control Women's Health: the Miseducation of Obstetrician-Gynecologists* (Boston: Houghton Mifflin Company).

Scully, D. and Bart, P. (1973) 'A Funny Thing Happened on the Way to the Orifice: Women in Gynecology Textbooks', 78 *American Journal of Sociology* 1045–9.

Showalter, E. (1987) *The Female Malady: Women, Madness and English Culture, 1830–1980* (London: Virago).

Simms, M. (1980) *Abortion in Britain before the Abortion Act: a Survey of the Historical Evidence* (London: Birth Control Trust).

Simms, M. (1981) 'Abortion: the Myth of the Golden Age', in Hutter, B. and Williams, G. (eds) *Controlling Women: the Normal and the Deviant* (London: Croom Helm).

Simms, M. (1985) 'Legal Abortion in Great Britain', in Homans, H. (ed.) *The Sexual Politics of Reproduction* (Hants: Gower).

Simonnot, D. (1993a) 'Avortements: le retour a l'étranger', *Libération*, 3 March.

Simonnot, D. (1993b) 'Avortement: la loi Veil appliquée a reculons', *Libération*, 16 March.

Skegg, P.D.G. (1974) 'Justification for Medical Procedures Performed Without Consent', 90 *Law Quarterly Review* 512–30.

Smart, C. (1976) *Women, Crime and Criminology: A Feminist Critique* (London and Boston: Routledge and Kegan Paul).

Smart, C. (1989) *Feminism and the Power of Law* (London: Routledge).

Smart, C. (1990a) 'Law's Power, the Sexed Body, and Feminist Discourse', 7 *Journal of Law and Society*, No. 2, Summer, 194–209.

Smart, C. (1990b) 'Law's Truth/Women's Experience', in Graycar, R. (ed.) *Dissenting Opinions: Feminist Explorations in Law and Society* (Sydney: Allen and Unwin).

Smart, C. (ed.) (1992a) *Regulating Womanhood: Historical Essays on Marriage, Motherhood and Sexuality* (London and New York: Routledge).

Smart, C. (1992b) 'Disruptive Bodies and Unruly Sex: the Regulation of Reproduction and Sexuality in the 19th Century', in Smart, C. (ed.) *Regulating Womanhood: Historical Essays on Marriage, Motherhood and Sexuality* (London and New York: Routledge).

Smart, C. (1992c) 'The Woman of Legal Discourse', 1 *Social and Legal Studies* 29–44.

Smith, J.C. and Hogan, B. (1988) *Criminal Law* (London: Butterworths).

Steel, D. (1971) 'Foreword', in Hindell, K. and Simms, M. (eds) *Abortion Law Reformed* (London: Peter Owen).

Steinberg, D.L. (1991) 'Adversarial Politics: the Legal Construction of Abortion', in Franklin, S., Lury, C. and Stacey, J. (eds) *Off-Centre: Feminism and Cultural Studies* (London: Harper Collins Academic).

Thomson, M. (1994a) 'After Re S', 2 *Medical Law Review* 127–48.

Thomson, M. (1994b) 'Women as Walking Wombs', *Socialist Lawyer*, No. 21, Spring, 12–13.

Thomson, M. (1995) 'Women, Medicine and Abortion in the Nineteenth Century', 3 *Feminist Legal Studies* No. 2, 159–83.

Thomson, M. (forthcoming) *Reproducing Narrative: Gender, Reproduction and the Law* (Aldershot: Dartmouth Publishing Company).

Thoss, E. (1993) 'Obstacles to Medical Abortion Provision in Germany', in Furedi, A. (ed.) *Medical Abortion Services: European Perspectives on Anti-progestins* (London: International Planned Parenthood Federation).

Tunkel, V. (1979) 'Abortion: How Early, How Late and How Legal?', *British Medical Journal* 253–6.

Tunnadine, D. and Green, R. (1978) *Unwanted Pregnancy – Accident or Illness?* (Oxford: Oxford University Press).

Turner, B.S. (1987) *Medical Power and Social Knowledge* (London: Sage).

United Kingdom Multicentre Trial (1990) 'The Efficacy and Tolerance of Mifepristone and Prostaglandin in First Trimester Termination of Pregnancy', 97 *British Journal of Obstetrics and Gynaecology*, June, 480–6.

USPDA (Union Suisse Pour Décriminaliser l'Avortement) (1990) *RU 486: Interruption de grossesse précoce: pour le droit de la femme de choisir le méthode* (Berne: Union Suisse Pour Décriminaliser l'Avortement).

Villmoare, A.H. (1991) 'Women, Differences and Rights as Practices: an Interpretive Essay and a Proposal', 25 *Law and Society Review*, No. 2, 385–410.

Warnock, M. (1985) *A Question of Life: The Warnock Report on Human Fertilisation and Embryology* (Oxford: Blackwell).

Weeks, J. (1989) *Sex, Politics and Society* (Harlow: Longman).

Wells, C. (1993) 'Maternal Versus Foetal Rights', in Feminist Legal Research Unit (ed.) *Body Politics: Control v Freedom: the Role of Feminism in Women's Personal Autonomy* (Liverpool: University of Liverpool).

Widdett, C. and Thomson, M. (1997) 'Justifying Treatment and Other Stories', 5 *Feminist Legal Studies* 77–89.

Williams, G. (1958) *The Sanctity of Life and the Criminal Law* (London: Faber and Faber).

Williams, P. (1988) 'Alchemical Notes: Reconstructing Ideals from Deconstructed Rights', in Lobel, J. (ed.) *A Less than Perfect Union* (New York: Monthly Review Press).

Winn, D. (1988) *Experiences of Abortion* (London: Macdonald Optima).

Woodside, M. (1963) 'Attitudes of Women Abortionists', 11 *Howard Journal of Penology and Crime Prevention*, No. 2, 93–112.

Young, A. (1993) 'Decapitation or Feticide: the Fetal Laws of the Universal Subject', 4 *Women: a Cultural Review*, No. 3, 288–94.

Young, G. (1981) 'A Woman Inside Medicine: Reflections from the Inside', in Roberts, H. (ed.) *Women, Health and Reproduction* (London, Boston and Henley: Routledge and Kegan Paul).

Zola, I.R. (1972) 'Medicine as an Institution of Social Control', 20 *Sociological Review* 4.

Zola, I.R. (1977) 'Healthism and Disabling Medicalization', in Illich I. (ed.) *Disabling Professions* (London: Marion Boyars Publishers Ltd).

Index